Published by Christian Art Publishers
PO Box 1599, Vereeniging, 1930, RSA

© 2024
First edition 2024

Designed by Christian Art Publishers

Cover designed by Christian Art Publishers
Images used under license from Shutterstock.com

Scripture quotations marked NIV are taken from the Holy Bible,
New International Version®, NIV® Copyright © 1973, 1978, 1984, 2011 by Biblica, Inc.®
Used by permission of Zondervan. All rights reserved worldwide. www.zondervan.com

Scripture quotations marked NLT are taken from the Holy Bible, New Living Translation,
copyright © 1996, 2004, 2015 by Tyndale House Foundation. Used by permission
of Tyndale House Publishers, Carol Stream, Illinois 60188. All rights reserved.

Scripture quotations marked NKJV are taken from the New King James Version®.
Copyright © 1979, 1980, 1982 by Thomas Nelson, Inc. Used by permission.
All rights reserved.

Scripture quotations marked ESV are taken from the Holy Bible, English Standard Version®.
ESV® Text Edition: 2016. Copyright © 2001 by Crossway, a publishing ministry of
Good News Publishers. Used by permission. All rights reserved.

Scripture quotations marked MSG are taken from The Message, copyright © 1993, 1994,
1995, 1996, 2000, 2001, 2002 by Eugene H. Peterson. Used by permission of NavPress.
All rights reserved.

Printed in China

ISBN 978-0-638-00043-6 (Faux Leather)
ISBN 978-0-638-00105-1 (Hardcover)

Christian Art Publishers has made every effort to trace the ownership of all quotes and poems
in this book. In the event of any question that may arise from the use of any quote or poem,
we regret any error made and will be pleased to make the necessary correction in future
editions of this book.

© All rights reserved. No part of this book may be reproduced in any form without
permission in writing from the publisher, except in the case of brief quotations in critical
articles or reviews.

24 25 26 27 28 29 30 31 32 33 – 10 9 8 7 6 5 4 3 2 1

ROOTED IN
Faith

January

January 1

Joy Unlimited

Rejoice in the Lord always. I will say it again: Rejoice!
Philippians 4:4 NIV

We have just had our New Year's parties and celebrations. New Year's resolutions are fresh! We feel ready to say goodbye to last year and welcome a new year.

Unfortunately joy, excitement and resolutions about the new year generally decrease. Most of it is based on our own efforts and trusting in our own ability to be different this year. While people who do not know God are resilient and have the potential to do great things, Christian joy and excitement are permanent.

Paul writes from prison. His freedom is curtailed. He adds a word to joy that seems unrealistic: rejoice *always*...How is this possible? Always? Certainly, this is not possible in a life with so many challenges and uncertainty. The answer lies in the other words that are added: rejoice *in the Lord* always.

To rejoice in the Lord means that we will be joyful because Jesus is Lord over all creation! He sits at the right hand of God. As Paul reminds us earlier in Philippians 2:9-11, all powers and forces are subjected to Jesus.

It does not matter what your circumstances or expectations are. Those who believe in the Lord still see the forces and adversity but are joyful because our Lord has overcome them all.

Lord, give me this joy and vision, in Jesus' name. *Amen.*

January 2

An Alternative Reality

> The One enthroned in heaven laughs; the Lord scoffs at them.
> Psalm 2:4 NIV

John Constable, a painter from the 18th-19th century, said: "I never saw an ugly thing in my life: for let the form of an object be what it may—light, shade, and perspective will always make it beautiful."

It can easily happen that we look at the powers and authorities around us and lose hope. We have all felt at some stage that we are close to losing hope. It may feel like other authorities are in control of our country instead of God. Psalm 2 reminds us that someone else is on the throne. Even if it appears as though someone else controls everything, God is still on the throne.

Psalm 2 begins with a kind of sarcastic tone. It is as if the poet wants to ask the nations and kings what they are up to. What are you trying to do with your little plans? It is all in vain! All people should understand that they should submit to the God who is on the throne.

Will you remember? Don't be scared when authorities flex their muscles. Keep the right perspective. Let us look at God's painting of reality! Jesus, the Lord of the universe, is on the throne (Eph. 1:20-22). He has absolute power. Try to smile with Him about people who think that they have absolute authority and the last say. Your Lord is King!

Lord, give me the right perspective in life, in Jesus' name.

Amen.

January 3

The Purpose of Wisdom

The proverbs of Solomon...To know wisdom and instruction, to perceive the words of understanding, to receive the instruction of wisdom, justice, judgment, and equity.
Proverbs 1:1–3 NKJV

The intention of the poet is to teach us wisdom (1:2). Wisdom is not meant for exceptional people. The poet says that young people, those who have no knowledge yet, yes anyone, can have a heart of wisdom (1:4). Some of us think that we are wise already. The poet says that we can become even wiser through his teachings (1:5). This wisdom is not a secret or out-of-this-world experience. It is about things that are extremely important to our society—what is right and just and fair (1:4).

This divine wisdom makes us concerned about a political system that promotes injustice where some people are treated better than others. We strive to see a society in which every person can take his or her God-given place with dignity. We are not only responsible for what we do but also for what we do not do. If you are a wise person, you will not be silent about injustice.

Someone said that knowledge leads us from the simple to the complex; wisdom leads us from the complex to the simple. May God grant you the wisdom to be able to discern what is best so that you may be pure and blameless for the day of Christ (Phil. 1:9–10).

Spirit of God, give me wisdom, in Jesus' name. *Amen.*

January 4

Wisdom from God

> The fear of the LORD is the beginning of knowledge;
> fools despise wisdom and instruction.
>
> Proverbs 1:7 ESV

I know young people who are wise and old people who are fools. Wisdom does not come with old age. How much wiser have you become in the last month? How much did your judgment on important matters improve in recent years?

We can have many degrees, diplomas and other qualifications and be very intelligent. We can have a vision for the future and make good economic and political predictions. We can be very successful in our profession. This does not mean that we have wisdom.

What is wisdom? We focus on what is fair, equitable and transparent. It teaches us to act with prudence and discretion (1:4-5). Wisdom is clearly worship in everyday life. Wisdom is to live in God's presence. It means to realize that everything we do and say is open before God. It is to live for God in all our relationships, in our work and in what we believe.

Where do you learn this kind of wisdom? Benjamin Franklin remarked that the doorstep to the temple of wisdom is a knowledge of our own ignorance. Wisdom comes from outside. What is its source? It starts when we listen to God (Prov. 1:7; 2:6; Job 28:28; Mic. 6:9). So, if you lack wisdom, ask the Lord and He will give it to you (James 1:5). He does it willingly.

Lord, teach us to number our days so that we may gain wisdom, by the power of Your Spirit. Amen.

January 5

God Completes What He Started

> ...being confident of this, that He who began a good work in you will carry it on to completion until the day of Christ Jesus.
>
> Philippians 1:6 NIV

This is one of Paul's letters from prison. It overflows with a good attitude and warmth. It was written as a letter of thanks for the help this congregation gave him.

As with most of his letters, he begins with a word of thanks to God. Who else should get the credit for the goodwill of people? He thanks the Lord for their cooperation in preaching the gospel (1:5). It is a source of joy (1:4). Therefore, the whole congregation, elders and deacons should hear of Paul and Timothy's gratitude to the Lord (1:1).

However, God does much more than that. If He has begun to work in our life, He does not leave us to ourselves to stand in the service of the Lord in our own strength. On the contrary. God enables us to walk the path all the way (1:6). He Himself completes what He has begun in people's lives (1:6).

This is how great God's grace is! If He had to leave us to ourselves to do good, we would never be able to do it. But He does not let us down. Every time something good appears in our life, it is the work of His persevering grace.

Father of grace, to You be the praise of all that is good in my life.

Amen.

January 6

Keep On Doing It

> "Ask and it will be given to you; seek and you will find; knock and the door will be opened to you. For everyone who asks receives; the one who seeks finds; and to the one who knocks, the door will be opened."
> Matthew 7:7–8 NIV

It is in my nature to be impatient. Things must be done quickly. With prayer it is different. When we pray, we leave our concerns in the hands of God. Yes, sometimes God takes much longer to answer than we expected. It is as if He sometimes says, "Wait a bit. Not now. At the right time."

Unfortunately, we sometimes ask for things that we think will be good for us. However, the Lord may have a different opinion. He knows it is dangerous for us. This is also an answer to prayer. God said no.

Prayer is ultimately a conversation with God—to ask things according to His will for our lives. It means that everything we want should be tested against the most important question: Will what I ask serve the purpose of God for my life? Will what I ask be the best for His kingdom? If I am sure about it, I may keep on asking. He will answer. The first lesson on prayer is this: Keep on doing it. Don't stop asking, seeking, knocking...

Spirit of God, teach me Your will so that I may say, "Let Your will be done." In the name of Jesus. *Amen.*

January 7

The Grace of Discipline

*Just as a parent disciplines a child, the LORD
your God disciplines you for your own good.*
Deuteronomy 8:5 NLT

These days we hardly measure distances when we travel. We rather measure the time it will take us to get from one point to another.

The distance between Egypt and Israel—even by foot—could not take forty years, but it did. The Israelites wandered through the wilderness. The reason? They had to learn discipline. They had to learn what obedience was (8:2, 5).

It is always hard to teach our children discipline. Sometimes there are tears and some form of punishment if they do not stick to the rules of the household. Yet, it is always an act of love by a parent who really cares.

The primary discipline that Israel had to learn was that one's path is determined only by God's Word (8:3). Through God's miraculous care, they had to learn that everything they had is a surprising gift from the Word of the Lord (8:6-10). Like Israel, we can forget how it came about that we are free. It may happen that we say: it was our own effort (8:17). That's when we live the way we want to.

The hardship in our lives is not without reason. It helps us to be totally dependent on the Lord. It teaches us to live from His hand. When we forget the Leader, the Caregiver, the Deliverer, we are actually saying that we do not need Him. And then we are on our own.

Lord, remind me of You, even if my life has to take detours. In Jesus' name. *Amen.*

January 8

Shadows Will Depart

> Your sun will never set again, and your moon will wane no more; the LORD will be your everlasting light, and your days of sorrow will end.
>
> Isaiah 60:20 NIV

Some days are diamonds. Some days are stone. These are the words of a song by John Denver. We know this feeling. Sometimes the rocky days are more than days. They are seasons and years, and then decades. Where is God then?

The Israelites knew everything about darkness. They were in exile. The prophet says that it will get better. The only reason why it will get better is that God is their God. He will drive away the darkness with His presence (60:2).

The sun and moon were often worshiped as gods by the nations around Israel. God, however, is not like the sun that rises and sets, or the moon that fades (60:20). He is an eternal light.

Jesus, the light of the world, expelled the darkness from people's lives (John 8:12). Wherever He went, He took away sadness and healed sickness. At the end of Revelation, He is the bright Morning Star (Rev. 22:16). The day of His return meant the end of suffering, pain and death (21:3-4).

Clement of Alexandria said that God changes sunsets into sunrises. On a Scottish castle there is an inscription: When Jesus comes, the shadows depart. Remember that He is with you today.

I worship You, Eternal Light, through Jesus Christ our Lord.

Amen.

January 9

Trapped or Free

My son, if sinful men entice you, do not give in to them...
How useless to spread a net where every bird can see it!
Proverbs 1:10, 17 NIV

As children, we often tried to catch birds in a trap. It was fun and we often wondered how a bird could be so stupid as to get caught. The birds' craving for food drove them to walk into the trap.

It is not just birds that are caught in traps. We are also caught. The context of these verses in Proverbs 1:10-19 is crime. People steal. You might say that you are not a thief. Well, sometimes our business transactions are not completely honest, because one has to be tough in the business world. Sometimes we underpay people, because we want more for ourselves. Friends tell us that this is the "going rate" for this type of work.

When we reject the authority of God in our lives, we often reject the teaching of God. If we were once touched by the Spirit of God and have learned the wisdom of the Spirit, we cannot be blind to the traps of life that the devil and sinful people set for us. Are our actions in accordance with divine wisdom, namely fairness and justice?

Do not be foolish and walk blindly into a lifestyle that may cost you your life (1:17-19). We will only be happy if we rather leave the baggage of our sins at the Cross instead of deliberately choosing to sin.

Spirit of God, deliver me from the foolishness of walking into the trap of sin with open eyes. In Jesus' name. *Amen.*

January 10

Under Construction

And this is my prayer: that your love may abound more and more in knowledge and depth of insight, so that you may be able to discern what is best and may be pure and blameless for the day of Christ.
Philippians 1:9-10 NIV

Roads under construction are very frustrating, but they are necessary. So is suffering. Paul has a different perspective on this. For him, his suffering is not something he has to bear, but an opportunity to defend and testify to the gospel. It is part of a journey with God that continues throughout life.

God began the good work in us and will complete it when Christ comes (1:6). We grow in our relationship with Christ. Therefore, Paul prays for increasing growth in understanding and discernment so that we will know what God really expects of us (1:9-10).

There are people who believe that we can achieve perfection in this life. Well, even if they do not always openly say it, they sometimes act as if they are already perfect! On this side of Jesus' return, however, we are still on our way. God is not done with us. That is why Paul says that we will be blameless only at the return of Christ (1:10-11). It will not be because we ourselves have become perfect. No, through Jesus Christ we will be in the right relationship with God and He will receive the glory (1:11). Before His return, we are still under construction!

Spirit of God, form me in Your hands so that I may discern what is important. Amen.

January 11

The Focus of Our Faith

The woman, fearing and trembling, knowing what had happened to her, came and fell down before Him and told Him the whole truth.
Mark 5:33 NKJV

So many people wish to get to Jesus to be cured of the disease that has occupied and taken over their lives. We confess that Jesus alone can do it. As Jesus listened to the woman, He also heard the despair of the people bringing the worst possible news about Jairus's daughter.

Jesus had compassion on the woman and Jairus. Jesus healed the woman and Jairus's daughter. The crowd saw God's healing power, yet He had more in mind. These events were just signposts of the real revolution and healing that God was to accomplish through Jesus' death and resurrection. We should not confuse signposts with the destination.

Discipleship is about following Jesus' example. There is a close link between faith and these events. Through this story, Jesus challenges this woman, Jairus, the messengers, His disciples and every reader. The challenge is this: Is Jesus, who is the Lord over sin, sickness, death and all powers, the object of our faith? And if we listen honestly and sincerely value every human being—like Jesus—the ultimate goal is to help everyone to come to the confession that He is the Son of God.

Lord, let us show Your compassion so that people will come to faith in You, our Lord and Savior. Amen.

January 12

Let God Interrupt You

> While Jesus was still speaking, some people came
> from the house of Jairus, the synagogue leader.
> "Your daughter is dead," they said.
> Mark 5:35 NIV

Cynical readers could accuse this woman of having caused the death of the young girl. She, after all, interrupted Jesus' journey on His way to a sick child. If she were not so selfish, Jesus could possibly have arrived at the child in time. Yet, Jesus gave her the opportunity to tell her story. I cannot imagine how long this story would have felt for Jairus.

God often interrupts our journey through people. The compassion of Christ in this story challenges us to open our eyes and ears. Everyone has a story. Sometimes there are success stories, but if we are honest, we have to admit that there are more stories of struggle, defeat, fear, being pushed to the margins of society, excluded from groups, as well as feelings of worthlessness. There are many stories of unspeakable pain.

We are called to take time to listen, to stand still, to let urgent matters wait so that broken people can be heard.

> Lord, help us to listen well, to see well, so that the interruptions on the journeys of our lives become opportunities. In Jesus' name. *Amen.*

January 13

Divine Authority

*Jesus kept looking around to see who had done it.
Then the woman, knowing what had happened
to her, came and fell at His feet and, trembling
with fear, told Him the whole truth. He said
to her, "Daughter, your faith has healed you.
Go in peace and be freed from your suffering."*
Mark 5:32–34 NIV

This woman is healed without Jesus laying a hand on her. Rather, she laid a hand on Jesus. Again, we see that there is fear and uncertainty. Jesus makes it clear that He is not some magical miracle worker. It is through faith that she discovered Him as the One who has power over disease. He assured her of a permanent cure, because she trusted Him.

Who is Jesus? What does He do? Typical of Mark, the authority of Jesus is emphasized. The purpose of the gospel is that people will recognize that Jesus is the Son of God (1:1). The centurion's confession at the end of the Gospel (15:39) makes it clear.

Mark attributes those things that only God can do to Jesus. Jesus has absolute divine authority. He has the power to forgive, to save, and to heal people's illness. He has power over the forces of nature and finally conquers death. Mark said to his readers that Jesus is God. Jesus knows everything; He knows that someone touched Him. He has the authority to heal people.

B. H. Streeter said that God is not a mere spectator. Christ is the image of the unseen God. It means that God does not stand outside our suffering.

Lord, thank You that You care about all people, also about me.

Amen.

January 14

God Wants You

> What can we bring to the LORD? Should we bring Him burnt offerings? Should we bow before God Most High with offerings of yearling calves? No, O people, the LORD has told you what is good, and this is what He requires of you: to do what is right, to love mercy, and to walk humbly with your God.
> Micah 6:6, 8 NLT

Many people think that they have done their part when they have given money or shared their talents for a cause.

The Israelites believed that sacrifices were enough, however, God was not interested in substitutes for the real thing. We should love the Lord our God with *all* our heart, soul, and strength (Deut. 6:5). There are no half-measures. We offer our bodies as living sacrifices, holy and pleasing to God (Rom. 12:1). There is a huge difference between giving our talents and giving ourselves!

God does not want a portion of ourselves. He does not want something—He wants all of us. This is an act of worship, not substitutes for worship. This act of worship demands that we put God first, walk with Him, and treat people with mercy. Paul describes this as a sacrifice of ourselves—an act of worship (Rom. 12:1).

Lord, take my life and use it in Your service as it pleases You.
Amen.

January 15

Changing Every Day

Therefore, I urge you, brothers and sisters in view of God's mercy...Do not conform any longer to the pattern of this world, but be transformed by the renewing of your mind.
Romans 12:1-2 NIV

To change is always difficult. Everything around us changes so quickly these days. We struggle with it. Some people never want change.

We find change even more difficult in our relationship with God. Change is a daily process in a Christian's life. Paul uses the word that we know in English as a *metamorphosis*. We are being transformed by God when our lives become a living sacrifice in His service.

In this life we will not reach what we are supposed to be, but it is not a reason to resist change. G. K. Chesterton correctly wrote that people who see no need for change think so not because they can't see the solution, but because they can't see the problem.

We are not what we are supposed to be! Anyone who understands this gives themselves into God's hands. It has been said that some people change when they see the light, others when they feel the heat.

Why do we change? We become clay in His hands, because we have seen the light. We change because we have discovered the grace and mercy of God. We let go of our control. We know that if He changes us, we will be different.

Lord, thank You for the light of Your love which changes us day by day, through the power of Your Spirit. *Amen.*

January 16

Desperation

> Is Your love declared in the grave, Your faithfulness in Destruction?
> Psalm 88:11 NIV

Everything is dark around me (88:6). I am tired of life. I do not expect any positive outcome in the near future. I feel that God and my own people are far away (88:8, 18). I feel abandoned and desperate (88:14–15).

This poet feels like many people feel today—he has no answers (88:14). He is at a dead-end street. This psalm is one of the darkest. Unlike other similar psalms, it does not end with praise, but with loneliness and hopelessness. Amid this terrible sense of the distance between the poet and God, a desperate feeling that there is no future, he prays to God.

Prayer is the deepest form of dependence and faith. God alone can help (88:1). The poet asks question after question about God's faithfulness in life and death (88:10–14). He did not expect any positive answers to these rhetorical questions.

The psalm is not without comfort. It teaches us that we do not need to pretend before God when we suffer. We may bring all our questions, and hopelessness before the Lord. We may even protest with Him and argue about our suffering.

Mother Teresa once said, "My secret is simple: I pray."

Lord, from the depths of darkness I call to You. Please hear my prayer. In Jesus' name. Amen.

January 17

Hope in Dark Times

Is Your love declared in the grave, Your faithfulness in Destruction?
Psalm 88:11 NIV

This psalm ends without hope. There is nothing in the psalmist's circumstances that gives hope. All he can do is complain. He can only hope that God will hear. This sounds very pessimistic. Sometimes, however, we are in seasons of disorientation in our lives. We lose hope. We see no outcome. And then hope breaks through again and new insights are born.

As Christians we read this psalm and see beyond the disorientation. The desire of the poet that his prayer will not be in vain (88:2), has been answered. We read the psalm after the death and resurrection of Jesus. Remember that the Son of God exchanged places with us on the cross, so that God will never be far away from us.

Although you may sometimes feel that God is absent, please look at the cross. It is the symbol of God's eternal presence with us. Because of the cross, we can say with Paul: God is for us (Rom. 8:31-32). We now know that God is not far away. Jesus bore our loneliness by suffering in our place. We know that death can no longer separate us from God's faithfulness, because even in death we belong to Him (Rom. 14:7-9). Is there a greater comfort in suffering?

> Jesus, thank You that You were abandoned by God in my place, so that God will always be close to me. In the name of Jesus Christ.
>
> *Amen.*

January 18

A Teachable Spirit

> "For the simple are killed by their turning away, and the complacency of fools destroys them; but whoever listens to me will dwell secure and will be at ease, without dread of disaster."
> Proverbs 1:32-33 ESV

My father studied theology. He knew the Bible inside out and was very knowledgeable in theology. Then he lost his way. A conversation with him about God was always very difficult. He believed he knew everything. He no longer had a teachable spirit.

The poet calls this attitude complacency. People cover their ears. They go their own way. They are self-righteous. Whoever goes his or her own way, says the poet, takes the road leading to a catastrophe—calamity, disaster, distress and trouble (1:27). If you end up on that sidetrack, you can reach a point of no return (1:28).

The poet says that it does not need to be the case, because "whoever listens to me will live in safety and be at ease, without fear of harm" (1:33 NIV). When we realize that we are ignorant, that we need advice, the doors to God's wisdom open. The author of Hebrews warns us that today is very important, "So, as the Holy Spirit says: 'Today, if you hear His voice, do not harden your hearts as you did in the rebellion'" (Heb. 3:7-8 NIV).

A committee of one is the best. Decisions are usually unanimous! But it is not an option for Christians. There is always another party involved when we make decisions. In Proverbs 1, it is God.

Spirit of wisdom and understanding, please teach me wisdom by listening to Your voice. In Jesus' name. *Amen.*

January 19

Be Fit!

*For physical training is of some value, but godliness
has value for all things, holding promise for both
the present life and the life to come.*
1 Timothy 4:8 NIV

My son and son-in-law did a grueling mountain bike race, the Desert Dash, in Namibia, crossing the oldest desert in the world. It is over a distance of 393 kilometers and hundreds of people take part in it annually in December. Some take part in teams and others solo. It is mountainous, sandy, stony. It is difficult. Preparation for this race is intense. It requires focus.

Being fit and exercising is very important and healthy. Our ultimate goal with exercise is to have a healthy body.

Being healthy in your faith also requires exercise. How good would our Christian life be if we were as disciplined with our spiritual exercise as we are at preparing for a grueling race? Martin Luther said that the Christian life does not mean that you *are* pious, but that you *become* pious. It does not mean that you *are* healthy but are *getting* healthy. The Christian life is not rest, but exercise. A true craftsman is never satisfied. Lazy people become satisfied very soon. Believers are always strengthening their faith.

Are you satisfied with your faith fitness? Now is the time to pay attention, because our faith life is a long journey. Without exercise, we may become spectators, instead of participants.

Lord, enable me to exercise my faith every day, by the power of Your Spirit. Amen.

January 20

Faith Is Not an Insurance Policy

> "Do not fear, for I have redeemed you; I have summoned
> you by name; you are Mine. When you pass through
> the waters, I will be with you..."
> Isaiah 43:1-2 NIV

What does our faith in God mean? You probably have an insurance policy or two. We need it. When we die, the people left behind must be well cared for. When someone breaks into your home or steals your car, we should be able to replace these things. Of course, insurance policies do not prevent people from breaking in and stealing. It does not keep death away from us.

Faith is in some sense like an insurance policy. Unfortunately, people sometimes think that their faith can prevent the hardships and crises in their lives. They have a wrong understanding of what faith is. God's love for us does not mean that we are free from trials. Isaiah says that we will still go through rivers and fires in our lives. However, we may know that the Lord formed us with His hands and therefore also continues to hold our lives in His hands (43:1-4). Faith means knowing that His love carries us through trials. When disaster strikes, as it often does, you have the insurance of God's love—the assurance that He will walk with you through the fire and pain.

Jesus came to do just that. On the cross He took all the suffering of the world upon Himself. Through His suffering, we have the assurance that He understands our suffering and is with us in all trials.

Lord God, thank You that Your love carries us through trials, through Jesus Christ our Lord. *Amen.*

January 21

The Keeper of Our Life

For to me, to live is Christ, and to die is gain.
Philippians 1:21 NKJV

As I read this passage, I often think about Narda, a remarkable woman I knew. She understood that death cannot deprive us of the quality of God's love for us. At her funeral, I could read Philippians 1:21 with confidence because my friend saw it as her "motto."

Shortly before Martin Luther's death, he wrote: "When we die, it does not mean real death, but rather the foretaste of God's season. The cemetery is not just a place of keeping the dead, but a field full of seed, God's seed; not a collection of skeletons, but a place full of summer promises..." Indeed, death is a gain because it means the eternal presence of God (1:21).

Now, as we read in Philippians 1, Paul did not have it easy. He was in prison and used the cell as his pulpit. Still, this situation advanced the gospel. Here the imperial guard discovers why Paul was willing to be put in prison (1:12–13) and it helps others to preach the gospel with greater boldness (1:14).

It does not matter where we are or what our circumstances are. Our purpose in life and death is to honor God. Because He has claimed our lives, we are safe, even if we suffer or die.

> I praise You, Faithful Lord, Keeper of my life. Thank You that through the resurrection of Jesus Christ, I have new life.
>
> *Amen.*

January 22

A Compassionate Heart

"Then a despised Samaritan came along, and when he saw the man, he felt compassion for him."
Luke 10:33 NLT

The Good Samaritan felt compassion for the man. The Message paraphrases, "When he saw the man's condition, his heart went out to him." He was filled with sadness and empathy for the man lying in pain and distress.

Good Samaritans are not common in our society. Religious people ask, "Who is my neighbor?" They want to define who should receive love and care. Good Samaritans say, "I want to be a neighbor to someone today."

Caring for someone is the loving attention we give to people who are suffering. We do not do this because they need it to stay alive. We do not care because the medical funds pay for it or because it provides jobs for people. We do not care for people because the law forbids us from practicing euthanasia or because someone's condition could be used for medical research.

We care because the person who is suffering belongs to God. To care for someone is to stand by a dying person and be a living reminder that that person is truly a beloved of God.

Yes, we are living reminders of God's incredible, unlimited and unconditional love, shown to us in Christ's self-sacrificing love.

Father, make me an instrument of Your care and love today. In Jesus' name. Amen.

January 23

True Neighbors

> "Which of these three do you think was a neighbor
> to the man who fell into the hands of robbers?"
> Luke 10:36 NIV

Who is my neighbor? Is it the person living next door? Some neighbors are not the most pleasant people to have around. But this question involves much more than my next-door neighbor. The question asked to Jesus was an attempt to draw boundaries. We do this when we try to define our neighbor. If the expert in religious law could get a simple definition of his neighbor, it would have been easy.

Jesus breaks the mold of our limited thinking about the needs of our fellow human beings. The question is not who is my neighbor, but rather are we willing to be a neighbor to people in need (10:36). Shakespeare takes it a bit further, as in this parable: "'Tis not enough to help the feeble up, but to support him after."

The parable of the Good Samaritan emphasizes our resistance getting involved where there is a need. We always find a reason why people in need may not be helped. The man caused his own mess. He has to get out of it himself. He should have known that the road was dangerous and full of robbers. We have our own people to take care of. Our budget does not provide for that. And then we walk past those in need, because it does not fit into our boundaries of what a neighbor means. Christians are neighbors. Be one today!

Lord, help me to be a neighbor today when someone needs me. In Jesus' name. *Amen.*

January 24

Learning Wisdom

> My son, if you accept my words and store up my commands
> within you…then you will understand the fear of the LORD
> and find the knowledge of God. For the LORD gives wisdom,
> and from His mouth come knowledge and understanding.
> Proverbs 2:1, 5–6 NIV

I am sure that you struggle to become wise. I know I struggle. We experience many things in life. Sometimes these experiences are painful. Yet, in spite of these experiences, we do not necessarily become wiser. We have to admit that wisdom does not necessarily come with age. It is said that we can learn wisdom by looking at a good example. Yet, in spite of the wisdom of others or good examples, we do not gain wisdom that easily.

The poet says that God is the ultimate source of wisdom. The challenge is to be open to His work in our lives (2:2–3). It does not help to wait to become wise. No, we have to look for it as if we are searching for a treasure, cry out for it, and work hard to find it.

Paul says that all the treasures of wisdom are to be found in Christ (Col. 2:2–3). Jesus is the best example of wisdom. May we be led by Christ, the source of our wisdom.

Lord, teach me Your wisdom, as I follow the example of Christ.

Amen.

January 25

Choices

For the LORD grants wisdom! From His mouth come knowledge and understanding. He grants a treasure of common sense to the honest.
Proverbs 2:6-7 NLT

Most of us drive somewhere every day. We must keep our eyes open in order to drive safely. The different paths we take in life are of course full of smaller side lanes—temptations, obstacles and wrong paths. The turnoff is sometimes so close to the right road that we do not see the difference.

We know how much grief wrong choices bring. David's sin and Peter's denial caused major difficulties. This could have been avoided if their self-interests had not taken the central stage in their lives. Thomas á Kempis wrote that those who strive to withdraw from obedience, withdraw from grace.

A choice for wisdom can prevent disasters, but wisdom is also a source of blessings. Wisdom allows us to see what it is to know God and to obey Him (2:5). It promises God's protective hand over our life (2:8). It fosters positive values of fairness, discretion and integrity in your life (2:9-11). God's wisdom enables us to withstand temptations and remain on track (2:16).

The Lord is the source of this wisdom. Paul reminds us that the greatest wisdom is to accept the wisdom of God, Jesus Christ, our righteousness, sanctification and redemption (1 Cor. 1:30). We fall and sometimes stumble, but if we stick with Jesus, we have the assurance that our sins are forgiven.

Wisdom of God, Jesus Christ, thank You for saving me so that I can walk the right path of wisdom, by the power of Your Spirit.

Amen.

January 26

Come, Lord Jesus!

> The Spirit and the bride say, "Come!" And let the one who hears say, "Come!" Let the one who is thirsty come; and let the one who wishes take the free gift of the water of life.
> Revelation 22:17 NIV

Infectious diseases are fresh in the minds of our generation. Several outbreaks of these diseases have caused the world to come to a standstill. Masks, travel bans, quarantine and tests before and after travel became part of our vocabulary. It was exhausting!

The last chapter in the Bible also speaks about being infectious, but in a very different way. In this chapter, Jesus assures us that He will return (22:7, 12). The tense in the Greek language indicates that He is about to come. He is coming!

Based on this assurance, the Holy Spirit leads us, His bride or church, to pray for this return (22:17). At its core, this prayer of the church is the same as the prayer for the coming of the Kingdom in the Lord's Prayer. It is also reminiscent of Romans 8:18-30 where creation, man and the Spirit sigh because God's new world has not yet arrived.

The prayer that Jesus will return soon is not just a vertical call to Jesus. This is immediately followed by a horizontal call to people. You see, the way we pray for the coming of the Kingdom should be infectious! It is a testimony to others so that they can come too.

Are your prayers and dedication to God's kingdom so contagious that people will join you with this prayer?

Come, Lord Jesus, come soon!

January 27

Sin Runs Deep

*Behold, I was brought forth in iniquity,
and in sin did my mother conceive me.*
Psalm 51:5 ESV

Sorry seems to be the hardest word. We all know how difficult it is to admit that we have failed or caused hurt. We rather try to justify why we have done it. The hardest part is to admit that the mistake is ours, nobody else's. It is my sin, my mistake, my failure!

This psalm was written by David after the prophet Nathan visited him. He had committed adultery and murder. Bathsheba was pregnant because of this and Uriah, her husband, had been killed.

The prophet confronted him with these sinful acts. David does not try to justify himself, he just feels guilt and contrition after this visit. He expresses the depth of sin in his life. Sin is not just something he did wrong; he is sinful in his very being. He was sinful even from before his birth.

When we come to such a point in our lives, a very important thing happens. We realize that we cannot live without God's grace. Without a proper awareness of the depth of our sin, we can never understand how necessary God's grace is. There are times when we have to sink into the depths of our misery to understand the truth.

This happened to David. The best place one can end up is in the pit of hopelessness. There we discover God's grace and forgiveness in a new way.

Lord, thank You for the truth of Your love that I discovered in the lows of my life. Amen.

January 28

The Privilege of Suffering

*For it has been granted to you on behalf of Christ
not only to believe in Him, but also to suffer for Him...*
Philippians 1:29 NIV

These are not really words we like to hear. Suffering is not pleasant. Yes, we must not forget that our salvation is always God's work (1:28). We do not believe it because we want to—it is a privilege! However, we do not like to hear that this privilege also includes suffering. We suffer, believe and live according to the gospel. We fight with one heart for the gospel because God has given us the privilege to do so (1:29-30). This is part of our walk of life that is in harmony with the gospel (1:27). It also confirms we still have to grow a lot. After all, we must continue to increase in understanding and discernment (1:9). We still need to grow in faith (1:25).

Living in accordance with the gospel is in this passage directly related to the unity that must exist in the congregation (1:27). They must be especially united in the way they stand together for the gospel. This will have two consequences. On the one hand, it will confirm their salvation in Christ. On the other hand, the world will see that they (the world) live far from God (1:28).

We are in the service of the Lord. The road may be difficult, but the end goal is His honor. What a privilege!

Father, thank You for taking us into Your service. Let our lives be in harmony with Your gospel. Amen.

January 29

Become More like God

> Let love and faithfulness never leave you; bind them around your neck, write them on the tablet of your heart. Then you will win favor and a good name in the sight of God and man.
> Proverbs 3:3-4 NIV

I must confess that sometimes I do not feel as if I'm growing, but rather moving backward. Sometimes my spiritual life blows hot and sometimes cold. Sometimes it is only lukewarm. Sometimes there are highs and sometimes lows.

The wisdom that God gives causes a shake-up in our lives. If God teaches us wisdom, there will always be some movement in our lives. Positive growth takes place as we sit at the feet of God, hear His voice and live near Him. Stagnation occurs when we turn our backs on Him. Without God's wisdom, a downward curve of negative "growth" is the result. Positive growth, an upward curve, is the result of fellowship with God.

What is this positive growth? The poet says that learning God's wisdom means faithfulness and loyalty to what we learn (3:3). Love and faithfulness, or loyalty, must be the characteristics of those on the path of wisdom.

Love and faithfulness? It sounds exactly like the qualities of God (Exod. 34:6). What does it mean? It is simple: God calls us to be like Him. Something of God should be in our lives. It is clear that the New Testament calls us to be like Jesus—the epitome of God's love and faithfulness (John 1:14-18).

Spirit of God, help me to grow in fellowship with God, through Jesus Christ. Amen.

January 30

Listen to His Word

Let love and faithfulness never leave you; bind them around your neck, write them on the tablet of your heart. Then you will win favor and a good name in the sight of God and man.
Proverbs 3:3-4 NIV

Christians hunger and thirst for righteousness. They always long for the redeeming Word. This is not natural. In themselves they are destitute and dead, therefore help must come from the outside. Where does it come from? It comes daily in the Word of Jesus Christ, bringing us redemption, righteousness, virtue and blessedness.

God's wisdom is the source of growth. Listen to what Peter said, "His divine power has given us everything we need for a godly life through our knowledge of Him who called us by His own glory and goodness. Through these He has given us His very great and precious promises, so that through them you may participate in the divine nature, having escaped the corruption in the world caused by evil desires" (2 Pet. 1:3-4 NIV).

When Paul speaks to the young Timothy, he also knows that growth and wisdom only comes from God. He says, "As for you, continue in what you have learned and have firmly believed, knowing from whom you learned it and how from childhood you have been acquainted with the sacred writings, which are able to make you wise for salvation through faith in Christ Jesus" (2 Tim. 3:14-15 ESV).

If you want to share in wisdom, it is simple: Listen to His Word.

Spirit of wisdom, make me full of love and faithfulness, in Jesus' name. *Amen.*

January 31

A Good Tradition

You must remain faithful to the things you have been taught. You know they are true, for you know you can trust those who taught you.
2 Timothy 3:14 NLT

How many sermons have you heard in your life? How many Christian weddings, funerals, baptisms or conferences have you attended? Although all sermons and messages are not equally inspiring and life-changing, some aspect of the gospel was mentioned in all of it. What effect did it have on you?

The famous theologian Thomas à Kempis said that four things are needed for peace and true freedom: Do another's will, not your own; always choose to have less rather than more; seek the lower positions in life and put to death the idea of being recognized and important; and pray that the will of God be fully embodied in you.

In Paul's two letters to Timothy, all these aspects are mentioned. We need to rethink the direction of and priorities in our lives, our titles and social standing, the way we handle our possessions, and what really gives direction in our lives.

Why? Because our lives are under new management. We follow the age-old message that was inspired by the Holy Spirit (3:16). Our faith is based on His Word. We do not have to look for other sources of inspiration or for direction, because the "Holy Scriptures...are able to make you wise for salvation through faith in Christ Jesus" (3:15 NIV).

Lord, let me live close to Your Word, by the power of Your Spirit.
Amen.

February

February 1

Your Kingdom, Not Mine

> Trust in the LORD with all your heart; do not depend on your own understanding. Seek His will in all you do, and He will show you which path to take.
> Proverbs 3:5–6 NLT

These verses capture everything written so far in the book of Proverbs and what is to come. This is what life is about. This is wisdom. Know the Lord and He will show you how to live. Ask God's advice and He will give you the right advice in your marriage, the way you raise your children, grow your business, approach your friendships, treat your parents—yes, in all areas of your life.

How do we desire to have this guidance every day! We need it! Life is not simple. Relationships are not easy. Amid all of these realities, we want to go His way—the right way! We give up our own wisdom and acknowledge and trust that only He knows the right way (3:5). It is hard. It is sometimes very painful! But if we do it, we will walk on God's right path. This is what Jesus taught us in Matthew 6:33 (NKJV) when He said, "Seek first the kingdom of God and His righteousness."

Not my kingdom or my will—no, my name is not important. It is about YOU, Lord! When this is our attitude, the Lord will provide what we need. There is no need to worry.

When I was a student we sang Proverbs 3:6 along with John 3:16. God loves you. His Son is the source of life. Trust Him and He will show you the right way.

Lord, I sacrifice all my dreams, ambitions and ideas before You in exchange for Your wisdom. Amen.

February 2

His Ways Can Be Hard

> ...in all your ways submit to Him, and He will make your paths straight...My son, do not despise the LORD's discipline, and do not resent His rebuke, because the LORD disciplines those He loves...
> Proverbs 3:6, 11–12 NIV

I must confess that there have been many times when I turned to the Lord for help in making decisions, but the road was not always easy after that. The right way is not always the easy way. The poet says that the Lord will make our paths straight, but it does not mean it will be easy. His advice is not "simple". He emphasizes that it may even include discipline (3:12).

Why is the right way not the easy way? The key is in the words "in all your ways submit to Him". In *all* our ways? *Submit* to Him? This means that we should put God first in every decision we make, every path we choose, in every relationship, in the knowledge we share, and in our jobs and business transactions. What this essentially means is that we will have to crucify ourselves. Self-denial is the path of wisdom.

We could say that the container in which pure water comes is of no importance. The vase does not matter, as long as we have the water. So what is it to me whether the will of God be presented to me in tribulation or consolation, since I desire and seek only the divine will?

Lord, in all my ways I want to honor You, even if it means suffering, in Jesus' name. *Amen.*

February 3

Mirror Images of His Love

Therefore if you have any encouragement from being united with Christ, if any comfort from His love, if any common sharing in the Spirit, if any tenderness and compassion...
Philippians 2:1 NIV

This is how it should be: a community of believers, a community of comfort, a community of ministry to one another. We only really give shape to the gospel when we have learned to serve one another.

It seems that sometimes there was a difference of opinion among the believers. Paul encourages them to be united. Despite differences, one vision is important. This vision is to serve one another. This only happens when we put our own interests aside. When everyone decides to serve one another, we have one vision.

Our own interests are set aside when God's purpose is our purpose (2:3-5). Of course, this is not something that comes naturally. That is why Paul says that this attitude is born from something God has done in our lives. We experienced the comfort in Christ, His love and fellowship with the Spirit (2:1). The love of Christ was to give Himself away for us. His love led Him to His death (2:8).

Our love and care for one another should be a mirror image of this. Since we have experienced this, let us begin to serve.

Lord, let me live the gospel today by serving those around me, to the glory of Your name. Amen.

February 4

God Always Cares

*"I am the God of your father—the God of Abraham,
the God of Isaac, and the God of Jacob."*
Exodus 3:6 NLT

Sometimes we forget God's plans for our lives. It happened to Moses. He was saved by an Egyptian and brought up in an Egyptian palace. When he grew up, he defended his people. He even defended one of his fellow Israelites who was treated badly. By killing the Egyptian, he had to flee.

Years passed. He was minding his own business until this day in the desert when God intervened because He is faithful. It is not about Moses or the needs of the people; it is about His own conscience. God did not forget His promises.

God saw and heard how hard it was for His people (3:7, 9). Their cries of pain touched His heart. It bothered Him and He could no longer see the needs of the people and do nothing about it. Therefore, He "comes down" to set them free (3:8). And Moses is part of this! He is not going to get away!

God engages ordinary people in the fulfillment of His promises. We cannot mind our own business and think that God has forgotten about His plans for us.

God does not look at the world "from a distance", as the song goes. He is involved in our needs. He not only saves them from slavery, but also creates a new future. We see this in a most excellent way in God becoming a human being in Christ.

Lord, reveal how You want me to be involved in Your acts of liberation, in Jesus' name. Amen.

February 5

Excuses

> But Moses said to God, "Who am I that I should go to Pharaoh and bring the children of Israel out of Egypt?"
> Exodus 3:11 ESV

I read the following about how unwilling people are to serve God: at 4 years—too small to think about God; 7 years—too playful to think about God; 18 years—too young and arrogant to think about God; Wedding day—too happy to think about God; Family—too busy to think about God; Sickness—too sick to think about God; Work—too many worries to think about God; Old age—too old to think about God; Death—too late to think about God.

We have so many excuses as to why it is not the right time to devote our lives to God. Moses fled after he committed a murder and spent many years looking after the sheep of his father-in-law. It was just his daily routine. But God never forgets His plan for our lives. God stopped Moses on his way to nowhere. He engages Moses in His plan.

However, it is not enough that God finds and sends Moses. This time Moses does not run away. This time he drags his feet. He finds many excuses as to why the Lord cannot use him.

Sometimes we complain that God does nothing in this world. It is not true. We are often the reason why things do not happen in the world. We often stand in God's way. What prevents you from serving the Lord fully?

Lord, I am in Your service. Use me, in Jesus' name. *Amen.*

February 6

Not Suited for the Task?

> But Moses said to God, "Who am I that I should go to
> Pharaoh and bring the children of Israel out of Egypt?"
> Exodus 3:11 ESV

Comfort zones are dangerous. It is dangerous because it makes us lazy and prevents growth. Everything becomes predictable. The routine becomes deadly. Later on, we do not live anymore—we just exist.

By appearing to Moses, God interrupted his life. Now he has many objections as to why the Lord cannot use him. Why me? Who am I really? We hear the same objection from Gideon (Judg. 6:15), Saul (1 Sam. 9:21) and Jeremiah (Jer. 1:6). We are always too young, too small, too few, too powerless to hear God's calling. We easily declare ourselves incompetent. Our first response when God calls us out of comfort zones is this: "I have to get away!"

Of course, Moses did not have a bad reason why he felt that way. His past does not look very good. He is a murderer in Egypt. Does the Lord really want him to go back now? Moses piles up the excuses: "Who am I? The people will not believe me. I stutter and cannot speak. Send somebody else!"

One can understand that Moses could have been afraid. Our past and inabilities sometimes make us feel that we are not suited for this task. The problem is us, not God. Remember, your inabilities are not a disqualification. They are a requirement to serve God. It prevents us from going in our own strength.

The answer of the Lord is wonderful: "I will be with you" (Exod. 3:12 NLT). This is all we need to know!

Thank You, Lord, for the assurance that You are with me.

Amen.

February 7

Who Are You, Lord?

> "Suppose I go to the Israelites...and they ask me,
> 'What is His name?' Then what shall I tell them?"
> Exodus 3:13 NIV

Family names are out of fashion in many cultures. People give names to their children without even thinking about the meaning or origin of the name. This was not the case in Israel. When you knew someone's name in the Ancient Near East, you knew his or her being.

As we have seen before, Moses had many objections when God called him. One of the most important objections was this one: "If people asked me who has sent me, who are You? It is fine that You promised to go with me, but tell me who You are, Lord. What is Your name?" Moses would go, but he wanted to know the Lord's "limits". Essentially, he wanted to be in control in the situation because he wanted to know how far this God would go with him.

In Exodus 3:14, God reveals Himself in His name: "I AM WHO I AM." Someone translates it this way: "I am there, wherever it may be, I am really there." What the Lord is saying is this: "Who I am and what I do will be clearly confirmed in the future." His name is a promise of His active presence. His name is full of promise. He keeps His promises and will always keep them (3:15). In Jesus the Lord shows who He is: Immanuel, God with us. He is there when He sends us.

Immanuel, thank You for being with us when we fulfill Your task in the world. Amen.

February 8

Whose Fault Is It?

> Faith comes from hearing the message, and the message is heard through the word about Christ.
> Romans 10:17 NIV

The gospel is so simple. Everyone who calls on Jesus' name is saved (10:13). Why Jesus' name? Simply because there is no other way. The sacrifice of Jesus Christ was enough to reconcile people with God. That is why we believe in Him.

On the other hand, it is not that simple. There are millions of people who do not believe. Why not? Paul reverses the whole sequence. He starts at the end and moves to the beginning of it all: the word about Christ. Christ is the messenger and the message. People heard it. They did not keep it to themselves. They shared it and others heard it. By hearing about it, people believed and called upon Christ. People cannot call upon the Lord if they do not hear the gospel. It is as simple as that. People are lost if they do not believe in Jesus.

Whose fault is it? Yes, it might be that people reject the gospel. The other scenario is that people like us do not share the message of salvation. If our colleagues or family or people at the ends of the earth never hear about Jesus from us or through us, how can we blame them for not believing.

Do you have a passion for the lost world?

> Father, make me an instrument so that the gospel will be preached to all, in Jesus' name. *Amen.*

February 9

God Surprises Us

> As He passed by, He saw Levi...sitting at the tax office. And He said to him, "Follow Me." So he arose and followed Him.
> Mark 2:14 NKJV

We should retell the stories of the past so that we will not repeat the same terrible mistakes. Stories serve to make us understand who we are. They help us to discover our identity. The Gospels are stories that were retold so that we can see ourselves in them.

The story of Levi teaches us, first of all, who we are. Think of Levi's suprize when Jesus called him. Tax collecting was the work to which the greatest social stigma was attached. Levi, therefore, was not the most loved person around. The Jews thought that tax collectors were unpatriotic, collaborators with the enemies, the oppressors, and, therefore, traitors! Taxes went to the Romans. Parasites, enriching themselves! On a religious level, they were unclean. They were avoided. Spare a thought for the tax collectors!

They also became the oppressed. They were exploited by the people above them and despised by the people below them. But... Levi's past and his background and religious impurity did not prevent Jesus from associating with him. How surprising is the grace of God!

This is our story. Our story is the story of grace despite sin. Let us never forget our story! Then we will also be filled with more mercy when we look at other people.

Lord, thank You for the story of Your grace in my life despite my sin, in Jesus' name. Amen.

February 10

No Spectators Allowed

Therefore God has highly exalted Him and bestowed on Him the name that is above every name...
Philippians 2:9 ESV

A Bredero Festival was held in Amsterdam to commemorate a poet born centuries ago. There were many attractions: 17th century arguments between neighbors, marriages, beggars, a popular civil battle and the hanging of a person on the Grimburg Wall. The interest in the execution was tremendous.

We can easily be spectators of others' pain. Jesus' suffering confirms that God is not a spectator. Jesus entered our need. He took our needs upon Himself and freed us from the powers of sin. However, Paul says more than that. Jesus' suffering eventually culminated in His glorification as Lord over the powers of evil. This is the perspective for our lives and actions. Jesus, who died as a slave, is now Lord. God gave Him a name above all names. Everyone must bow before Him now!

When we discover this gospel, we no longer remain at a safe distance. Everything we do is focused on acknowledging that He is the Lord. When we acknowledge His rule, we look at one another with the attitude of Christ. Mother Teresa said: "It hurt Jesus to love us, for He died on the cross to teach us how to love. And this is the way we too must love: until it hurts."

This is the style of Christians who say, "Jesus Christ is the Lord!"

Lord, teach us to bow before one another because we acknowledge Your rule. *Amen.*

February 11

The Fruit of Wisdom

> Blessed are those who find wisdom, those who
> gain understanding, for she is more profitable than
> silver and yields better returns than gold.
> Proverbs 3:13-14 NIV

What is the most valuable possession you have? Your house, car, marriage, children or investments? We find security in different things—money, possessions or relationships. Yet, the poet discovered that wisdom is more valuable than any precious possession (3:14-15).

What are the advantages of this wisdom? In Solomon's time, it was very concrete. The poet says that people who have wisdom will be blessed with wealth, honor and a long life (3:16). God will protect this peaceful life (3:23-26). It is certain, whoever finds wisdom is like someone who has discovered more than a great treasure.

It sounds very simple. Is life really that simple? I have known people who lived near the Lord but died early. I know people who served the Lord with their possessions and were declared bankrupt.

We know that life is not so simple. And yet it is simple. Jesus the Sinless, suffered innocently. His life shows that not everybody who serves the Lord will experience prosperity, peace and protection. Who served God with more commitment? The good news is that Jesus' innocent suffering secured a much greater blessing than material prosperity. The blessing that we share is more than a long life. It is eternal life. The blessing is more than wealth. It is a treasure in heaven. The blessing is more than a quiet night. It is resting in God.

Jesus Christ, true wisdom of eternity, thank You that I share in all Your blessings, only by grace. *Amen.*

February 12

The Power of Love

Do not envy the violent or choose any of their ways.
Proverbs 3:31 NIV

Power. This word should not be part of the vocabulary of the church of Jesus Christ. It is one of the greatest temptations for every leader. How strange it is to see leaders in churches looking for better and bigger positions! Every time the church and believers have chosen to use power, love went out the back door. Power and love are mutually exclusive!

The poet says that the evil man, the wicked and the arrogant scoffers, are abusing their power. In contrast, those who are humble and have a spirit of wisdom, choose to show love (3:27).

Karl Barth said that God's omnipotence is not power in itself, but the power of love. The only one who has power is the Lord of the church, Jesus Christ. All power belongs to Him who gave up His life and rose from the dead (Matt. 28:18–20). This is the power of His love.

Our response to this love is to love the same way. Our commitment to God is often tested by whether we help those who are hurting (Luke 10:25–37; James 1:27; 1 John 3:16–18). This is the power of love. It requires that we stand next to and with those who suffer hardship and need help.

What power will you use today? The power of love? This is wisdom. The power to control others? It is foolish and wicked.

Lord, let Your love in me have a powerful effect, by the power of Your Spirit. Amen.

February 13

Live by the Spirit

But the fruit of the Spirit is love, joy, peace, forbearance, kindness, goodness, faithfulness, gentleness and self-control. Against such things there is no law...Since we live by the Spirit, let us keep in step with the Spirit.
Galatians 5:22–23, 25 NIV

What happens to you when you read these words? Paul describes the life of a Christian in Galatians 5 as a struggle between our flesh and the Spirit of God. Without the Spirit, the life described in Galatians 5:19-21 (NLT), is quite natural, "...sexual immorality, impurity, lustful pleasures, idolatry, sorcery, hostility, quarreling, jealousy, outbursts of anger, selfish ambition, dissension, division, envy, drunkenness, wild parties, and other sins like these." No one has to go on a course to learn these things. It comes naturally. People who do not have the Spirit of God, do not feel guilty about it. This is life!

When we are under the control of the Spirit, our sinful nature does not disappear from the scene. We keep on struggling with it. We feel guilty when the fruit of the Spirit is not evident in our lives. We want more love, joy, peace, patience, kindness, goodness, faithfulness, gentleness and self-control.

Someone wrote that if moral behavior were simply following rules, we could program a computer to be moral. We are not computers. We live by the Spirit. He creates in us an intense hunger for this fruit in our lives.

Spirit of God, bring our lives under Your control, in Jesus' name.

Amen.

February 14

Revolutionary Love

> Never pay back evil with more evil. Do things in such a way that everyone can see you are honorable. Do all that you can to live in peace with everyone. Dear friends, never take revenge. Leave that to the righteous anger of God…
> Romans 12:17-19 NLT

Jesus would certainly have known that something was wrong in society. Yet He never advocated that a new political regime should be established by force. He came to bring a new revolution, but not a political one.

How often do we see this strategy: burning cars and violent protests, rebel forces and freedom fighters who believe that change through violence is the only solution. Of course, we reject oppressive forces and the emotional, physical, spiritual and political oppression and exploitation of God's people and His creation.

We are to be revolutionary, but our revolution lies on another level. The revolution Jesus had in mind was a radical change of heart. It involved conversion away from selfishness toward the willing service of God and of people in general. Jesus called for the love of our enemies, not their destruction, a readiness to suffer instead of using force, forgiveness instead of hate and revenge.

When we are in the center, our revolution hurts others. When Jesus is the center, our revolution makes room for other people. They love even their enemies. This is the way of the cross.

Lord Jesus Christ, teach us to be as revolutionary as You were by the power of Your Spirit. Amen.

February 15

This Love Can Change the World

> "You have heard that it was said, 'You shall love your neighbor and hate your enemy.' But I say to you, Love your enemies and pray for those who persecute you…"
> Matthew 5:43-44 ESV

Love hurts. Is this true? Should love hurt? On the one hand the answer is "no". Love "is patient, love is kind. It does not envy, it does not boast, it is not proud. It does not dishonor others, it is not self-seeking, it is not easily angered, it keeps no record of wrongs" (1 Cor. 13:4-5 NIV). Love always seeks the best for the other. Even if they have made a mistake, love "bears all things, believes all things, hopes all things, endures all things" (1 Cor. 13:7 NKJV).

Jesus teaches us that we should even love our enemies and pray for them. Love hurts! It means sacrificing yourself. It requires that we should not love in a human way. We need to reflect God's character (Matt. 5:43-48). We often have an attitude of an "eye for an eye" and a "tooth for a tooth". We want revenge. Love hurts because it requires us to be like Jesus. It requires us to take the way of the cross—to crucify ourselves. It hurts!

> Spirit of God, fill us with Your love, so that we shall show it unconditionally, in Jesus' name. *Amen.*

February 16

I Hide with You

The godly will rejoice in the LORD and find shelter in Him.
And those who do what is right will praise Him.
Psalm 64:10 NLT

John Calvin wrote that false statements, blasphemy and slander sometimes do much more harm than physical theft. This kind of theft harms our neighbor's dignity. Therefore, if we obey God, we must uphold our neighbor's dignity.

The poet has experienced this form of theft with the tongue—underhandedness, dishonesty and plotting (64:1-6). It left him vulnerable. He had only one place he could turn to—God. He could only hide in the safest place he knew—God (64:10). He knew that God would ultimately make sure that justice is done (64:7-9). Then people will recognize that those who judge over another's life are not the actual judge.

We are completely vulnerable when other people slander us. Yes, it is not right. People murder our spirit, steal our enthusiasm and vision through their talk, but ultimately, they are not the judges of our lives. Yes, it can spoil our future, but ultimately, it cannot change our destination. Hide with God. Talk to Him. It is the only safe place. He will set things straight!

Lord God, You know how hard I find it when people steal my dignity. Help me, Lord. Amen.

February 17

Tuned into God's Will

> Give careful thought to the paths for your feet and
> be steadfast in all your ways. Do not turn to the
> right or the left; keep your foot from evil.
> Proverbs 4:26-27 NIV

Thomas Merton said that the most dangerous person in the world is the contemplative person who is guided by nobody. Why? Because his own visions are all he trusts. An interior voice attracts him and he will not listen to other people. This person believes that anything that makes him feel warm inside is the will of God. Then he says, "The sweeter and the warmer the feeling is, the more he is convinced of his own infallibility."

Many have compared faith to a pilot who must listen to the voice from the control tower. Although the pilot cannot see the person in the control tower, he must trust the directions. If he does not obey the instructions of the control tower, it can be fatal. Maybe you think that you can live without the instructions of God's control tower. Do you listen to His instructions? What are the main adjustments required to be in tune with God's way?

If you want to walk in God's way, you have to listen to Him. Whoever listens to His advice is preserved from the destructive influences in his or her life (4:23-24). It will prevent you from going through life without direction, by following the evil thoughts in your heart.

Spirit of God, make my ears open so that I will be able to go the way that You show me, instead of my own, in Jesus' name.

Amen.

February 18

The Work of Marriage

Let your wife be a fountain of blessing for you. Rejoice in the wife of your youth...Why be captivated, my son, by an immoral woman, or fondle the breasts of a promiscuous woman?
Proverbs 5:18, 20 NLT

The poet describes the consuming power of desire. It makes us no longer think clearly (5:6, 20). Desire makes it difficult for us to control ourselves (5:23). Jesus says that if we desire someone, we are already guilty of adultery. Extramarital relations have become "normal". We are all exposed to this temptation. This is the path of destruction (5:6, 22-23). Sometimes it leads to huge financial losses and intense emotional struggle (5:10-14).

God created marriage. It is not the creation of governments. Marriage is hard work. Sometimes people believe that they will get better treatment from someone else and it often leads to undesirable relationships. The grass on the other side of the fence is not greener. Do not believe this lie.

The pain caused in your life and the lives of the people around you is something that you will have to carry with you for the rest of your life. John Donne said, "Love built on beauty, soon as beauty, dies." Our spouse is the best place to experience joy and satisfaction. All the privileges and joys of sexuality and security can be found there (5:15-19).

Let us therefore give serious attention to our own marriages and pray that the Lord will build marriages and preserve them.

Father, protect marriages and families and let us work hard to have good families, by the power of Your Spirit. Amen.

February 19

Work Hard

> ...continue to work out your salvation with fear and trembling, for it is God who works in you to will and to act in order to fulfill His good purpose.
> Philippians 2:12-13 NIV

To live as redeemed is our commission. This means that in the midst of a world where the Lord is not acknowledged, we will live in such a way that God's light will be visible (2:15).

How do we do that? We do this by sharing the Word of Life through our actions and by living with integrity (2:15). Yes, we give our life, our whole life, as a sacrifice to God (2:17). However, our commission is embedded in His grace. Our faith, our commitment, our light, our integrity are all thanks to God's amazing grace in our lives. We live for Him because He makes us willing and able to carry out His will (2:13).

There is a unity between the command and the gift. The one cannot do without the other. God does not give something so that we can keep it to ourselves. God does not ask for something He has not given. But never, yes never, is the command something we can fulfill in our own strength. It always rests in the wonderful grace of God. Augustine said: "Give what You command and command what You will." That is why the command is such a serious matter.

Father, give what You ask, and then ask whatever You want.

Amen.

February 20

Judgment Begins at Home

> "Judge not, that you be not judged. For with the judgment you pronounce you will be judged, and with the measure you use it will be measured to you. Why do you see the speck that is in your brother's eye, but do not notice the log that is in your own eye?"
> Matthew 7:1–3 ESV

Do not judge. Is it Jesus' intention that we should in no way judge between right or wrong? Should we just accept that people can do whatever they want to do? Should we be silent about injustice and sin? No. Jesus was quite judgmental. The religious people of His time found His words so offensive that they organized a whole campaign to get rid of Him.

What did Jesus mean then? All judgment begins with us. Before we are able to see the splinter in someone else's life, we must first see if we are not guilty of something much worse. Jesus challenged His followers not to make a mockery of our judgment of the sins of others.

We have the task to see what sin is and to judge sin. Yet, as Thomas á Kempis said, we seldom weigh our neighbor in the same balance with ourselves. When we measure others' lives, we must be prepared to meet the same standards. Are we willing to do it?

> Lord, enable me to consider other people with more love and humility, for the sake of the honor of Your name. *Amen.*

February 21

Don't Let Judgment Harm God's Cause

*"Do not give what is holy to the dogs;
nor cast your pearls before swine…"*
Matthew 7:6 NKJV

Don't judge me! Judgment, or so some people think, is against the Bible. People would quote Matthew 7:1 (NIV), which says, "Do not judge, or you too will be judged."

We judge when we gossip. We judge when we think we are better than other people. We judge when we withhold our love. Judgment is like mud against a clean wall. It may not stick to the wall, but it does leave a mark. Before you judge your friend, first stand in his shoes.

Should we not judge at all? It is unavoidable, but Jesus immediately adds two requirements. Firstly, would we be able to live according to the standards that we set for others? When we judge, the same standards apply to us (7:2)! Secondly, we need to examine ourselves. Maybe we first need to deal with the sin in our lives before we try to help others (7:3-5). Benjamin Franklin rightly said, "Clean your finger, before you point at my spots."

Followers of Jesus should behave in such a way that the dogs and the pigs (symbolic of those who do not know God) are unable to point fingers at us. Judging each other without dealing with our own sin and not living up to the same standards we set for others, is throwing our lives, along with God, before their feet to be trampled upon.

Lord, let my conduct be to Your honor, in Jesus' name. Amen.

February 22

The Same Rules for Everyone

"For in the same way you judge others, you will be judged, and with the measure you use, it will be measured to you."
Matthew 7:2 NIV

Some psychologists say that conflict between a parent and a child is often the result of a similar personality in the parent and the child. The child that is most like us is often the child whom we criticize most!

We should examine our own hearts because those things that bother you about others, may also be present in yourself.

We all know how easy it is to judge others. If people do not act the way we want them to, they are wrong. We are right. So, we all have a list ready according to which we judge others' actions. It is either right or wrong!

What would happen if the Lord took that same list and said, "Well, let us test your life against the demands and rules you made for your children, your friends and enemies"? Jesus says that we should prepare ourselves for this kind of thing to happen! The requirements or measuring instruments that we apply to the lives of others will be the same that God will apply to our lives. It is not unfair. It is not ridiculous or spiteful. We wanted others—our children, parents, colleagues, friends, husband or wife—to comply with it!

When you honestly look in the mirror of God's Word, will you be kinder in your judgment of others?

Lord, forgive me for Christ's sake, because I am just as broken as those whom I criticize. Amen.

February 23

Sharing Love, Sharing Hope!

> Hope does not put us to shame, because God's
> love has been poured into our hearts through
> the Holy Spirit who has been given to us.
> Romans 5:5 ESV

Some days are good. We cope well. Other days are bad and then we just need a lot of support. H. F. Kohlbrugge asked why the Holy Spirit is called our Comforter. He said it's because He transfers those who long for God out of their hellish existence and dark prison to the sweet light of grace and gives the right word at the right time. This is grace.

The Holy Spirit is the instrument of certainty and grace in our lives. This is what Paul means when he says that God has poured out His love into our hearts through the Holy Spirit. The love that has been poured out in our hearts by the Holy Spirit is not a mystery. It is described virtually verse after verse (5:1-11). It is *God's* love that is poured out in our hearts. This love is the *peace* He gives us (5:1), the *free access*, the *acquittal* of *sinners* on the basis of the atoning death of Christ (5:6-10).

We have hope in times of trouble. God loved us before we could love Him. God chose us before we could make a choice for Him. The Holy Spirit is therefore like someone who hands out wonderful news and lets us share in God's unconditional, indescribable and boundless love.

Spirit of God, thank You for the good news I so desperately need today. Amen.

February 24

All People Should Praise Him

*Praise the LORD, all you nations; extol Him, all you peoples.
For great is His love toward us, and the faithfulness
of the LORD endures forever. Praise the LORD.*
Psalm 117:1-2 NIV

My mom used to ask me two questions every night: Did you brush your teeth? Did you read the Bible and pray? Neither of these things is something that children like to do. If I forgot to read the Bible, Psalm 117 was usually my choice. Why? Well, that's because it's the shortest chapter in the Bible.

Little did I know that Psalm 117 has very rich perspectives. First of all, it is a call to praise the Lord. This call is all-encompassing. All nations should praise the Lord. No one is excluded. The Lord revealed Himself especially to Israel. It was especially His people who had to bring praise to Him. Now, all nations are included.

Secondly, this is not a general call to praise God. The reason is given: God's love and faithfulness. These words are a brief summary of the entire history of God's involvement with the people of Israel. This involvement is that God decided to commit Himself to people by grace. It begins with the covenant with Abraham and runs throughout the Exodus from Egypt, the entry into the Promised Land, and all the other saving deeds of God—all the way to our Savior, Jesus Christ.

God saves not just for our sake, He saves so that all people would praise God for it.

Lord, grant that all nations will rejoice in the salvation that You bring. Amen.

February 25

In Step

> Since we live by the Spirit, let us keep in step with the Spirit.
> Galatians 5:25 NIV

John Livingstone said that we should let God be our only rule, Christ our only hope, the Holy Spirit our only guide, and the glory of God our only end. John Livingstone was a minister of a congregation in Ireland about 400 years ago. It is the same congregation I served in as a minister for over ten years. It made me think about the emphasis of some of the Reformers: *sola gratia* (only grace), *solus Christus* (only Christ), *sola Scriptura* (only Scripture) and *sola fide* (only faith). Not us—God should get all the honor. To God alone be all the honor—*soli Deo gloria*!

The Old Testament emphasizes that we should love the Lord our God above all things (Deut. 6:4–5). There is no other God apart from Him. He is the only true God. Jesus, admired by all religions, said that His highest purpose in life is to do the will of His Father in heaven (John 4:34).

To glorify God means to be guided by the Spirit of God. He leads us to a life of love, joy, peace, patience, kindness, goodness, faithfulness, gentleness and self-control (Gal. 5:22–23). Is there a better order in life? He loves us and guides us. Walking in step with Him will bring glory to Him and a meaningful life for us.

> Lord, free us from ourselves so that we can learn that Your guidance and rule is the best for our lives and the lives of those around us, in Jesus' name. *Amen.*

February 26

Laziness

Go to the ant, you sluggard; consider its ways and be wise!
Proverbs 6:6 NIV

My generation grew up with the idea that we have to work hard. There was no time for playing games.

There are many lazy people. Paul says that if someone does not work, he or she cannot eat (2 Thess. 3:6-10). All of us are sometimes guilty of having "a little sleep, a little slumber, a little folding of the hands to rest" (Prov. 6:10). Should we expect that anything can happen by itself? No, a lazy person cannot expect success.

Lazy people are inferior to even the smallest creature. What do ants do? Ants instinctively know that they must take precautions for the bad times. They collect food. Do they need constant motivation and bonuses? Do they need a manager to motivate and encourage them all the time? No, "It has no commander, no overseer or ruler, yet it stores its provisions in summer and gathers its food at harvest" (6:7-8).

Whoever confesses that Christ is the Lord works not only to make good provision for the future. Our motivation is different. We are in service of Christ, our Lord. We work not to be seen by people, but for the sake of His honor (Col. 3:22-24). This is our calling.

Holy Spirit, make me hardworking and faithful in the work You have given me, in Jesus' name. Amen.

February 27

Making Yourself Poor

> Therefore disaster will overtake him in an instant;
> he will suddenly be destroyed—without remedy.
> Proverbs 6:15 NIV

Poverty—there is no shortage of it in the world. From Proverbs it is very clear that people are the main cause of poverty.

Firstly, we can impoverish ourselves by putting up security for others. We can impede our own ability to help others when we take responsibility for debt in an irresponsible way. However, this is not a warning against helping people in need (6:1-5). God hates it when we harm our neighbor (6:16-19).

Secondly, we can impoverish ourselves by being lazy. Paul says that we must work hard, then we will have something to give to the poor (Eph. 4:28).

Thirdly, people can end up in poverty if we purposely make them poor. If we pay our workers too little or intentionally deceive them, we steal from our neighbor. If we do this, we should not expect anything good (Prov. 6:12-15). The fall will come. It is certain. God warns us through His Word that this fall may be permanent. There might be no remedy.

John Chrysostom remarked that feeding the hungry is a greater work than raising the dead. Followers of Jesus are always looking for the benefit of others. The last judgment in Matthew 25:31-46 emphasizes this one thought: How we treat our fellow human beings is how we have dealt with Christ.

Spirit of God, teach me good judgment, so that I can serve others with my energy, goods and gifts, in Jesus' name. Amen.

February 28

The Right Attitude

*All the others care only for themselves and
not for what matters to Jesus Christ.*
Philippians 2:21 NLT

What is your *attitude*? It is a word that is often used in various forms in this letter. Sometimes it is "one mind" and sometimes the *attitude* of Christ.

Paul is referring here to an attitude of Timothy and Epaphroditus. Epaphroditus risked his life to help Paul (2:30). When he visited Paul, probably on behalf of the congregation, Epaphroditus became very ill. After God healed him, Paul sent him back to the congregation. Timothy, who is now on his way to the congregation, is also someone with the right attitude (2:20). This attitude is described as that of Jesus Christ (2:21).

These two people are examples of what Paul already described in Philippians 2:1-5. They show the attitude of Christ. We should not push our way to the front of the queue. Let others go before you. Think of others before you think of yourself. Two people whose lifestyle testifies to this are on their way to the congregation in Philippi.

What is your attitude? If your congregation wanted to send someone who understands this, would it be you? We who are comforted by Christ and understand His love for us, follow Christ in His footsteps. He gives us the strength to do so. This is how the world sees that Christ really makes a difference.

Spirit of Christ, fill me with the attitude of Christ. *Amen.*

February 29

Are We Different?

> Of course, your former friends are surprised when you no longer plunge into the flood of wild and destructive things they do. So they slander you.
>
> 1 Peter 4:4 NLT

The difference between Christians and non-Christians is vague. Is a person who has Christian "values" and Christian "convictions" necessarily a Christian? If someone belongs to a church, does it mean that he or she is a Christian?

It is a fact that the readers of Peter's letter often experienced verbal abuse and were pushed aside by the society in which they lived. Why? Because they were Christians. They were different. Previously, they were pagans (4:3). Now their lifestyle is so different that people could clearly see it. Peter's readers experienced abuse and marginalization because they did not "plunge into the flood of wild and destructive things they do" (4:4). When we break with sin, it does not only require separating oneself from sinful human desires, but also from the company of the sinful.

The psalmist speaks about this difference in Psalm 1. It is when people do not go with the flow of the wicked, sinners and mockers, but are planted in the Word of God.

I wonder if it is still the case with us. Are we so genuinely Christian that people notice us? Are we subject to slander and gossip because our lives differ so much from our confession as Christians?

Spirit of God, make us different from the world, in Jesus' name.

Amen.

March

March 1

The Program of Ministry

> Jesus went throughout Galilee...proclaiming the
> good news of the kingdom, and healing every
> disease and sickness among the people.
> Matthew 4:23 NIV

The ministry and atoning work of Christ show that God said no to suffering. Matthew says that Jesus' ministry consisted of two basic elements, namely preaching and miracles, which included the healing of people. Jesus healed sickness and pain, cast out demons, and fed hungry people. His ministry improved people's quality of life.

His atoning work also shows that God is opposed to the death and sorrow that result from sin. By His death He atones for the sin He did not cause. Through His resurrection, He overcomes death, which was not part of God's good creation. When Paul speaks of the atonement of our sins and the victory over evil, he does not separate the two aspects (Col. 2:14–15). What Jesus did shows how holistic God's act of salvation is. It is not just a "spiritual" liberation, but includes dealing with everyday realities like cancer, viruses, heart disease and death.

So God says no to suffering and death. Let us join with God in the fight against suffering and death in the world by supporting medical research, praying for doctors and nurses, starting to improve the quality of life of children, poor people and those who have been pushed to the margins of life. This is what following Jesus means.

Father, give me a passion for improving the quality of life of those who need it today, in Jesus' name. Amen.

March 2

Prepared to Suffer

> "Students are not greater than their teacher, and slaves are not greater than their master...And since I, the master of the household, have been called the prince of demons, the members of my household will be called by even worse names!"
>
> Matthew 10:24–25 NLT

To follow Jesus is to walk where He walked, to say what He said and to do what He did. What happened to Jesus will also happen to His followers.

Followers of Jesus continue His ministry here on earth (10:7-8). When we proclaim the gospel of the kingdom of God and help all people in every form of need, not everybody will like it. Jesus' ministry, His undivided love for the kingship of His Father, His passion to touch the lives of every person, and His compassion for those who were marginalized are part of the Christian life. How can we divide our lives into compartments and think that there are some areas where we would rather not use the name of Jesus?

Jesus says in Matthew 10 that we will be hated by everyone for the sake of His name because we associate with Him—even by closest family members. Following Jesus will not always be easy, but a student is not above his teacher...

Are you on board?

Lord, use me in Your service more and more, in Jesus' name.

Amen.

March 3

Loyalty to Jesus or Something Else?

"I am sending you out like sheep among wolves...But when they arrest you, do not worry about what to say or how to say it. At that time you will be given what to say, for it will not be you speaking, but the Spirit of your Father speaking through you."
Matthew 10:16, 19–20 NIV

Martin Luther wrote in one of his sermons that living in the kingdom of God is to be in the midst of your enemies. When we want to be among friends, we should sit among roses and lilies—not with the bad people but the devout people.

Jesus reminds us that we will be persecuted for the sake of His name (10:16-18). Loyalty to Jesus Christ will even divide families (10:21, 36-38). The words of Jesus are shocking, "You will be hated by everyone because of Me, but the one who stands firm to the end will be saved" (10:22 NIV). It is no surprise that people will treat believers this way (10:25)—after all, Jesus was killed!

However, Jesus also gives comfort. He gives His Spirit so that we can say what is necessary in these circumstances. He also says, "Are not two sparrows sold for a penny? Yet not one of them will fall to the ground outside your Father's care. And even the very hairs of your head are all numbered. So don't be afraid; you are worth more than many sparrows" (10:29-31 NIV).

Lord, make us faithful to You in all circumstances, for the sake of Jesus Christ. *Amen.*

March 4

He Remembers You

> "Are not two sparrows sold for a copper coin? And not one of them falls to the ground apart from your Father's will."
>
> Matthew 10:29 NKJV

Is everything that happens in this world God's will? I am sure that our common sense would say, "No!" So many atrocities in history were the result of despotic leaders, racist attitudes, ethnic cleansing and plain cruelty.

One terrible misconception that exists is that everything that happens is God's will. One of the verses in the Bible that is often quoted to confirm this is Matthew 10:29, namely that no sparrow will fall to the ground without it being the Father's will. Unfortunately, this verse has been mistranslated in many translations. The Greek text does not have the word "will". It says that no sparrow will fall to the earth without the Father knowing about it.

Luke writes something different: "Are not five sparrows sold for two pennies? Yet not one of them is forgotten by God" (Luke 12:6 NIV). In short, God is there when the sparrow falls. God does not forget the sparrow. God does not cause the sparrow to fall or even allow it to fall. However, He is present with the sparrow—and with us—when we suffer.

It makes a huge difference to the way we think about suffering. If God does not forget sparrows in their suffering and death, He will definitely remember us! Where is God when I suffer? The Bible says that God stands by you and will not let you down.

Thank You, Lord, that You do not forget us when we suffer, in Jesus' name. *Amen.*

March 5

Error in Judgment

Free yourself, like a gazelle from the hand of the hunter, like a bird from the snare of the fowler.
Proverbs 6:5 NIV

Emotions can sometimes be good, but sometimes very dangerous. Sometimes my reason can be positively influenced by my emotions so that I make a good decision with my heart. But sometimes my emotions can negatively affect my capacity to make reasonable decisions.

The poet emphasizes how we often plunge ourselves into the biggest mess by our own doing. We can provide surety for someone and then be captured in a net like a bird. We can make promises to someone and then be trapped like a gazelle in the hand of a hunter (6:5). By providing surety for someone who cannot repay their debt, it might happen that we land up in the power of someone else and have to carry the burden of other people (6:3).

What should we do when we plunge ourselves into trouble? The poet says that we should admit it to the person involved. It is the only way to get rid of the burden. Maybe we will find a gracious person.

We read about such a person in Matthew 18. It refers to God. He wrote off our debt unconditionally. If we call ourselves Christians, we should also be prepared to write off others' debts. Maybe we will also find someone who is willing to excuse us for our error in judgment and who would be willing to write off our financial debt.

Lord, keep me sober in my mind that I would not destroy myself through errors in judgment, in Jesus' name. Amen.

March 6

In the Center

*But they will be destroyed suddenly, broken in
an instant beyond all hope of healing.*
Proverbs 6:15 NLT

"I am the Lord my God! I am in the center of my world. There is no room for others." This is what is written in Proverbs 6:12-19. It sounds like the Ten Commandments' second table. Nearly all of it is there. Fraud and lies are the main course on this menu (6:12-14, 17, 19). Everything is geared towards hurting a fellow human being and to do things that will benefit oneself. This is why the poet describes it as proud and malicious behavior (6:17-18). This behavior has one purpose: to break relationships between people (6:18-19).

This person is called wicked and a troublemaker (6:12). He has lost his way and has evil intentions in his heart (6:18). He is a fool. Do not think of your neighbor or the colleague at work. If one of *our* actions is on this list, *we* are guilty of everything. The violation of one commandment is disobedience to all (James 2:10-12).

This passage challenges us with the way Christians are supposed to go, because we follow Jesus. Not us, but Christ is the center of our lives by His Spirit. Not our interests, but the interests of our fellow human beings are the most important (Phil. 2:3-4). Where love rules, there is no will to power.

Lord, let me promote reconciliation and justice through my actions, by the power of Your Spirit. Amen.

March 7

It Is Not about Me

*You must have the same attitude that Christ Jesus had.
Though He was God, He did not think of equality
with God as something to cling to.*
Philippians 2:5-6 NLT

It was 1986 and I had just been appointed as minister in a rural town about 800 km from the place where I grew up. It was a dry and dusty town, far away from my beloved Table Mountain. I missed the beautiful surroundings of my student town of Stellenbosch with its mountains and vineyards. I asked myself: *What am I doing here? How long will I have to stay here?*

I was preparing a series of sermons. The passage was Philippians 2. As I read it, I could sense that the Spirit of God was speaking to me about one of the biggest issues in my life. I was moaning while I was reading that Christ made Himself nothing and became like a servant. I was reluctant to be where I was, while I read verse 8 (NLT): "He humbled Himself in obedience to God and died a criminal's death on a cross."

The church does not need brilliant personalities but faithful servants of Jesus and the fellow believers. It is not about us, but about Him.

Lord, teach me every day that it is never about me but always about You, by the power of Your Spirit. Amen.

March 8

Will the World Be a Better Place?

> ...so that no one can criticize you. Live clean, innocent
> lives as children of God, shining like bright lights in
> a world full of crooked and perverse people.
> Philippians 2:15 NLT

Someone remarked that we should be the change we would like to see in the world. The philosopher Immanuel Kant said that we should act in such a way that the principle of our deeds can very safely be made a law for the whole world. Wow! I wonder what the world would look like if my lifestyle was made a law by which others had to live! Would this be a better or worse place?

We can complain and be unhappy about the deteriorating values and morals of the world, but change starts with us. Using Paul's image about stars, we see how bright stars shine when it is very dark. Since we live in a dark world, our lives should be so different that people can see the light through us.

If you could, what would you do to change the world? Should the political, economic and moral-ethical systems change? Should our family change? Should our marriages change? What about our workplace or school or congregation?

Maybe we cannot change the whole world, but let's set ourselves the goal of living today as if God is going to make our lives, our priorities, our values and principles the rule for the society in which we live. Will the world be a better place if everyone lives like you?

Lord, let my life with You be like a shining star in the darkness around us, in Jesus' name. Amen.

March 9

God's Power in Jesus

> While Jesus was still speaking, some people came from the house of Jairus, the synagogue leader. "Your daughter is dead," they said. "Why bother the Teacher anymore?" Overhearing what they said, Jesus told him, "Don't be afraid; just believe."
>
> Mark 5:35-36 NIV

The story in Mark 5:21-43 is like a sandwich. It starts with a request that Jesus should please come to a sick girl, the daughter of Jairus, a Jewish leader. It ends with the astonishing miracle that Jesus raises the dead.

Between the two "slices" of the sandwich, we find another story. It is a strange one. A woman with a chronic disease that would make anyone who touches her unclean, realizes that there is only one way out—Jesus' healing power.

He also has the power to raise someone from the dead. It is this authoritative Christ, the One with power over disease and death that takes time out on His journey towards urgent business to help someone. It is God in Jesus who turns around and pays attention to people who are most desperate. He was her only hope. Likewise, Jesus is the only hope of Jairus and his family. It seems that all is lost when Jesus tarries, but because He is the Son of God, it is not. He alone has power over life and death.

Like the woman who trusted Him, Jesus calls Jairus to keep believing, even if it all seems hopeless. Every reader of this story should hear the call to trust Christ, the authoritative Son of God.

I trust You, Jesus, Son of God, even when everything seems lost.

Amen.

March 10

He Guides Well

He leads me beside peaceful streams...He guides me along right paths, bringing honor to His name.
Psalm 23:2-3 NLT

Martin Luther once said, "I know not the way God leads me, but well do I know my Guide. "This is one of the main themes of this psalm. Knowing the Guide well will enable you to follow Him today without fear.

A friend told me that he often takes people on hikes. He asks the people to follow him, otherwise they might get lost. Sometimes, he deliberately takes a longer road to see what they do, while there was clearly an easier way. They followed him because they trusted him. They knew that if they did not follow him and trust him, they would not reach their destination.

The psalmist speaks of his trust in the Lord. The Lord is like a shepherd leading His sheep to the best places so that they can be best cared for. He walks out in front of them and with the stick in His hand, He protects them from wild animals and danger. The sheep run after Him, not knowing where they are going to end up.

Jesus said that He is the Good Shepherd. He guides us to an abundant life in Him. Even more, He protects us in such a way that nothing can snatch us from our Father's hands (John 10:28). Our final destination is eternal life!

Lord, let me follow and trust in You, the Guide of our lives.

Amen.

March 11

Safe in God's Hands

Yea, though I walk through the valley of the shadow of death, I will fear no evil; for You are with me; Your rod and Your staff, they comfort me.
Psalm 23:4 NKJV

Someone once said that when the path of life is steep, you should remember to keep your mind straight. Yes, the danger is that one can completely lose perspective if things go wrong. We may come to a point when we feel that life is not worth living. Sometimes it is the result of circumstances beyond our control.

Sometimes it is our own fault. We may feel that we have become unfaithful to the Lord because we just don't have the energy to pray. It makes us feel even worse about ourselves. We should trust God, but it is hard to do so.

The dark depths of our lives do not have the last say. Whether we can hold on to God is not the deciding factor in times of suffering. Sometimes we have to understand the more important truth: God will not let us fall out of His hands. Faith is to know that God holds onto us. Faith is to know that we are safe in God's hands. When we know this, our focus is right. He is our Shepherd, our Comrade, our Guide.

Your thinking can only stay the same on the steep path of life when you know that God is holding you even though things are completely messed up.

Thank You, Lord, that no matter how dark the depths are, we are safe in Your hands. Amen.

March 12

Satan, Sin and Self

So I find this law at work: Although I want to do good, evil is right there with me...What a wretched man I am! Who will rescue me from this body that is subject to death? Thanks be to God, who delivers me through Jesus Christ our Lord!
Romans 7:21, 24-25 NIV

Someone wrote that there is an unholy "trinity" in our lives—Satan, sin and self. To be liberated from this "trinity" is God's grace. We rejoice in Jesus Christ. He saved us from this oppressive regime! This does not mean that we are left on our own again. The Christian journey is increasing in dependence. We realize more and more that Jesus, and only Jesus, is our hope and salvation.

As we grow we will not necessarily be happier. The opposite is true. It may mean greater unhappiness. Why? As we grow, we become more sensitive to our brokenness and sin. We become more aware of the distance that separates us from the ideal, from what we should be. Therefore, we become more unhappy in ourselves. Sin becomes a much bigger issue for us. Guilt weighs much heavier on us.

It sounds very pessimistic, however, this is not the final word. When we come to God with all of this, we find new strength to fight the battle of life, sure of the final victory. Thus, we know our past. We know the present struggle. However, we also know that the victory is won! We have the strength to fight because Jesus walks with us on our journey towards the final victory.

Lord, thank You for the certainty of victory through Jesus Christ our Lord. Amen.

March 13

He Speaks to Me

*For their command is a lamp and their instruction
a light; their corrective discipline is the way to life.*
Proverbs 6:23 NLT

When we read all the consequences of sin in the book of Proverbs, we should realize the need to sit at the feet of wisdom and learn from history. God warns us about the unhappiness that we can experience because of our disobedience.

The clear warning against the temptation to commit adultery is a timely warning. Over the centuries, this lifestyle destroyed many people's lives. To succumb to the temptation of extramarital sexual temptation is to play deliberately with your life (6:25-29, 32). It does not only cause tremendous stress for the other spouse (6:33-35). It also shows how self-destructive our desires can be (7:22-23). This is why the poet pleads, as he has already done (2:16-19; 5:1-13), that we should not ignore the life experience of the teacher. The wisdom teacher saw these things happening.

Please accept today that God has good intentions for your life. He knows what is best for you. God gave us His Word. His Word is a light for our path and a lamp for our feet (Ps. 119:105). Trust the guidance He is giving you. Jesus, the Word of God, is the Vine and we are the branches (John 15:1-8). If we remain in Him, we will bear the right fruit.

Lord, thank You for the light of Your Word. Enable me to obey it, in Jesus' name. Amen.

March 14

Wisdom Brings Life

For those who find me find life and receive favor from the LORD.
Proverbs 8:35 NIV

Today, we have two options: either succumb to temptation, which leads to death (8:36), or listen to wisdom and find life.

How do you find wisdom? It is a gift from God (2:6). This gift requires that we realize that we only truly live once we serve the Lord. We live when we turn our back on all that is bad (8:13). We live once we discover that God's wisdom is worth more than anything else (8:10-11).

For Christians this means that we have found eternal life in Jesus Christ, the Wisdom of God. Of course, eternal life is not only the life that awaits us in the future. It also means to experience new life in Christ and to live this life. In Christ we indeed find all the hidden treasures of wisdom (Col. 2:3).

For us as Christians, wisdom means to recognize Him as the only Lord in our life. So, Paul says, "For this reason, since the day we heard about you, we have not stopped praying for you. We continually ask God to fill you with the knowledge of His will through all the wisdom and understanding that the Spirit gives, so that you may live a life worthy of the Lord and please Him in every way: bearing fruit in every good work, growing in the knowledge of God." (Col. 1:9-10 NIV).

Lord, thank You for the abundant life we have through Jesus.

Amen.

March 15

Jesus, All for Jesus

"Most assuredly, I say to you, you seek Me, not because you saw the signs, but because you ate of the loaves and were filled."
John 6:26 NKJV

In John 6:28-29 (NLT), the people ask Jesus, "'We want to perform God's works, too. What should we do?' Jesus told them, This is the only work God wants from you: Believe in the One He has sent.'"

William Barclay, in his commentary on John's gospel, wrote that the crowd that followed Christ wished to use Him for their plans, dreams and purposes. People want Christ's gifts without Christ's cross. What is in our minds, he says, is to use Christ instead of allowing Him to use us.

To believe in Jesus is to follow Him where He leads us unreservedly. It means to follow the way of the cross. On this journey, our will and dreams become subject to His will.

A few centuries ago, Bernard of Clairvaux described different degrees of love. At first, we love ourselves for our own sake. Then we love God for our own benefit. After that, we love God for the sake of God Himself. The fourth degree is when we love ourselves for God's sake. At this point, our will dissolves in His will like a drop of water poured into wine loses itself.

People follow Jesus for different reasons, but mostly for the benefit it has for themselves. Is it all for Jesus, or is it about us?

Bread of Life, let me eat the bread of Your will. *Amen.*

March 16

Our Greatest Ambition

*It has always been my ambition to preach
the gospel where Christ was not known.*
Romans 15:20 NIV

Christianity has become such a general concept. It says almost nothing. Many people claim to be Christians, but they have no concern for the message and teaching of Christ. There are congregations with large investments and beautiful church buildings. In some cases, they achieved this because they looked after themselves very well. For some pastors and members of the congregation, it is a great honor to serve in such a church.

Is this what Christianity means? No. When we listen to Paul, he has an intense desire that people who do not know Christ, should come to know Him. For many of us living in comfortable "Christian" societies, it is inconceivable that there could be people in the world who have never heard of Jesus. In each town there are one or more churches with one or more pastors. Sunday after Sunday people go to church and day after day we hear the gospel on the radio or the internet. We have a Bible in our own language. Yet there are still thousands of unreached peoples in the world. These people need the good news of God's grace in Jesus. We have the ability to reach them.

Should this not be our biggest ambition—to help the gospel be preached where people have not yet heard of Christ? This is why we are Christians! This is our passion!

Spirit of God, use me to let Your light shine in the darkness of unbelief, in Jesus' name. *Amen.*

March 17

New Beginnings

> Again the Israelites did evil in the eyes of the LORD...
> The angel of the LORD appeared to her and said,
> "You are barren and childless, but you are going
> to become pregnant and give birth to a son."
> Judges 13:1, 3 NIV

Augustine remarked centuries ago, "It is not that we keep His commandments first, and then that He loves; but that He loves us, and then we keep His commandments." This grace is revealed to the humble, but hidden from the proud.

Samson's story begins with the suffering of Israel because of their sins. There is not a single trace of remorse, repentance, sadness or prayer to the Lord. In spite of this, God brings salvation and liberation through Samson, the broken man.

The story of the birth of Samson reminds us that God gives a new beginning by His grace. God alone should get the honor for our salvation.

The Lord remains faithful, even when we are unfaithful. Eventually He sends His Son to a world that does not recognize Him (John 1:11). This is the story of the gospel of Jesus Christ. When we were powerless, Paul says, Jesus died for the ungodly. He did not wait for us to become righteous, instead He died for His enemies (Rom. 5:6–10).

God gave a new beginning with the story of Samson. He gives a new beginning to you today. Forget about yesterday and live for Him today!

> How great is Your grace, O Lord! Deliver us from evil, in the name of Jesus Christ. *Amen.*

March 18

Black Swans

*Praise be to the God...the Father of compassion and the God
of all comfort, who comforts us in all our troubles, so
that we can comfort those in any trouble with the
comfort we ourselves receive from God.*
2 Corinthians 1:3-4 NIV

These days we hear of so-called "black swans". This refers to radical and unexpected changes that have a massive impact on society—emotionally, economically and politically. COVID-19 is a good example. When I arrived in Namibia at the beginning of the 1990s, our congregation reached out to churches in South Africa with a project called 2 Corinthians 1:4. We wanted to help people to know that God is with His church amid radical changes. We could comfort them with the comfort God gave us. We could tell them that God is in control.

We can be grateful when we have experienced hardships. We do not choose for radical and unexpected changes, but when we look back on it, we sometimes understand more about God, ourselves and other people.

Paul also looks back on his suffering and finds meaning in it. He now understands better how to encourage others because God encouraged him in difficult circumstances. Someone writes that to suffer is to know many languages—it gives the suffering person access to many people.

I know that suffering is not pleasant, but when we suffer, we may find meaning in it. Perhaps we are thus learning the language to assist others in their suffering.

Lord, use my suffering in Your service, so that others may be comforted by it, for the sake of Jesus Christ. *Amen.*

March 19

Respect

Show proper respect to everyone...fear God, honor the emperor.
1 Peter 2:17 NIV

Those in power want people to recognize them and even pray for them irrespective of the way they represent the interests of all citizens. A former South African president while at a church conference said that the Bible has a message for the governments and governed of the world. Thus, he said, we read in Romans 13 that every person should be subject to the governing authorities. There is no authority except from God. Rulers are not a terror to good conduct, but to bad conduct. He explained that we should do what is good, and we will receive the approval of the ruler who is God's servant for our good.

Should we honor those in power even if we strongly disagree with their actions? Peter wrote to people who did not live under a Christian government. The Christians were a small minority in society. Discrimination against them was part of their lives. Yet, Peter, the Jew, does not call his readers to oppose the Roman authorities. Rather, he emphasizes that it is God's will to be subject to every human authority.

It is difficult, especially when the authorities are corrupt, often do stupid things, and do not properly punish the people who do wrong. Yet we must continue to obey the authorities, because we are not citizens of our country in the first place. We are foreigners and strangers—without rights. We are citizens of heaven! Therefore, we act as citizens of God's kingdom. This will make people realize that the Lord is alive (2:12).

Lord, bless all in authority today, in Jesus' name. Amen.

March 20

So Many Standards!

Fear of the LORD is the foundation of wisdom. Knowledge of the Holy One results in good judgment.
Proverbs 9:10 NLT

There are so many voices in the world claiming to be the truth. It is so hard to distinguish between right and wrong.

Wisdom has to be learned. We learn it in relationship with God. We should listen to the Word of Wisdom (9:1-6). When we are attentive to the voice of the Lord, it will teach us steadily to distinguish between the many voices of the world and make the right decisions. If we don't listen, we have no understanding (9:13-18).

Paul emphasizes it when he says that we can discern the will of God when we surrender ourselves to God. In surrendering to Him, He renews our minds (Rom. 12:2). Then we shall experience life as a feast with God, "Wisdom…calls from the highest point of the city, 'Let all who are simple come to my house!' To those who have no sense she says, 'Come, eat my food and drink the wine I have mixed'" (Prov. 9:1-5 NIV).

Augustine was right, "For there is a joy which is not given to the ungodly, but to those who love Thee for Thine own sake, whose joy Thou Thyself art. And this is the happy life, to rejoice to Thee, of Thee, for Thee; this is it, and there is no other."

Thank You, Lord, that You bring me to the right understanding by the power of Your Spirit. Amen.

March 21

Give Him the Glory

Lazy hands make for poverty, but diligent hands bring wealth.
Proverbs 10:4 NIV

The "Proverbs of Solomon" are from Proverbs 10 to 22:6. Earlier in the book, faithfulness in our daily activities was emphasized (6:6-11). The author of this group of proverbs makes it clear that people who do not work, could eventually become poor.

There is not always a link between poverty and laziness, or between wealth and hard work. We can get possessions through injustice (10:2). Yet, a wise man works hard. Others try shortcuts to get rich quickly. These shortcuts sometimes include exploitation of others. No, there must be a fair balance between our work and the income we receive.

However, wealth is not primarily the product of hard work. The poet says that wealth is in the last instance a gift from God (10:22). If He does not bless us, we can toil as much as we like, but we will not prosper. Without God's blessing, we cannot make fair, good decisions or have the energy to work. He should get the honor for every blessing in our lives. It is not our deserved reward.

Thank Him today for every blessing, every piece of bread and every cup of water. Then, as Samuel M. Shoemaker once wrote, work will have a different meaning, "When we begin to look upon work, business, money, as potential sacraments through which God can work, we shall make better use of them."

God bless me with strength, wisdom and health to do my work in Your service and to Your glory. Amen.

March 22

My Biggest Desire

What is more, I consider everything a loss because of the surpassing worth of knowing Christ Jesus my Lord, for whose sake I have lost all things. I consider them garbage.
Philippians 3:8 NIV

Nikolaus Ludwig count von Zinzendorf's words are well known: "I have but one passion: It is He, it is He alone." These words express something of what Paul also writes here.

Paul could have stepped into the high positions at any Jewish company. He has the right background. He also met every possible religious requirement of the Jews (3:4-6).

Now his energy is channeled in another direction. In the past, external things mattered. People had to be circumcised first before they could belong to God's people (3:2). After the Lord took possession of his life, he no longer served God with outward appearances, but in the Spirit (3:3). This means that the Spirit now lives in his life and has awakened in him this passion—to get to know Christ better (3:8).

What are you set on? Does it matter to you where you come from, what your background is and how long you have been serving in the church? Are you perhaps spiritually arrogant because you are important in the church and society? No more wasting your energy on unnecessary things! Christ has set us free from outward things. It is all garbage!

Spirit of God, fill me with an overriding desire to know You better.
Amen.

March 23

Arrested by God

*Not that I have already attained, or am already perfected;
but I press on, that I may lay hold of that for which
Christ Jesus has also laid hold of me.*
Philippians 3:12 NKJV

We are often chained to the past. This can include the "good old days", but also our past failures. Paul thinks about both these issues. He had a good reputation and was passionate about his heritage. However, he says that God "laid hold of" him. It happened on the road to Damascus while he was still persecuting people who believed in Jesus. All the things he had done in the name of his religion—arresting them and approving their killings—must have been a massive burden. But all the things of the past were taken care of and God forgave him. He is now on a new journey. He lives in the present and knows that he will reach the goal that God has set before him. He leaves the past behind him.

What makes you feel sick? Your past and failures? There are an awful lot of people who get sick because they keep thinking about the things that went wrong in their lives. They are anxious about the future because they think that the Lord will punish them.

The past is the past! Your future is with God! Run the race in the present.

Lord, thank You for Your grace that gives me hope, in Jesus' name. Amen.

March 24

Spiritual Maturity

> Let all who are spiritually mature agree on these things...
> Philippians 3:15 NLT

There is a constant movement in our Christian life. We will increase in insight and discernment (1:9-11), and in faith (1:25).

In Philippians 3:12-13, we are like athletes. We are on our way. We threw our excess clothes aside. We know that our goal has not yet been reached. On this journey, we will realize more and more that we have been acquitted by God's grace (3:9). The past is behind us. Our desire is to understand what it means to be dead to sin (3:10). We will also understand that, because we believe in Christ, we may suffer for what we believe. It does not matter because we have been given a new life through the resurrection of Christ (3:11).

This is why we run full speed. God "laid hold of" us—we are His (3:12). All of this is His wonderful gift. We run this race because we belong to Him.

Spiritual maturity means that we will realize that we are still on the way (3:15). We are not there yet! To grow, to run, to exert ourselves, is to discover every day that His grace is enough for us.

> Lord, You who are always the same, grant that I will know myself; grant that I may know You. (Prayer of Augustine). *Amen.*

March 25

Everyday Worship

"Not everyone who says to me, 'Lord, Lord,' will enter the kingdom of heaven, but only the one who does the will of My Father who is in heaven."
Matthew 7:21 NIV

I helped out for some time in a church where there was no minister. It was not the same denomination as mine. It had a fixed way of doing things during the service. Many people may find it very ritualistic. The content of what they do is beautiful, but they repeat the same thing Sunday after Sunday.

We may be very critical of such a way of worship. Jesus just spoke about the danger of worship that is not about God, but about show (Matthew 6). Yet, He did not speak out against what we do. He wants us to test where our hearts are. The religious things we do are not necessarily an indication that our hearts are in the right place. Faith is a way of life. Our thoughts, words and deeds should be imbued with the love for the Lord and for our fellow human beings. If we live one day in the service of the Lord and another day in the service of ourselves, we have not understood what faith in God means.

Our worship should therefore be seen in our everyday lives. To put it differently, our worship is about doing what God's Word is saying—everywhere and at all times! Charles Spurgeon said that faith is not meant for the bedroom, but the living room. In other words, it should be lived in everyday life.

Holy Spirit, give me an obedient life, in Jesus' name. *Amen.*

March 26

Extraordinary Graces

*The fear of the LORD adds length to life,
but the years of the wicked are cut short.*
Proverbs 10:27 NIV

Is it true that service to God leads to a long life, but the people who do not serve Him will have a short life? This idea is also expressed in Psalm 1. Does this mean that all who die young are unbelievers? Does this mean that old people are all believers?

Our experience is different. Proverbs and Ecclesiastes hold different views. Ecclesiastes says that the wicked and the righteous go the same way (Eccles. 9). Psalm 73 grapples with the problem that the wicked have a good life, while people who serve the Lord sometimes experience hardship. The life of Job is a good example that sin leads to punishment and a good life to reward.

Who is right? Proverbs and Psalm 1 or Job and Psalm 73? Both. Many of the words of Ecclesiastes were written from the perspective of a destroyed temple and exile. Young and old, righteous and godless, all lost their lives. Job's friends had to repent from their one-sided view. The Bible gives us different perspectives on God. Sometimes one perspective speaks to us in certain circumstances and another perspective in another circumstance.

Matthew Henry said that extraordinary afflictions are not always the punishment of extraordinary sins, but sometimes the trial of extraordinary graces.

Christians will experience many disappointments and losses in this life. By serving Jesus, we live in the presence of One who will accompany us through the ups and downs of life.

Lord, let me rest in Your care even when things do not make sense, in Jesus' name. Amen.

March 27

Words

The words of the godly are like sterling silver;
the heart of a fool is worthless.
Proverbs 10:20 NLT

The South African author C. J. Langenhoven was also a parliamentarian. Once he remarked in parliament that half of the members were donkeys. The speaker said he should withdraw his statement. Langenhoven agreed and said, "Half of this parliament are not donkeys."

Words cannot be taken back. Gossip is like feathers blown by a strong wind. Words are powerful. Sometimes we use words of encouragement so that we can serve our own interests. A husband can say nice words to his wife to get what he wants. Sometimes people can make you feel good about yourself so that they can strike a good business deal. The nice words of the wicked might be like messengers of bad things (10:6, 11, 18). Behind the words are hatred and violence. We have to weigh every word we hear.

The primary goal of Christians is to love (10:12). Words driven by love are like the finest silver (10:20). George Herbert said that good words are worth much and cost little. It builds others up. Each word has value (20:19). Spirit-filled people know that. Paul says, "Do not let any unwholesome talk come out of your mouths, but only what is helpful for building others up according to their needs, that it may benefit those who listen. And do not grieve the Holy Spirit of God…" (Eph. 4:29-30 NIV).

What is the purpose of your words—to serve others or yourself?

Lord, let my words be driven by love, in the name of Jesus Christ.

Amen.

March 28

How Do You Treat People?

*If you bite and devour each other, watch out
or you will be destroyed by each other.*
Galatians 5:15 NIV

Wars among nations cover the headlines. Some nations are depicted as the bad ones and some as the good ones. Some are the aggressors and some are the victims. Though there is some truth in it, there is also a bigger truth to keep in mind: They are all people Christ died for. We can demonize people and nations, but this is not what God wants us to do.

God made us to be His representatives on earth. He made us so that He could pour out His love on us. We have an inalienable dignity. Because of this, we must never look at others in another way than that they are God's creation. All people have this dignity. Paul says that life in freedom before God is first and foremost a life of love towards God's people around us (5:13–26).

There are many people who are broken today because we forgot to treat them as people of God. We labelled them and, in this way, excluded them from our love and even God's love. In doing so, we actually turned against God's purposes. We hurt His people.

When we bow before God, let us not have blood on our hands by thinking that others are not worthy of God's care and love.

Lord, help us to realize today that our journey with You is a journey with Your people. Amen.

March 29

You Are My Everything

> Keep me safe, O God, for I have come to You for refuge.
> I said to the LORD, "You are my Master!
> Every good thing I have comes from You."
> Psalm 16:1-2 NLT

One of my friends was a missionary in Afghanistan. He met many "secret" Christians there. These people could not tell anybody about their faith, because it could mean the end for them. Some of them lost everything for the sake of Christ. My friend said that Jesus is all they had, but for them it was enough.

The psalmist asks for God's protection. There is nothing worth more for Him than the Lord. He says that there are many idols in the land that can pull his attention away from God. However, he came to the realization that he could not live without the Lord. The Lord is his life. God alone gives meaning!

Have you ever tried to do without the Lord? Maybe you are doing it at the moment. Perhaps God is not part of your plans and life. Sometimes it happens that we are forced to think of God. Usually, it happens because we are experiencing a crisis. Maybe the Lord is just like an emergency parachute—we only use it in case of emergencies! Someone said that there are no atheists in trenches.

C. S. Lewis wrote, "Once a man is united to God, how could he not live forever? Once a man is separated from God, what can he do but wither and die."

Father, thank You for the meaning You give to my life, through Jesus Christ our Lord. *Amen.*

March 30

My Citizenship

For our citizenship is in heaven, from which we also eagerly wait for the Savior, the Lord Jesus Christ, who will transform our lowly body that it may be conformed to His glorious body, according to the working by which He is able even to subdue all things to Himself.
Philippians 3:20–21 NKJV

Where I currently work, it is better to obtain residency to do my job unhindered and without a visa. After many documents and tests, I got it. I am still a citizen of my country, but can now work unrestricted and live here for as long as I choose. Yet, like a rubber band attached to one end and pulling back to the place of its origin, one's heart always pulls back to your homeland.

Where is it? Christians are citizens of heaven. The image used here is of a colony in a foreign land. Here the culture, language, customs and lifestyle of the fatherland apply.

The church is such a heavenly colony on earth. We are citizens of the heavenly colony on a strange piece of land. We speak the language of heaven, even though the world around us speaks a different language and even though the world around us lives a different kind of life. We are governed by the loyalty to our heavenly homeland. Here Christ is the Lord and here applies the lifestyle and customs of the Fatherland! Here our highest loyalty is to Christ!

It means that we live with commitment here and now. We would like to see something of heaven on earth. We do not avoid the world. We live life to the fullest!

Lord, enable me to make visible something of Your kingdom here on earth, by the power of Your Spirit. Amen.

March 31

Our Longing

For our citizenship is in heaven, from which we also eagerly wait for the Savior, the Lord Jesus Christ, who will transform our lowly body that it may be conformed to His glorious body.
Philippians 3:20–21 NKJV

The life of John Calvin was full of tragedies. His mother died when he was four years old. His wife, Idelette, died only nine years after their marriage at the age of forty. All their children died in infancy. He himself was not healthy and died at the early age of 54 years.

Calvin had a constant longing for heaven. At one point he asks whether we will not be comforted by the fact that we are called back to our heavenly homeland by death from exile. It is an echo of Augustine's words: "I sigh with unspeakable sighs on my pilgrimage…and I remember Jerusalem with my heart lifted up there…"

It is the language of being on a journey. Christians have a constant longing, a serious desire for the return of Jesus Christ (3:20). It is especially related to our desire that God will put an end to the limitations, finitude and suffering. Our whole being is focused on the power of God that will recreate us into a new immortal existence.

O God, I also long for my homeland, my eternal home with You.

Amen.

April

April 1

Seeing Christ in Me

*The fruit of the righteous is a tree of life, and
the one who is wise saves lives.*
Proverbs 11:30 NIV

We are instruments of salvation and a source of life. Whoever looks at us should see something of God. People will see it when we live according to God's will.

What is the will of God? A lot of proverbs in this chapter are about how we acquire and use our possessions. Some slyly acquired their possessions (11:1, 6). Some people store necessities so that the price can rise and poor people suffer as a result (11:26). This was the sin of the rich fool in Luke 12:13-21. People like him are heartless (11:17) and are despised by society (11:26).

We become a source of life and blessing when we manage our possessions in such a way that it benefits others (11:24-26). Remember God's blessings in your life. Become a source of life and salvation for the poor with the goods you manage on God's behalf. Don't trust in uncertain riches (11:28).

In a famous prayer attributed to St. Patrick, one of the main missionaries in Ireland's history, we read, "Christ in the mouth of every man who speaks of me, Christ in the eye that sees me, Christ in the ear that hears me..."

Lord, let the way I handle my belongings help people to think of Christ, by the power of Your Spirit. *Amen.*

April 2

God's Creation

The godly care for their animals, but the wicked are always cruel.
Proverbs 12:10 NLT

Animals were one of the sources of life in the days of Israel. Animals were used to plow the fields and served as draft animals. This is why people cared for their animals. It was foolish to do otherwise.

There is, however, a bigger reason why God wants us to look after animals. It is because God has created them. We share life on planet earth. God has given us the responsibility to ensure that His creation is well cared for.

Not everybody likes animals. They lose hair, make a mess and are sometimes very noisy. However, if we remember that they are part of God's plan for the world, we can never treat their lives with contempt; we can never allow animals to be destroyed in a pointless way. The whole universe matters to God.

An image that will always stay with me is how many beggars in the streets of many countries have a dog with them. Very often that dog is the only warmth and friendship the person experiences. The way the beggar sometimes cares for that dog is often an example of what God expects of us.

Albert Schweitzer said that we will never find peace until we extend the circle of our compassion to all living things.

Lord, teach us to care for all creation and for the animals that You have placed in our care, in Jesus' name. Amen.

April 3

Planning My Spiritual Life

> I want to know Christ—yes, to know the power of His resurrection and participation in His sufferings, becoming like Him in His death, and so, somehow, attaining to the resurrection from the dead.
> Philippians 3:10-11 NIV

Life is a rat race. We have to do certain things; we just don't have a choice. Then the longed-for holidays come at last! Some of us sit down and plan it carefully. What about our spiritual life? Is there a place for spiritual strategic planning? There are many events in our lives with God that we cannot plan, but there are many things we can plan. In short, where do we want to be in our lives with God by the end of the year?

Maybe we need growth in our knowledge of the Bible, or in our life with the Spirit of God, or in our discipline, or in following Jesus, or in our life of prayer. Dorothy Canfield Fisher wrote that if we would only give the same amount of reflection to what we want to get out of life as we do to the question of what to do with two weeks' vacation, we would be startled at our false standards and the aimless procession of our busy days.

Paul describes our lives as one with direction (3:12-14). It is not aimless. It is like a carefully planned race towards the finishing line. We plan our journey with one single purpose—to come to know Him better.

Lord, help us to plan our spiritual journey with more passion than we plan the rest of our lives, by the power of Your Spirit.

Amen.

April 4

How Much Do You Weigh?

> But whatever were gains to me I now consider loss for the sake
> of Christ. What is more, I consider everything a loss because
> of the surpassing worth of knowing Christ Jesus my
> Lord, for whose sake I have lost all things.
> Philippians 3:7-8 NIV

In the old days, shops did not have electronic scales. People determined the weight of an item on one side of the scale by putting a solid weight on the other side of the scale.

Paul weighs his old status and his new life. When he places his old, impressive status and religious qualities on the scale, it weighs less, no, nothing in comparison with Christ. Therefore, he could let go of all these things for the sake of Christ. What does it mean? It means that we share in everything Christ experienced. It means to die with Him every day (3:10).

We weigh everything. When we have to make choices and decisions, we ask ourselves if it stands in the way of a true, intimate relationship with Christ. When we look at our traditions, our background, even our religious principles, we weigh them. Does it weigh anything in comparison with Christ? If so, we know what to do. We consider them rubbish.

What weighs heavier than Christ in your life?

> God of grace, I have only one desire, and that is to know You, for the sake of Christ Jesus. *Amen.*

April 5

Look Away!

If God is for us, who can be against us?
Romans 8:31 NKJV

Life can hurt people so much that they cannot rely on God's love. Others may feel so guilty about personal and collective guilt that it draws their heart away from God. Still others can suffer from the general brokenness of creation that they are no longer sure of God's closeness. Illness, failure, rejection, suffering, sin and guilt of the past can do all of this to a person.

It seems Paul understood that. His words free us from the tendency to look at ourselves when we feel guilty about sin. This is exactly what the devil wants us to do. He is the prosecutor. He wants to see that we are struggling with guilt. He wants to convince us that God does not forgive. He especially wants to pull a veil over our vision of Calvary. He wants us to be blinded by our sin so that we no longer see Jesus on the cross.

Against this satanic strategy, Paul says that we should look away from ourselves. We should see what happened on Calvary. Jesus died. He has risen. He lives. God has justified us! And even if Satan accuses us many times, Jesus, our pleading Advocate, is at the right hand of the Father interceding for us every time (8:33–34).

Thank You, Father, that You are for us, through Jesus Christ our Lord. *Amen.*

April 6

Do You See the Cross?

If God is for us, who can be against us?
Romans 8:31 NKJV

When life is difficult, when every possible thing goes wrong, the temptation is to look at our situation and conclude that God does not love us anymore. In Romans 8:35-39 Paul expresses the magnitude of circumstances that we face. When, in these extreme situations, we feel like we are going to be overwhelmed, we begin to believe the lie that He is no longer with us.

Nothing is further from the truth. God's love is so strong that nothing—not the pain in our lives, not the guilt accusing us, not the brokenness that we see, yes, not even death, can separate us from Him. Nothing in this life or in death can ever snatch us from His presence (8:38-39).

How do we know God is for us? Clean the glasses of your vision. Do you see the cross? Remember that He bore your sin by His own Son. Is this not proof enough that God loves us and will never abandon us?

Thank You, great God, that You are on our side, through Jesus Christ our Lord. *Amen.*

April 7

A Happy Ending

> ...despite all these things, overwhelming victory
> is ours through Christ, who loved us.
> Romans 8:37 NLT

I do not like a movie that has a sad ending. There are enough sad and tragic stories in everyday life. We want something positive—good stories and good outcomes. Yet, we know that we cannot escape tragedy or hardships. Life does not always have a happy ending. Sometimes people's lives go completely wrong and they die alone, without people around them to comfort them.

While saying this, every Christian may know that our lives are heading for a happy ending, despite the ups and downs in our lives. There is a proverb that goes something like this: "God promises a safe landing, not a calm passage."

When Paul writes to the Romans about their suffering, he sings a song of praise. He sings this song because he knows that the chains of God's love for us cannot be broken. These chains are of blood—Christ's blood. He makes a list of all the possible things that can happen to us. He even leaves the list open by talking about things that might still go wrong in the future. One could probably add many more things. However, the end is certain—nothing can nullify God's love for us. We will be more than conquerors!

This is probably why many of us like a movie with a good ending. The difference is that movies are stories. Our life story is based on the foundation of God's promises and love for us.

Father, thank You for the happy ending You have promised to all who believe in You, in Jesus' name. Amen.

April 8

Nothing Can Separate Us

For I am convinced that neither death nor life, neither angels nor demons, neither the present nor the future, nor any powers, neither height nor depth, nor anything else in all creation, will be able to separate us from the love of God that is in Christ Jesus our Lord.
Romans 8:38-39 NIV

Someone wrote that he once witnessed the simple funeral of a country farmer. A few men carried the humble coffin to a cemetery. They filled the grave with sand and covered it with patches of grass. Then one of them took two pieces of wood and made a cross, and stuck it in the ground. He writes that the simple, unadorned wooden cross symbolized that where death is affirmed, hope finds its roots.

Jesus' death and resurrection gives us hope in the midst of death, powers and life-threatening circumstances. We are not being reincarnated in a never-ending cycle of life, death and resurrection. Through Jesus Christ, we are being made alive by the power of the Spirit of God in this life. When this life ends, we will live forever in the presence of the God who made us and who has recreated us by His grace. Our lives do not start when we are born and end when we die.

Who can ever separate us from the love of Christ (8:35)? Nothing. Nothing!

Lord, thank You for Your wonderful love that never ends.

Amen.

April 9

Patience Amid Struggles

*This calls for patient endurance and faithfulness
on the part of God's people.*
Revelation 13:10 NIV

We are supposed to live in a free world, but it is not always the case. There are so many oppressive governments in the world. No opposition is tolerated. The prisons are filled with those who have opposed the ruling political system. Even in the so-called free world, there is little freedom. Christianity and its values are not tolerated. When Christians speak out against some lifestyles, they are considered to be intolerant and even silenced.

People may feel that God's order is no longer served by the government. In Revelation 13, we have such a government. It describes the wicked Roman Empire and its leader. Christians suffered greatly under these intolerant and godless systems. They were marginalized and even killed. The system was evil and driven by Satan himself.

How should Christians respond in such a situation? One thing is certain: We should definitely not give up our faith in Jesus Christ. John sums it up briefly: You need endurance and faithfulness (13:10). Even if the government says that your faith is not the only one, we should not water down what we believe about Jesus as the Way, Truth and Life. He is the Lamb of God, the Alpha and Omega. He will return and things will change for the good. In the meantime, we should remember that God still has the world and your life in the palm of His hand. No authority can snatch us from His hand.

Lord, help me to remain faithful to You in all circumstances, by the power of Your Spirit. Amen.

April 10

Wasted Energy

Give all your worries and cares to God, for He cares about you.
1 Peter 5:7 NLT

One of the quotes that helped me most in my life was the one by William R. Inge: "Worry is interest paid on trouble before it becomes due." We have this terrible tendency to see problems and trouble even if there is no immediate threat. It wears us down. We are anxious about something that has not yet happened and will probably not happen. We are sometimes also worried about something we can actually do nothing about.

We do not know if we might be alive tomorrow. We do not know if we might lose everything tomorrow. Does it help to worry about it? Jesus says that we cannot prolong our life by a single hour by worrying about it (Matt. 6:27). The psalmist says in Psalm 131 that he does not worry about things that are beyond his ability.

The readers of Peter's letter were under pressure about many things. They were a minority in society. They experienced discrimination and sometimes oppression by authorities and employers. In this context, Peter reminds them that the Lord will take care of them. Therefore, they should give all the things they are anxious about to the Lord.

Energy is very precious. Do not waste your energy on worry. It consumes everything. You need your energy to live a meaningful life in the Lord's service today. Let go of your urge to take control of everything. Leave it to the Lord. He will take care of it (Ps. 37:5).

Lord, take care of me and my anxiety today, in Jesus' name.

Amen.

April 11

Do You Have Something to Say?

*God's purpose in all this was to use the church to display
His wisdom in its rich variety to all the unseen rulers
and authorities in the heavenly places.*
Ephesians 3:10 NLT

Religion kills. So many atrocities have been committed in the name of religion. It also kills in another way. It makes people satisfied with themselves. If I have performed my religious duties, I feel good and can go on with the rest of my life. Religion kills a living, vibrant relationship with God.

Christians are not religious in this way. We celebrate a relationship with the living God. We follow Jesus! Paul says that the miracle of our salvation is like a secret revealed. All people are included and all people should hear about this. He cannot be silent about the revelation of this beautiful message. God did not just give Paul this task. This message is made known by the church to every power and authority over which Jesus Christ has won the victory.

The church becomes the bearer of the gospel for all people. As part of the church, we must do everything in our power to be channels through which the Lord can reveal the secret of His love. Someone wrote that people not going to church cannot be reached by a church that does not go to the world.

Why are we silent? John Stott wrote, "Nothing shuts the mouth, seals the lips, and ties the tongue like the secret poverty of our own spiritual experience." The reason we do not testify is simple: We have nothing to testify about.

Lord, renew my life with You, so that I will be an active witness of Your grace, in Jesus' name. Amen.

April 12

Words of Life or Death

The words of the reckless pierce like swords,
but the tongue of the wise brings healing.
Proverbs 12:18 NIV

The old saying, "Sticks and stones may break my bones, but words will never harm me," is not entirely true. Words have destructive and constructive power.

The wicked are like people at war; their words are like an ambush (12:6). Like a criminal stabs someone with a knife, the words of wicked people pierce the hearts of others. You can never take the advice of a wicked person seriously (12:5). They will be ruined by their own words (12:13). A fool is someone who does not listen to wisdom (12:1). They think they can manage on their own. In contrast, the words of people who listen to wisdom bring healing. When someone is worried or depressed, your words may encourage such a person and build them up (12:25). Your words are like a force that can bring relief in difficult circumstances (12:6).

What we say is very important. When we say, "I love you," we can give another person new life, new hope, new courage. However, when we say, "I hate you," we can destroy another person. Therefore, we have to watch our words.

Are you someone at war or are you bringing healing with what you say?

> Lord, please help my words to be uplifting, by the power of Your Spirit.
>
> *Amen.*

April 13

Build Others Up

*The words of the reckless pierce like swords,
but the tongue of the wise brings healing.*
Proverbs 12:18 NIV

Paul writes in Colossians 4:6 (NIV), "Let your conversation be always full of grace, seasoned with salt, so that you may know how to answer everyone." In Ephesians 4:29 (NLT), we find an echo of what the poet says, "Don't use foul or abusive language. Let everything you say be good and helpful, so that your words will be an encouragement to those who hear them." James warns against the power of the tongue (James 3). If our goal is to praise God with our words, it can never be used to break down people who are made in God's image (James 3:9). The wisdom that comes from God is indeed aimed at a lifestyle that is "peace-loving, considerate, submissive, full of mercy and good fruit, impartial and sincere" (James 3:17 NIV).

What force will your words have today? Remember that it can destroy lives. It can cause permanent damage, or it can bring healing to people who have been hurt by life. If you listen to God's advice, you will weigh your words.

Father, use my words today to build others up, by the power of Your Spirit. Amen.

April 14

Hope!

*If in this life only we have hope in Christ,
we are of all men the most pitiable.*
1 Corinthians 15:19 NKJV

Paul writes to people who have rejected faith in God and live without hope in the resurrection of Christ. These people rejected the fact that Christ was raised from the dead. Therefore, their attitude was simple: "Let us eat and drink, for tomorrow we die" (15:32 NKJV). It is a life without hope.

What is the meaning of life without the resurrection of Jesus? The scientist Pascal was right when he said that without Christ, the world could not continue. Without Christ, the world would either have to be destroyed or would degenerate into a kind of hell. It would be a hell without a gospel, good news, a Bible and without the church. It would be a world without faith, hope, full of lies, with bondage to sin. Yes, we would have been lost (15:14-18).

But that's not the case with us. Peter says that through the resurrection of Jesus we have a living hope that looks beyond this world (1 Pet. 1:3-10). The resurrection wipes our spectacles so that we look at life with new eyes. This life is not the last—we have hope!

Lord, thank You for the living hope we have, through Jesus Christ our Lord. *Amen.*

April 15

God's "NO" to Death!

"Where, O death, is your victory? Where, O death, is your sting?"
1 Corinthians 15:55 NIV

I wonder about the influence of the COVID-19 pandemic on families. We have not really seen the long-term effects on people who lost loved ones during this pandemic. In many cases, people could not even say goodbye to their loved ones because they could not see them. Postponed or delayed grief could become a massive mental health issue as the years go on. Death ripped people out of their lives. All that is left are memories. There are now more questions than answers.

Is this what God wants? No. God's stance against death is clear! God could no longer tolerate this strange invader, death. Therefore, He won the victory over death through His Son (Rom. 5:17). This is why Paul mocks the powerlessness of death in 1 Corinthians 15:54-55. It is like a bee without a sting. Death is no longer dangerous, because Christ died for our sin. Whoever trusts in Him, can join in the song of victory.

God said "yes" forever to life through the resurrection of Jesus Christ. Death is dead now. Yes, the pain of losing someone is immense. Not to say a proper goodbye is indescribable. Yet, to have hope that this is not the last reality, can carry us through even this pain. Faith and hope in the Risen Christ is the only stable foundation for our lives amid the turmoil of life.

Father, thank You for Your victory over death through Your Son, Jesus Christ. *Amen.*

April 16

The Nearness of the Lord

The Lord is near.
Philippians 4:5 NIV

Sometimes I spend more time worrying than experiencing peace. Worries deprive me of joy. Maybe sometimes life gets too much for you, too. Worries, says Hans Iwand, want to convince us that God is not near.

We must remember where Paul is when he writes these words. He is in prison. It is not the most comfortable place to be happy! Apart from his imprisonment or house arrest, he has other worries. He is concerned about the apparent division in the congregation caused by some people (4:2-3). Amid his worries, he calls the congregation to rejoice (4:4).

What is the motivation for our joy, peace, unity and goodwill? It is in the words: "The Lord is near" (4:5 NIV). These words can have two meanings and Paul deliberately leaves them open. One is that Jesus will come soon. This was the expectation of the early church. The other meaning is that He is close to us. He never leaves us. When we disagree with each other, the Lord's nearness changes our attitude.

When our heart and mind make us morbid about the worries for which we have no answer, the Lord's nearness opens a different perspective on our suffering. His presence and the fact that He will make everything new, dispels the discontent and brings peace that we cannot explain. It enables us to focus on the beautiful things in life and to live as God wants us to live (4:8-9).

Lord, thank You for being near, for Christ's sake. *Amen.*

April 17

Our History, My Story

Shout joyful praises to God, all the earth!
Psalm 66:1 NLT

Sometimes friends tell us about the way God did great things in their lives. It can make us envious. Why is God so good to them and not to us? Psalm 66 says that the greatness of God means that He is there for His people in the small and big things. The first part is about what the Lord did for His covenant people (66:5-9). The people suffered and were trampled on by others who did not care for them (66:12).

The Lord did not let His people down. He helped and supported them through every difficult situation. He also used all the events as a test for His people (66:9-11). Based on God's great acts in the past, the psalmist calls people to shout for joy and proclaim that He is Lord over all the earth. Even His enemies should know this and bow before Him (66:1-4, 8).

Suddenly, however, the story of the past becomes the psalmist's own story. Everything changes to "I" and "me" (66:13-20). God answered his prayer, saved him and therefore he praises God. He now has the courage to call on the Lord in every situation.

You don't have to be envious about what God does in other people's lives. Think about God's acts in your life today. He is there. The more you thank Him about what He has done for you, the more you will see what He is doing now.

Lord, fill me with joy for what You are doing in my life, in Jesus' name. *Amen.*

April 18

Channels of Blessing

"All the families on earth will be blessed through you."
Genesis 12:3 NLT

One of the great characteristics of God is that He is willing to give new beginnings even when we have failed miserably. In my own life, God opened the door of His grace when I thought that it would be closed. We have to rejoice in God's grace! After the mess that man made of God's good creation, God started all over with human beings. God regretted that He made us. He gave a new beginning when Noah came out of the ark. Then things went wrong again.

The story of Abram is another new beginning. It is a strange one. Abram's wife is infertile and he is already 75 years old. God decides to start over with someone like that. He did this to make it very clear that God's new beginnings are always His choice and His grace. His new beginning for the world is not devised by us. He does it just because He is good. Even at this early stage in the Old Testament, it is clear what God's vision for the world is. All nations are included in His plan. He will not leave the nations now scattered over the whole earth to themselves.

Abram's purpose was to be a channel of blessing. Share in God's vision for the world! You are part of the blessed people who are now channels, through Christ. There are millions who have not yet received this privilege. Share the blessing you have received. This is our purpose!

Father, thank You that Your heart is so big that there is room for all mankind. *Amen.*

April 19

Is Suffering God's Will?

> So then, those who suffer according to God's will should commit themselves to their faithful Creator and continue to do good.
> 1 Peter 4:19 NIV

Maybe you find this verse shocking. Can there ever be suffering according to God's will? Is the suffering in this world His will? Does it not go against God's character of being just? Is the resurrection of Christ not the clearest expression of God's resistance against all death and evil? Yes. God is against death and suffering.

Yet, there is one kind of suffering which is the will of God. This is the suffering for the sake of Christ. When the New Testament speaks of suffering, it refers in most cases to suffering because we are committed to Christ. The people to whom Peter writes were but a small minority in the pagan community in which they lived. There they sometimes experienced insults, marginalization and discrimination.

Matthew 10 says that every person who follows Jesus may walk the same path as their Master. Therefore, do not be surprised if you suffer for the sake of Jesus. If they crucified Jesus, His disciples will also share in His suffering. We will not necessarily be crucified or killed like our Lord, but we will endure some suffering or rejection. Therefore, we can be happy about this kind of suffering. It helps us to cling to Jesus alone for life and death. It also reminds us that we share in the suffering of Christ.

Lord, I commit myself anew to You, even if it leads to suffering, for the sake of Jesus Christ. Amen.

April 20

Fake News?

An honest witness tells the truth, but a false witness tells lies.
Proverbs 12:17 NIV

Fake news and true news...one wonders if there is something like true news at all. Truth is rare. The truth lies buried among the ruins of many sides of a story. Proverbs 12 emphasizes that truth should always triumph. This is what God wants (12:2, 17, 19).

There is a Yiddish proverb that says, "A half-truth is a whole lie." If I distort the truth to suit myself, I am not righteous (12:5). Our words should reflect that we are people of God (12:22).

Earlier in Proverbs we read, "Keep your mouth free of perversity; keep corrupt talk far from your lips" (4:24 NIV). The Ten Commandments also emphasize that we should not give false testimony against our neighbor. Psalm 50:16 and 19 say that a person who understands God's grace is not supposed to be deceitful.

How often one lie leads to many other lies. When we are saved from death to life, our words and deeds must bring honor to God and represent Jesus (Col. 3:17).

In Ephesians, Paul says more or less the same thing: "So stop telling lies. Let us tell our neighbors the truth, for we are all parts of the same body" (Eph. 4:25 NLT). Let us now do everything in our power to stay with the truth. It fits Spirit-filled people.

Spirit of God, make me trustworthy in word and deed, in Jesus' name. Amen.

April 21

Watch Your Tongue!

*Those who guard their lips preserve their lives,
but those who speak rashly will come to ruin.*
Proverbs 13:3 NIV

I have often asked the Lord to guard my tongue. Perhaps you know the experience. You did not want to say anything, but you did before you could help yourself. It is one of the things we cannot undo—words.

We have already seen in Proverbs 12 how important words are. It is sometimes amazing how words can heal and unite people. Sometimes, however, we talk too soon, we promise too easily and respond too quickly. The poet says that it can lead to our downfall. Perhaps he was referring to an unreliable messenger that did not convey the right message (13:17). Perhaps he was referring to people who are gossiping and then caught out. Maybe he just refers to lies (13:5).

Perhaps, like Ecclesiastes warns us, our words and promises to God could be unreliable: "Don't make rash promises, and don't be hasty in bringing matters before God. After all, God is in heaven, and you are here on earth. So let your words be few...When you make a promise to God, don't delay in following through, for God takes no pleasure in fools. Keep all the promises you make to Him. It is better to say nothing than to make a promise and not keep it" (Eccles. 5:2, 4-5 NLT).

Watch your tongue today. God knows your words. In the end, we are not accountable to people, but to God.

Lord, help me to watch my tongue, in Jesus' name. *Amen.*

April 22

Speaking from the Heart

> Those who guard their lips preserve their lives,
> but those who speak rashly will come to ruin.
> Proverbs 13:3 NIV

Jesus emphasized that negative words also carry in it the seed of something far worse, namely murder: "You have heard that it was said to the people long ago, 'You shall not murder, and anyone who murders will be subject to judgment.' But I tell you that anyone who is angry with a brother or sister will be subject to judgment. Again, anyone who says to a brother or sister, 'Raca,' is answerable to the court. And anyone who says, 'You fool!' will be in danger of the fire of hell" (Matt. 5:21-22 NIV).

Words that destroy and kill, words that do not come from the heart but are mere lip service—this is what we regularly experience and speak. Words of healing are rare. We are called to make a difference in the lives of others with our words today.

Our children, our colleagues and the person who is unimportant in the eyes of the world need a kind word today by which he or she will be blessed. Then your life has meaning and gives meaning. After all, a person can prosper by using the right words (Prov. 13:2).

> Lord, let my words today come from my heart to bless people and bring glory to You, by the power of Your Spirit. *Amen.*

April 23

Your Help Makes a Difference

> I can do all things through Christ who strengthens me.
> Philippians 4:13 NKJV

In many ways, giving to others and serving one another are central aspects of the biblical message. This is what happened to the Philippians. Their help to Paul was one of the most wonderful experiences of his time as an apostle. They even sent for Epaphroditus to bring gifts for Paul and to assist him in prison. That is why Paul regards their help as "a fragrant offering" (4:18).

We do not realize what our help to others can mean to them. Paul's letter is full of words of joy over the love he has for the congregation. They helped him to bear his suffering. He is able to do all things through Christ who strengthens him, and because of their help. This is how people experience Christ's power. Through their help, Paul discovered that he is able to persevere (4:13-14).

Paul prays from prison that the Lord will provide in their every need (4:19). Yes, Christ gives strength, but He also uses people like us to give encouragement and to receive encouragement. Let us never underestimate the power of love for one another. We are His instruments!

There is a beautiful story of someone who gave a beggar not money, but a beautiful red rose. It brought tears to his eyes, because someone cared deeply for how he felt. We help and serve, because we care.

Lord God, open our hearts today to people who may need us, in Jesus' name. Amen.

April 24

The Best for the Lord's Work

*Then, having fasted and prayed, and laid
hands on them, they sent them away.*
Acts 13:3 NKJV

A Brazilian preacher visited South Africa and Namibia a few decades ago. He was intrigued and disappointed at the same time when he saw a box in the vestibule of one of the churches he visited. Outside the church where he was preaching, there were a lot of luxury cars. Yet on the box in the vestibule of the church was written: "Cents for missions." It simply looked like this church thought of missions as something optional. We give our leftovers or the money that is not important to us to missions.

The congregation in Antioch was so different. They were a "macro congregation" with five pastors. In their hearts was a burning ambition that the gospel of Jesus Christ would be heard amongst the nations. Who would they send? Normally, we would like to keep the best pastors for our congregation. Yet, they took time to fast and pray—to listen to God's voice. What did they hear from the Holy Spirit? I am sure there would have been many other candidates, but the Holy Spirit appointed two of their pastors to do full-time missionary work. They were not anyone. They were two of their best—Paul and Barnabas. God's work is serious work.

He wants the best—the best of our income and gifts and the best people. We exist essentially for those who have not heard the gospel.

Lord, guide us to give our best resources and people in service of the gospel, by the power of Your Spirit. Amen.

April 25

Religion or Relationship?

> "Watch out! Don't do your good deeds publicly, to be admired by others, for you will lose the reward from your Father in heaven."
> Matthew 6:1 NLT

Are you religious? Jesus speaks here to people for whom religious duties were very important. They prayed, fasted and gave alms to the poor. These were the pillars of piety. Jesus emphasizes that religion is about God.

Four times in Matthew 6 Jesus warns us not to be religious to impress people (6:1-2, 5, 16). This is a serious warning. Someone who has received the honor of people because they are so religious has already received their reward. There will be no further reward from God. We who live before God must constantly ask why we help the poor, pray in public or set ourselves apart to be with God in silence. Yes, we should also ask ourselves why we go to church, read the Bible, or participate in the activities of the congregation. Is it because we want people to say nice things about us? Do we want to be known as a good Christian? Does it speak of a close connection with God? Do we do it for personal gain?

A pure heart means to follow and serve the Lord with undivided motives. We focus on Him, not on the approval of people or to be honored by them. One of my friends wrote this to me: "Let us not confuse doing things for God with spending time with God; to confuse activity with intimacy; to mistake the trappings of spirituality for being spiritual."

Spirit of God, You are all that matters. *Amen.*

April 26

Life before God

*"But when you give to the needy, do not let your
left hand know what your right hand is doing,
so that your giving may be in secret."*
Matthew 6:3-4 NIV

Many Christians detest the term "religious duties". They are against all forms of outward religion that could be perceived as being legalistic. Some people might even respond to Matthew 6:1 by saying, "Because Jesus says that we should not fulfill our religious duties in public, I would rather do nothing."

Jesus was not against religious duties; He performed these duties Himself like all good and faithful Jews did. One must therefore not misunderstand Jesus. The Lord obviously expects us to practice our faith, and spiritual discipline is part of it. The point Jesus is making is that we should not do it to be seen by people. Jesus is not saying that we should not fulfill religious duties. Helping the poor is every Christian's calling. Our life before God is also about people! However, what we do as faithful people is a matter between God and us! Our help to the poor is something we do for God and in the presence of God. No one needs to know about it.

I know there are many poor people, but that should not stop us from doing our part before God to alleviate the need in our world. We serve God by serving people!

Lord, open my eyes today to help those crossing my path who are in need, by the power of Your Spirit. Amen.

April 27

Say "NO" to Appreciation

*"But when you do a charitable deed, do not let your
left hand know what your right hand is doing, that
your charitable deed may be in secret;
and your Father who sees in secret
will Himself reward you openly."*
Matthew 6:3-4 NKJV

The neediest people are often the most hospitable. We see in so many poor communities how they help each other and care for one another.

Sadly, it is not always the case with us who have enough and more than enough. When we help, it is often calculated and sometimes there's strings attached. We like to hear "thank you" if we did something for someone. We sometimes want public recognition that we are actually good people.

When you help people, you do it because you want to honor God through it, not to be honored. It is a matter between you and God.

Likewise, when we are helped, we should give recognition to the source of help, which is God who enabled others to help us. In all circumstances God should get the honor.

Lord, thank You for the goodness of others in my life, in Jesus' name. *Amen.*

April 28

He Knows!

"When you pray, don't babble on and on as the Gentiles do. They think their prayers are answered merely by repeating their words again and again. Don't be like them, for your Father knows exactly what you need even before you ask Him!"
Matthew 6:7–8 NLT

Why should we pray if God already knows what we need? This is not the point. Jesus does not say that we should not pray. Jesus says that we should not use prayer as a way of twisting God's arm. Some people think that by reciting prayers, using many words and using specific formulas, we will convince God to give us what we want. We must beg Him, convince Him, otherwise He will not give.

Behind this kind of thinking is an image of a god who is unwilling to look after his children; a god who wants to keep blessings away from those who need it. The living and loving God knows us and our needs. He likes to give, even before we ask. He already knows what our needs are.

Which parent would not listen to the needs of his or her child? It is wonderful when they want our advice and help. God likes to hear our voices, too. He listens to the shortest prayer, even our thoughts. He knew so well what we needed that He gave His Son and His Spirit (Rom. 8:26) to intercede for us when we sigh and struggle to find words. Charles Spurgeon got it right when he said, "Short prayers are long enough."

Lord, thank You that You are a willing Giver, through Jesus Christ.

Amen.

April 29

Fasting to Do God's Will

"When you fast, do not look somber as the hypocrites do, for they disfigure their faces to show others they are fasting. Truly I tell you, they have received their reward in full."
Matthew 6:16 NIV

What effect does your devotion to God have on the people around you? This is the wrong question. Our devotion is a matter between God and us. When we pray, help the poor and fast, it is about God. The point is simple: The purpose of spiritual disciplines is not to impress people.

Our spiritual disciplines should also not be done to impress God. They are rather an expression of love to God and others. Fasting is not a part of everyone's Christian lifestyle. Many people think that it belongs to the Old Testament dispensation and therefore no longer needs to be done. Yet, it is a very helpful way to set ourselves apart in order to dedicate ourselves to God.

Jesus says that if you dedicate yourself to God, you do not have to announce it or make a show of it. It is about Him. It also should not lead you to withdraw from the world. That is why the Lord says in Isaiah 58 that true fasting means to serve people in need. We dedicate ourselves to God so that He can send us out into the world.

The big question for all of us is this: Are we trying to impress people with our spiritual disciplines, or are our spiritual disciplines a selfless service to God and people?

Father, grant that my devotion to You may result in love for my fellow human beings. Amen.

April 30

Realistic Hope

*Hope deferred makes the heart sick,
but a dream fulfilled is a tree of life.*
Proverbs 13:12 NLT

Romans 5:5 tells us that hope will not disappoint us because God loves us. Yes, sometimes He will humble us, but He will never let us down or fail us. The poet says that a dream fulfilled brings joy and new life. It is wonderful! This is true in marriages, and in our life with our children, colleagues, employers, and employees. We can only try to meet expectations if we know what they are.

This is also true of our relationship with God. God has expectations. He asks obedience to His word, "Godliness guards the path of the blameless, but the evil are misled by sin…People who despise advice are asking for trouble; those who respect a command will succeed" (Prov. 13:6, 13 NLT).

We may also have expectations. The expectations that we have of God must be built on His Word. We have, through Jesus Christ, the firm hope that God will live up to His word. He fulfilled the promises of the Old Testament through Jesus Christ (2 Cor. 1:19-22). We have by His Spirit the assurance and guarantee that God will fulfill all His promises. He keeps His promises and we now can celebrate the eternal life in which we already share! The Bible tells us, "Whoever believes on Him will not be put to shame" (Rom. 10:11 NKJV).

Lord, thank You that we are people of hope through Jesus Christ and the Spirit, Your guarantee to us. *Amen.*

May

May 1

He Understands

*The heart knows its own bitterness,
and a stranger does not share its joy.*
Proverbs 14:10 NKJV

Galatians tells us that we should bear one another's burdens (Gal. 6:2). It means that we should share in someone's happiness but remind them that everything is God's gift. It also means that we should make every effort to bear the sadness and brokenness of others. Sometimes someone's pain is more bearable when we help to carry it (1 Cor. 12:26; Rom. 12:15).

We can only partly share in the experience of others. Sometimes people's bitterness or joy is so deep that he or she cannot put it into words (Prov. 14:10). Sometimes life just does not work out. Sometimes this is because of other people and circumstances beyond our control. We become bitter about it. No one can really share in this pain.

However, there is someone who completely understands what we go through. God's Son also bore the disappointment that life brings. He understands that life has a dark side to it. Our Savior has compassion for our brokenness (Heb. 4:15). Jesus' love fears no pain, no self-denial, no suffering if someone else can be helped. He understands.

> Savior, Friend, thank You for understanding me. Make my heart light, so I can live with joy, by Your grace. *Amen.*

May 2

Dwelling of the Holy Spirit

> Do you not know that your bodies are temples of the Holy Spirit, who is in you, whom you have received from God? You are not your own; you were bought at a price. Therefore honor God with your bodies.
> 1 Corinthians 6:19–20 NIV

The Greek philosopher Plato said that a person consists of two parts: a body and soul. The soul is an important and eternal part of us. The body is the prison of the soul and is inferior and temporary.

So many of us think this way and it has led to many skewed beliefs. We also easily separate physical and spiritual things. We would pay attention to people's "souls", while not caring for their physical needs. We believe that we have a so-called immortal soul while our body is temporary. This is not biblical.

Paul disputes this view by saying that the Lord bought us with His blood (6:20). The Spirit of God has chosen our body as a dwelling place (6:19). Paul could not be more radical.

We cannot separate body and soul. A person is a unit. We should not think that we can abuse our body and that it does not matter to the other "parts" of our existence. Our body also belongs to God. Our whole life belongs to God! Therefore, we must glorify the Lord with all that we are.

Lord, help me to honor You with my whole existence, in Jesus' name. *Amen.*

May 3

Under His Lordship

...no one can say, "Jesus is Lord," except by the Holy Spirit.
1 Corinthians 12:3 NIV

A spider in the middle of the web waits for its prey to be caught in the web and then takes hold of it. In many ways, this is a metaphor for our life. We are in the center of it, which is why the people around us suffer. We are uncontrollable in our self-centeredness!

Before talking about the gifts of the Spirit, Paul wants to clear up something. The gifts of the Spirit are not something you can work for. It is given to people who are under the new rule of Jesus Christ. As we read this chapter, we see that these gifts serve others and build them up. They are not victims because of our self-centeredness, but beneficiaries, because Christ is our Manager!

How did we come under new management? It was the work of the Spirit. As the Spirit taught us to call God our Father (Abba!), He taught us to say: "Jesus is my Lord." Calling Jesus Lord was one of the earliest Christian confessions (Phil. 2:11). Jesus, who was a human being here on earth, now reigns as Lord. He not only rules over all the powers but is also the Manager of my life. So, everything I do is under His control. This is the work of God's Spirit!

Spirit of God, manage my life today so that it will honor You, in Jesus' name. *Amen.*

May 4

The Guarantee

The Spirit is God's guarantee that He will give us the inheritance He promised and that He has purchased us to be His own people.
Ephesians 1:14 NLT

Buying a house or a farm takes a lot of time and money. Most banks would require a deposit based on the value of the property we would like to buy. In the New Testament times, people also had to give a guarantee for the land. This is what we call a deposit today. This deposit guaranteed that the rest of the payments would follow. In Ephesians 1, we are called God's property. The Holy Spirit is God's guarantee or deposit that He will give us the inheritance He promised.

Very often we associate the work of the Spirit of God with the gifts or fruit of the Spirit. We hear how preachers correctly emphasize these gifts and fruits. Yet, we seldom hear that the Spirit is also warming our hearts with the assurance that we belong to God. Our salvation is not something based on our feelings or quality of life. Our salvation is on the firm foundation of the Holy Spirit—God's guarantee that He will fulfill His promise. Your future is secure in God's hand!

Holy Spirit, thank You for the assurance we receive from You.
Amen.

May 5

The Seal

*When you believed, you were marked in Him
with a seal, the promised Holy Spirit...*
Ephesians 1:13 NIV

God as Father, Son and Holy Spirit is a mystery, but also a revelation. Oepke Noordmans, a Dutch theologian, says about the Trinity that God spoke (as Father), came (as Jesus Christ) and comforted (as the Holy Spirit). When it was not enough that He spoke, He came. When that was not enough, He comforted us.

How does the Spirit comfort us? We saw that the Spirit is our guarantee. In Ephesians 1:13, the Spirit is like a seal (see also Eph. 4:30; 2 Cor. 1:21-23). A king or emperor had a signet ring. When he sent a letter or document, he confirmed with his seal that the letter or document was actually coming from him.

In the same way, the Holy Spirit is God's seal on us, indicating that we are truly God's own. Nothing can erase this mark from us. We are real children of God! We are therefore assured of our future with Him. The Lord will never let us down. You may never think of yourself as anything other than God's property!

Thank You, Holy Spirit, that You have sealed us as our Father's property. *Amen.*

May 6

The Firstfruits

...we also who have the firstfruits of the Spirit, even we ourselves groan within ourselves, eagerly waiting for the adoption, the redemption of our body.
Romans 8:23 NKJV

If we have already driven in an expensive and luxurious car with all the extras, and we are suddenly forced to start driving a rust bucket, we will never be satisfied. We will always compare the two cars. Any car brings us from point A to point B, but it is so much nicer if it is done in comfort.

God has given a foretaste of heaven. We have received the Spirit as the firstfruit of what is to come. The firstfruits in the Old Testament were symbolic of the whole harvest that belonged to the Lord. When Paul calls the Spirit the firstfruit, he says to his readers: "God gives you the Holy Spirit as the first gift of the harvest. Heaven, in which there will be no pain, tears, death, sin and sorrow, belongs to God's children."

Christians also suffer in conflicts, in violent societies, with cancer and other illnesses. Everyone who has received the Spirit sighs because this world smells like death. Paul says that there is an intense longing in our hearts and in creation for the day when all of this rust bucket business in our lives—all the brokenness—will be replaced with a new reality, namely the fulfillment of our hope! Even the Spirit groans with us (8:26).

We will never be satisfied with the old car, because we have tasted the new world!

Thank You, Holy Spirit, that You sigh with us, in Jesus' name.

Amen.

May 7

We Will Be Raised

> And if the Spirit of Him who raised Jesus from the dead is living in you, He who raised Christ from the dead will also give life to your mortal bodies because of His Spirit who lives in you.
> Romans 8:11 NIV

The older I get, the more I become aware of my mortality. I know I have, humanly speaking, just a decade or so left here on earth. I am at that stage where when I buy something, I begin to ask if it will last until the end! I am not a pessimist. I say all of this with a smile on my face, because I know that this is not the last word.

Paul often uses the expression that we are in Christ or that Christ is in us. It means that everything Christ has done also applies to us. Christ died; we also died. Christ was raised; we too have been raised. This is the work of the Spirit of Christ in us (8:9). It means that we have received eternal life. Even though death is the necessary consequence of the sin of humanity (8:10), we share in eternal life through the Spirit of Christ. After all, Christ, the living Lord who overcame death and sin, dwells in us.

Therefore, we are no longer under the rule, the dominion, the government of death and sin. We no longer live, but Christ lives in us through the Spirit. This will last into all eternity! Death never has the last word! We have eternal hope!

Thank You, Lord, for the hope we have, by the power of Your Spirit. Amen.

May 8

No Fear

*The Spirit you received does not make you
slaves, so that you live in fear again...*
Romans 8:15 NIV

The concept we have of God determines our whole life. If we see God as a loving Father, it makes it easier for us to love Him. If we see Him as someone looking over our shoulder all the time to see if we step out of line so that He can punish us, we live in fear of Him.

Are you afraid of God? Only slaves are afraid of their masters. Children should never be afraid of their father or mother. They should respect them but should also know that this father and mother loves them so much that they just want the best for them.

This is how people in whom the Spirit of Christ lives feel about God. They call God their Father (8:15). This Father is filled with love and forgiveness. This Father is to them like a deliverer. When someone scares them with a god who is going to punish them, they hear from the Spirit of Christ in them that they are children who are no longer condemned (8:1). They no longer live in fear of God but follow the guidance of His loving Spirit.

They know that they will inherit heaven (8:17). They know that God loves them despite their brokenness. You do not have to flee from God—you are not a slave. You may love Him, for He loves you.

I love You, Lord, because You care for me in life and death, through Jesus Christ our Lord. Amen.

May 9

One Spirit

> For by one Spirit we were all baptized into one body...
> and have all been made to drink into one Spirit.
> 1 Corinthians 12:13 NKJV

If you put a tennis ball in water, it becomes wet, but the inside remains dry. If you put a sponge in water, it is filled with water. The whole inside is wet.

The words "baptized" and "drink" are synonyms in this verse. What does it mean to be baptized with the Holy Spirit? The Greek tense refers to something that happened once in the past. We are totally filled with the Spirit. There is not a part that remains our own.

What does it mean? Firstly, that we share in the events of Pentecost. The Spirit was poured out once and even though we live almost 2,000 years later, we also share through faith in those great events. Therefore, as a church, we should follow the guidance of the Spirit. Secondly, the church and every believer are under the rule of Christ. Just as the breath of God was first breathed into human beings, the Spirit of God has given new life under the rule of Jesus Christ. Just as baptism in the name of Father, Son and Holy Spirit in Matthew 28:19 means that we have been placed under the rule of the Triune God, we have a new owner of our lives—Jesus is our Lord!

You have been baptized with the Holy Spirit. Go live today as a new person who has Jesus as Managing Director of your life!

> Lord Jesus Christ, I accept Your authority over my life again today, by the power of Your Spirit. *Amen.*

May 10

Be Filled

*Do not get drunk on wine, which leads to debauchery.
Instead, be filled with the Spirit…*
Ephesians 5:18 NIV

I own my life. I am the master of it. I make decisions. Nobody else does it for me. This is the vocabulary of darkness. Yet, we see how some people with this kind of self-centered life give themselves over to other powers: alcohol and drugs, sexual immorality and greed. They are not in control!

The command in Ephesians 5:18 that we should be filled with the Spirit is closely related to Paul's warning that we should not give ourselves over to the control of something outside ourselves, like alcohol. Someone who indulges in alcohol is obviously under its control. When alcohol (or anything else besides the Spirit) controls us— even if it is for one day or evening—we become immoral, unethical and hard to live with. Ephesians 4:25-5:18 refers to this as a life of darkness, hatred, envy and bitterness. This is a life of chaos.

As a Christian, I am not the master of my life. It does not belong to me. The Spirit filled my life. The influence of the Holy Spirit fills me with love for people around me and with praise and devotion to God (5:19-20). I constantly ask if something is acceptable to the Lord (5:10, 17). In short, it means that such a life accepts the will of God above any other authority in our life. Not our own will, but God's will prevails in every situation. This is a life in good order.

Spirit of God, take control of my life, in Jesus' name. Amen.

May 11

Spiritual Zeal

Never be lazy, but work hard and serve the Lord enthusiastically.
Romans 12:11 NLT

Unmotivated, feet-dragging people are sometimes a terrible annoyance. I played cricket when I was younger. Between the overs, the field would change position. Very often, there was a player in the fielding side who always changed position terribly slowly. He always looked unmotivated. One wondered if he wanted to play cricket at all. There was no enthusiasm.

Christians cannot be like this player. Why not? Because people who live before God have a different motivation than people who live without the Lord. We give ourselves to God because we are held by His love (12:1). Let me be clear: God does not withdraw His love because we are sometimes slack. We do not deserve to receive God's love. Yet, we sometimes lose our drive and commitment in the service of the Lord, because we forget His love for us.

We do not serve the Lord to be noticed by Him or because we want to persuade Him to love us. He loves us. We are enthusiastic in His service because we are driven by the Spirit. What drives you? Are you perhaps dragging your feet in the service of the Lord? Think about His incredible love for you. May it fill you with zeal and spiritual fervor!

Lord, fill me with Your Spirit today, in Jesus' name. Amen.

May 12

Spirit of Love

What is important is faith expressing itself in love.
Galatians 5:6 NLT

Love, love, love…all you need is love. Those of us who are old enough will remember these words from a song by The Beatles. I have not done research about it, but my impression is that the majority of pop songs are about love. We need love! This, however, is also the problem.

Paul does not speak about needing love, but giving love. Needing love is natural. It is very self-centered. Giving love is unnatural. Giving love, Paul says, is the fruit of faith. Faith that does not bear fruit in love is no faith at all. Faith, life in the Spirit, becomes visible when it turns into acts of love. If one is connected to Christ by the Spirit, love for the Lord and each other will therefore be our lifestyle.

However, we don't always get it right. We often make mistakes and sometimes lose hope that God loves us. Yet, the Spirit, as a guarantee of God's love, keeps our hope alive (5:5). He constantly emphasizes not the quality of our life, not our works, but that Christ is our salvation: "For through the Spirit we eagerly await by faith the righteousness for which we hope" (5:5 NIV). The Spirit constantly reminds us of this firm guarantee of our salvation. The Spirit keeps our hearts burning for the day when God will finally declare that we are acquitted people.

Thank You, Spirit of God, for reminding us that we have been set free, in Jesus' name. *Amen.*

May 13

Listening to the Spirit

So, as the Holy Spirit says: "Today, if you hear His voice, do not harden your hearts as you did in the rebellion..."
Hebrews 3:7-8 NIV

It was not an easy journey when we traveled from Cape Town to Windhoek in Namibia. Restless children and the summer heat in January distracted us from enjoying the journey. When we reached our destination, it was like heaven. There were welcoming people and a cool swimming pool awaiting us.

One thing is certain about our Christian journey—it will end well. We will reach the Promised Land. The journey is not always easy. There are a lot of distractions. Sometimes we want to return from where we came. This is what the letter to the Hebrews is about. It warns us not to be like Israel on the journey to the Promised Land. Sometimes they wanted to return to the land where they were treated like slaves. They became rebellious. As a result, some of them never saw the Promised Land.

Christian pilgrims should not have nominal loyalty to Christian truths. It is not enough to occasionally show lip service to faith in Christ at worship services. Our commitment must be sincere and honest.

What is the key to completing the journey and reaching the Promised Land? The message is simple: Do not be distracted by the heat and the complaints around you—the voices of this world. Listen to the only One who can guide you on this journey—the voice of the Spirit!

Spirit of God, open my ears every day on this journey of life.

Amen.

May 14

Don't Let It Come In

So, as the Holy Spirit says: "Today, if you hear
His voice, do not harden your hearts..."
Hebrews 3:7-8 NIV

The little foxes spoil the vines (Songs 2:15). It has become an idiomatic expression to say that the things we do not regard as a big danger, have the potential to cause much damage. The letter to the Hebrews warns that we can become complacent or even careless about our way of life. Yes, it is true that we have a faithful God. We remember with fondness what God has done in the past. It often carries us in difficult times. Yet, it does not help to think that you can run the marathon of faith on yesterday's faith. For that you need exercise.

It seems there is a realistic chance that people who started the journey of faith, can forget the importance of a daily commitment to hear what God is saying. When we forget this, small things, small distractions, creep into our life of faith. Slowly but surely, bad habits can start to find a place in your life so that you finally have no more time or desire to walk the path with the Lord.

The Lord does not ask whether you accepted Him long ago. Instead He asks: "Today, when you hear My voice, what do you do with it?" (Heb. 3:7, 13, 15; 4:7).

Father, let me hear Your voice today, by the power of Your Spirit.

Amen.

May 15

Learn from the Past

> ...but the word which they heard did not profit them,
> not being mixed with faith in those who heard it.
> Hebrews 4:2 NKJV

One of my brothers once said that he would have liked to teach his son not to make the same mistakes he did. He soon realized that it did not work. It seems that his son could only learn when he made the mistakes himself!

The letter to the Hebrews tries to do what my brother did. He wanted them to learn from the mistakes of their forefathers. This was very serious because it was not just about a few lessons in life. This was a matter of life and death. He refers to Israel who had fallen away from God.

How does it happen? It does not happen all at once. It happens over time, slowly but surely. The letter refers to Psalm 95. It is about the rebellion of the people against Moses, the messenger of God (Exod. 17; Num. 20). Their rebellion was nothing but defiance of the Lord Himself. Because of their rebellion, hardship, unbelief and disobedience, they missed the land of rest and perished.

Apostasy begins when we stop listening to God. These people rejected the proclamation of God's word (Heb. 4:2, 6). The Holy Spirit spoke through it. This is the voice of God (3:7). Therefore, we must not reject Him who speaks to us (12:25). The author therefore constantly admonishes us to persevere and to look after one another (3:12, 4:1, 11; 6:11-12; 10:35-36).

Lord, open my ears to the Word so that I will hear Your voice every day, in Jesus' name. *Amen.*

May 16

Dangerous!

> How much more severely do you think someone deserves to be punished who has trampled the Son of God underfoot, who has treated as an unholy thing the blood of the covenant that sanctified them, and who has insulted the Spirit of grace?
> Hebrews 10:29 NIV

I am a Christian. I will stand for Christian values in society! How many times do we hear these words? The problem is not the words, but whether we really mean it.

What is a Christian? A Christian is someone who has responded to the grace of God in Jesus, the Son of God, and who listens to God's Spirit (10:26). This is a lifelong commitment. Yet, we often fail. Sometimes we fail miserably. Is there a way back? Have we committed the ultimate sin—the sin against the Holy Spirit? Hebrews 10 refers to intentional sin. It is not the individual mistakes of each day, nor some single deliberate transgression of a commandment, but rather the constant persistence with something intentional—to intentionally reject the only sacrifice of Jesus Christ. He described this Savior throughout the first ten chapters so clearly and distinctly.

When the gospel of God's grace is preached, we hear that only one perfect sacrifice has been made for our sins. This message the Spirit of grace conveys to us with love. When we deliberately reject this message throughout our lives, we insult the Spirit of grace. If we reject the Spirit's voice, there is no longer a sacrifice that can take away our sin. Who will save us then?

> Spirit of God, thank You for the message of hope and salvation. I accept it again today, in Jesus' name. *Amen.*

May 17

Be Part of the Solution

Don't let evil conquer you, but conquer evil by doing good.
Romans 12:21 NLT

In this world, we can either be part of the problem or part of the solution. How can we be part of the solution? You might be surprised when I say, by complaining! Go on complaining about the corruption, disorder and deterioration of society. Christians sometimes complain, according to Paul, because they have received the Spirit. We know of a better world that God has in mind. He will bring this about. After all, through the Spirit, we have a foretaste of God's future world (8:23) and groan with creation and the Spirit for a new world. We are dissatisfied with the mess in the world.

However, our complaints may never make us passive. We are called and equipped by the Spirit to do everything in our power to make the world a better place. We become part of the problem of the "bad" world when we are apathetic. Romans 12:9-21 speaks about the many ways we can make this world a better place—inside and outside the church—including no revenge, love without masks, giving bread to our enemy. The Spirit teaches us to put an end to evil with a godly lifestyle. The Spirit makes us part of the solution, not part of the problem.

Yes, complain! Then become active in doing something about the problem you are complaining about.

Father, make me an instrument of Your goodness in society, by the power of Your Spirit. Amen.

May 18

No Masks

Love must be sincere.
Romans 12:9 NIV

Fake news is all over the place. Sometimes we read about so-called "research" that someone did on the internet, which later turned out to be fake. We don't know what to believe anymore.

Fake love is also all around. It is much more hurtful and damaging than fake news. Every act of political power in this world to "help" nations is not born out of concern, but self-preservation or self-enhancement. On an individual level, we ask ourselves: Who really loves me without any conditions? Love must be sincere. It literally means that love never wears masks. We have learned from Christ what true love is. He sacrificed Himself for us. Therefore, Christian love bears this stamp. How do we know if love is sincere? Paul answers immediately: It hates what is evil and clings to what is good. Love hates evil. Love clings to the good.

Our love is not reserved for fellow Christians. Yes, as in a family, there must be brotherly love, help in times of need, unity, and compassion among us. However, this is not where love ends. The Spirit fills us with love that overflows into the world. When God changes me, I also think about how I can spread the kindness, goodness and love of God to those outside the boundaries of the church. We even love our enemies (12:20). We seek peace with all. We choose what is good. The enemies of the Lord are ashamed when our love is without limits.

Spirit of God, fill me with unconditional love for all people, in Jesus' name. *Amen.*

May 19

Good News

"The Spirit of the LORD is upon Me, for He has anointed Me to bring Good News to the poor...the time of the LORD's favor has come."
Luke 4:18-19 NLT

It looks like Jesus is taking sides in these words. Jesus is indeed taking sides. Yet He does not take sides against anybody, but for everybody. He announces in public worship that His year of mercy for the broken people of the world has arrived! The man of Nazareth has good news for the poor, the slaves, the jailbirds, the oppressed, the blind.

The year of God's favor refers back to a practice every 50 years where land was returned to people who lost it through debt when slaves were freed and all debt was written off. Jesus quotes from Isaiah 61:1-2. This was written during a time when the people lost their place of worship, their security, everything!

Jesus is taking sides with all people who desperately need Him. The year of grace of the Lord is not proclaimed to the materially poor, but they are also included in it. Nor is it preached to people in concentration or refugee camps, but they are included in it. All are included here: the spiritually and materially poor, the mentally and physically blind, the person who is physically and mentally captive or in exile. No matter how bad our condition is, Jesus' year of grace, His year of restoration, dawned on us when He came into the world.

Lord, I stand where You stand, with those who desperately need You, in the name of Jesus. *Amen.*

May 20

Reflecting His Love

"The Scripture you've just heard has been fulfilled this very day!"
Luke 4:21 NLT

Gandhi was attracted to Christianity, but the lives of Christians put him off. It is sad but also understandable. It is sad because our lives should reflect Christ. It is understandable, because many people who confess that they are Christians, are not.

When Jesus spoke after reading from Isaiah 62, He said that Isaiah's words were fulfilled. God's plan for a broken world was unfolding in His ministry. His entire ministry was focused on the total needs of people. He expelled the evil spirit with power and authority from the possessed of Capernaum (Luke 4:31-36), healed lepers, the paralyzed and blind. He gave bread to hungry people and raises a daughter from the dead. He gave God's forgiveness to a sinful woman washing His feet (Luke 7) and the sinful tax collector Zacchaeus (Luke 19).

When we follow Jesus as Savior and Lord, we continue His ministry of compassion. Mother Teresa said that the joy of living with God presupposes certain things. What are these? She then describes the life reflecting God's compassion and love: to love as He loves; to give as He gives; to help as He helps; to save as He saves; to live 24 hours a day in His presence; to touch Him in the poor and the afflicted.

Father, help us to reflect Jesus today, by the power of Your Spirit.

Amen.

May 21

Tamed or Untamed?

> For the flesh desires what is contrary to the Spirit, and the Spirit what is contrary to the flesh. They are in conflict with each other, so that you are not to do whatever you want.
> Galatians 5:17 NIV

In St Petersburg, Russia, there is a bridge with four sculptures of a man who tamed a horse in four stages. It reminded me of myself. I am not like the man, but like the horse—an untamed horse. We are wild. We need to be tamed. This is a lifelong battle that the Spirit of God is performing in our lives.

When we follow our own inclinations, we cause chaos. Galatians 5:19-20 describes this wildness and chaos of self-centered service. We make life "hell" for others. However, the Spirit is like the man taming our wildness. It is not our efforts, but the power of the Spirit that will change us.

We become like a sailboat. When the wind of the Spirit fills the sails of our Christian life, the wildness and rudderless existence make way for a life of harmony, care and genuine love. Paul therefore calls us to let our behavior be determined by the Spirit (5:25). We will not be like a wild horse or a boat without direction.

> Lord, today we give You glory for our salvation and we trust that You will fill the sails of our lives with the power of love, by the power of Your Spirit. *Amen.*

May 22

In Step with God

*I say then: Walk in the Spirit...If we live in
the Spirit, let us also walk in the Spirit.*
Galatians 5:16, 25 NKJV

There is an old story about a mother who saw her son marching at a military parade. Everybody was marching in time, but he was out of time. Then she said, "See, only my son is marching in time. All the others are out of time."

It seems like Christians are now like this one soldier—out of time with the rest of the world. Why? The values and lifestyle of the world around us have rapidly become immoral and ungodly. The values of Galatians 5:19-21 are reigning supreme around us.

Being in step with the Spirit puts us at odds with the values of the world. The Spirit produces fruit in us that does not come naturally (5:22-23). Christ lives in people who were justified by grace (2:20)! Faith leads to loving acts (5:6). Our freedom in Christ enables us to show love to those around us (5:14). We bear one another's burdens out of love (6:1-2). It is very difficult for us to get this right. No, it is not just difficult, it is impossible!

The Spirit of God carries His characteristics and rules of conduct into our lives. Our own efforts will come to nothing. On the other hand, we can do anything if God enables us to do it. St Augustine prayed, "Give what You command, and then command whatever You will."

Spirit of God, I want to walk in step with You today, in Jesus' name. Amen.

May 23

A New Body

Now you are the body of Christ, and each one of you is a part of it.
1 Corinthians 12:27 NIV

A toothache or headache is terrible. When we have a toothache or a headache, the whole body is affected. Paul understood this when he spoke about the church. We are like a body. When there is a problem with one part of the body, the whole body is affected.

It is so awful to see how much rivalry there often is between Christians. It must be painful to Christ, the Head of the body. He wanted us to live in unity and prayed for it (John 17:20-23). Very often there is disagreement about God's gifts. Paul writes that the Lord gave certain tasks to different people. These people are like body parts that fit together (1 Cor. 12:27-28). Not everyone can be the same.

Therefore, in 1 Corinthians 12:29-30, Paul asks questions that must be answered with "no" every time. Are all apostles? No. Are all pastors? No. Does everyone speak in tongues? No! Not everyone will speak in tongues because not everyone receives the same gifts (12:7-11). It remains important for Paul to respect the work of the Spirit in the church. Gifts are given, yes, but not the same gifts and none is better than the other.

Let us not judge one another. Let us respect God's choice and rejoice about the variety of gifts in one body.

Lord, thank You for the variety of gifts You have given to Your body, the church, by the power of Your Spirit. Amen.

May 24

God's Sculptor

And we all…are being transformed into His image with ever-increasing glory, which comes from the Lord, who is the Spirit…Though outwardly we are wasting away, yet inwardly we are being renewed day by day.
2 Corinthians 3:18; 4:16 NIV

Aging is a slow process. We do not really see the changes ourselves, because we see ourselves in the mirror every day. However, when we see a photograph from some years ago, we realize that things have changed radically!

Change is a natural part of life. There is, of course, a different kind of change—a very positive kind. This is the change the Spirit of God brings about in our lives. A person who walks with the Spirit of God never remains the same.

Paul says that we are being changed more and more to look like Christ. This is wonderful news! This is one of the most important tasks of the Spirit. He is God's chisel that cuts off the pieces of our lives that do not look like Christ. He is God's operating knife that cuts out the things that destroy us. Without this work of the Spirit of the Lord, our lives will perish.

Christians therefore never long for the "good old days". The old photographs do not matter! The changes the Spirit brings are all that matter. We want to grow, to mature in faith, so that we can be more and more like Christ.

Spirit of God, change me every day to become more like Jesus.

Amen.

May 25

Which Plant Do You Water?

Do not be deceived: God cannot be mocked.
A man reaps what he sows.
Galatians 6:7 NIV

I am not a gardener. When I was a child, I was forced to do work in the garden in the hot summer sun. Since then, I try to avoid anything reminding me of those days! But Paul reminds us in Galatians 6 that we are gardeners, whether we like it or not. We sow and reap. The philosopher Francis Bacon remarked that a person is a plant that either becomes a fragrant spice or a destructive weed. Therefore, he said, we should pay attention to which one gets water.

We can grow in two directions: One is the way of death, the other the way of life (6:8). It is fatal to build on our own nature. Human beings, whether religious, legalistic and moralistic, or living a sinful life apart from God, are never fertile soil. It is very volatile. We must acknowledge that humans are really just destructive weeds. When we water our human nature, there will be uncontrollable disasters for us and others.

However, the water of the Spirit also has a means of destroying weeds, namely Jesus' death and resurrection. The Spirit uses the redemptive work of Christ to destroy sin in our lives. It is written off in the eyes of God. Through the redemptive work of Christ, the Spirit makes the new life, the Christ life, visible in us. We can rely on the Spirit. When we water this plant, the end of it is clear: abundant life and joy from God's hand!

Holy Spirit, come and fill me today, in Jesus' name. Amen.

May 26

New Management

*Do not let sin control the way you live;
do not give in to sinful desires.*
Romans 6:12 NLT

Workplaces can be like hell because a manager can make life very difficult. Sometimes people just have no energy to go to work or develop depression because of this pressure. Imagine such a horrible life. If you can find a way out, you will take it. Nobody wants to work in such an atmosphere. Yet sometimes people are trapped in situations like this. Our job becomes a duty, not a pleasure. We do our job for only one reason: we have to, otherwise we will starve.

Then another company buys the one you work for. Your manager is fired. You get a new manager who makes you and the other staff feel like people. It is fun for you to go to work. Your workplace becomes a joy and energizes you. Will you then long for the old dispensation with your previous manager every day? Will you drive to his house every day after work and hang out with him for a bit?

Unfortunately, there are people like that in our life with God. We were liberated from the slave master of sin, but we still like to hang out with our old life. Paul calls us to stop visiting the old manager of our lives (6:14). We are God's new people who have come to life. We are under new management. Why then are you and I like slaves of our old lives?

Lord, enable me to break with the old manager and continue to live under new management with joy, in Jesus' name. Amen.

May 27

Wonderful Gifts

All these are the work of one and the same Spirit, and He distributes them to each one, just as He determines.
1 Corinthians 12:11 NIV

We all spend some time in front of the mirror. Normally it is not to inspect our bodies, but to shave or to put makeup on our faces. We almost never think about our body as long as it works well. We walk, talk, eat, play without giving it the slightest thought that our bodies are a complex system working together in harmony.

I often wonder if church leaders think about the church in this way. Sometimes they expect things from a part of the body that cannot perform that function. An eye cannot hear and an ear cannot see. Would we expect it from these body parts?

Unfortunately, we do not understand the gifts of the Spirit correctly. In 1 Corinthians 12:7 and 11, the words "each one" are used. The congregation members each receive an operation of the Spirit separately. One person does not receive everything. That is why we see all the time that Paul is using the words "to one" and "to the other".

Finally, the Spirit of God decides how He divides the gifts (12:11). It is the choice of God. Why does the Spirit do it in this way? So that we can use our gifts "for the common good" (12:7). We are called to serve one another with our gifts.

Thank You, Holy Spirit, that we differ. Help us to respect our differences and serve Your body, in Jesus' name. Amen.

May 28

We Suffer Together

Just as a body, though one, has many parts, but all its many parts form one body, so it is with Christ...Even so the body is not made up of one part but of many.
1 Corinthians 12:12, 14 NIV

Charles Spurgeon was a very famous and dynamic Baptist preacher in the 19th century. He got very ill. After a long period of illness, someone gave him something to eat. He then said that it tasted like grace. When our bodies are sick, we long for them to be well again. When one part is sick, it influences the whole body. Then we realize how important every part of the body is. When we get well, it feels like grace.

Paul writes to a Corinthian congregation that had become a sick body for many reasons. One of the reasons was that some people felt inferior about their own gifts. Apparently, they felt they could not make any contribution as their gift was not important enough.

I often hear people say, "No, let someone else do the work. They are more competent. I don't have their ability." This is the argument that Paul takes up in verse 14. The Spirit gives everyone a gift. They differ from each other. The one is not more important than the other.

No matter how small your gift is in your own eyes, it does not matter for the Lord and His church. You are making a contribution to the healthy functioning of the body. Without you, it will become sick. When you make your contribution, grace will be experienced.

Lord, let me be willing to share my gifts, in Jesus' name.

Amen.

May 29

Love

And yet I will show you the most excellent way.
1 Corinthians 12:31 NIV

The blood transfusion services perform an essential service to thousands of people. Give blood and save lives, they say. No description could be more accurate. People can have the most amazing skills and bodies, but without blood, the body is a corpse. This is what love is in the church of Jesus Christ. It is the blood of the body. It carries the necessary oxygen and life-giving elements to enable the body to function.

Paul again makes a list of the gifts. This time he does it for a different reason. He says that lovelessness draws a line through gifts. Even if we speak in tongues, without love it is just a terrible noise (13:1). Even if we prophesy on every occasion and claim extraordinary wisdom or knowledge, without love it means nothing. If we boast of a faith that heals others or does extraordinary things, but there is no love, it means nothing (13:2). Even if you give yourself to others in a sacrificial way by helping the poor or showing charity, if it is not driven by love, it is no good (13:3).

Sometimes it is awful to listen to the spiritual superiority of Christians. "If you have not yet experienced this or that gift, something may be wrong with you." Is it love that speaks like that? Without love, no gift is worth anything. Love is like the blood of the body. Without love, the body is dead.

Father, give us the love of Christ, by the power of Your Spirit.

Amen.

May 30

Love Despite...

Always be humble and gentle. Be patient with each other, making allowance for each other's faults because of your love.
Ephesians 4:2 NLT

People are different and disagree with each other. This is part of life. Therefore, we will always experience conflicts, wherever we work. We generally try to avoid conflict. However, life is not that simple. The longer we know each other, the more we also realize what others' faults and shortcomings are.

The church, society and good relationships do not depend on whether people understand each other. Understanding each other can never be the basis of any relationship. Only people who think alike could then live together.

The challenge for all Christians is to be humble and gentle, and to bear with one another. The Spirit teaches us to live with differences. It teaches us to create space for those who are not like us or think like us. This attitude is motivated by love, Paul says. Without love, it is impossible to live with people! This love is the fruit of God's Spirit in us. Mutual understanding is not the key to good relationships—mutual love is.

Spirit of God, teach me to love, in spite of misunderstandings, in Jesus' name. Amen.

May 31

There Is Enough for All

> It is a sin to despise one's neighbor, but blessed
> is the one who is kind to the needy.
> Proverbs 14:21 NIV

A relationship with God offers us security. People who are upright, experience reconciliation (14:9). To serve God provides a safe place for our children (14:26). Those who serve Him receive life as a gift (14:27).

What does it mean to serve God? The poet makes it simple. Our relationship with those around us is the place where it becomes clear what our relationship with God is. The people he refers to are especially those among us who are in need (14:21), the poor people (14:31). If we despise or oppress them, we sin. Moreover, it is an insult to God, because He made them (14:31). God is close to the people who are experiencing distress (Ps. 146).

The Lord comes to us in the form of people in need. The Final Judgment will show that we often stopped at the Lord Himself when we stopped to help people in need (Matt. 25:31–46). For as far as we have helped someone in distress, we were doing it to Jesus (Matt. 25:40). If we live this way, we honor God (Prov. 14:31).

> God of grace, free me from greed and teach me to be generous, by the power of Your Spirit. *Amen.*

June

June 1

A Refuge for Children

*Whoever fears the LORD has a secure fortress,
and for their children it will be a refuge.*
Proverbs 14:26 NIV

Family life is in a crisis and has been for decades. The number of children who come from broken homes is growing. Tomorrow they will be parents. What prospects do they have to be good parents if they themselves did not have a good example to follow? What prospects do they have to have a healthy family life if they were not exposed to a good family life? Please note, I do not think for a moment that people who are divorced are not Christians or have not served the Lord when they divorced. Sometimes the divorce was one of their biggest faith struggles.

The poet says that people who serve the Lord are giving their children stability. I know of cases where the example of parents so affected their children that they also serve the Lord today. Again, it does not always happen that parents who serve the Lord have believing children. Yet, these parents are giving their children the stability they need in their lives.

It is a myth to say that we will not influence our children in any way about religious matters. They have to choose themselves. If this is your view, you need to wake up. If you do not influence your children, the world will. The values of the broken world will be their guide.

Father, help me to influence my children with Your love, in Jesus' name. Amen.

June 2

For the Sake of Our Children

> Whoever fears the LORD has a secure fortress,
> and for their children it will be a refuge.
> Proverbs 14:26 NIV

Not everyone is blessed to have good parents. Not everyone grew up in a Christian home. Many of us grew up in a home where people went to church, but it was pure religious duty. There was nothing of God in it—just tradition.

If this was the case with you, you can change the way you raise your children. How? E. Stanley Jones remarked that religious education without conversion is like a course in marriage relations without marriage. The stability we owe our children is to live with Christian integrity. It does not mean that we are faultless; it just means that stability starts when we love the Lord with all our heart.

Deuteronomy 6:5-9 (NKJV) says, "You shall love the LORD your God with all your heart, with all your soul, and with all your strength. And these words which I command you today shall be in your heart. You shall teach them diligently to your children, and shall talk of them when you sit in your house, when you walk by the way, when you lie down, and when you rise up. You shall bind them as a sign on your hand, and they shall be as frontlets between your eyes. You shall write them on the doorposts of your house and on your gates."

Let us decide today to give our children the best gift—the security that we love the Lord. They need it in very uncertain times. It will make a difference in their lives!

Father of families, please help us to provide stability of faith to our children, by the power of Your Spirit. Amen.

June 3

The Symbol of Marriage

Live happily with the woman you love...
Ecclesiastes 9:9 NLT

When a bride wears her beautiful white dress on her wedding day, I sometimes wonder how long the beauty and happiness are going to last after the wedding. Will the bride and bridegroom continue to enjoy life together? Statistics say that many marriages end or become a place of strife and pain.

The poet says that we should enjoy life together. In Ecclesiastes 9:7-8 (NIV), he says, "Go, eat your food with gladness, and drink your wine with a joyful heart...Always be clothed in white, and always anoint your head with oil." Bread, wine, white clothes and oil on the hair were symbols of festivity in Israel. A proper party now and then is good, but is the author unrealistic when he says that we should always wear white clothes? Is it possible that life can always be a feast? How will our marriage always remain such a festive symbol? We should acknowledge that life and all its pleasures are a gift from God (2:24-25; 3:12-13; 5:17-18). These gifts include the person God gave to you. Our relationship will remain a feast if we always treat our partner as a gift from God.

After all, marriage is also a symbol of the eternal marriage between God and His people. Then we will all stand in white robes before the throne of the Lamb and partake of the wedding supper (Rev. 7:9-17; 19:5-10). Let your marriage symbolize this great feast that awaits us!

Lord, give joy in our relationships, in Jesus' name. *Amen.*

June 4

Path of Freedom

*"I am the LORD your God, who brought you out
of Egypt, out of the land of slavery."*
Deuteronomy 5:6 NIV

Millions of people over many centuries experienced the atrocities of slavery: losing their identity, their freedom and having to do what their master or owner told them to do. Israel experienced physical slavery. One terrible atrocity was added: all male babies had to be killed. Their future was being threatened. The Pharaoh wanted the people of God to be wiped out.

But God set them free! What a wonderful act of God's intervention. When someone sets you free from this kind of pain, you want to say thank you. God gave them a future; therefore, they should live as He wants them to live.

Our "thank you" is to obey God's guidelines for freedom. Every commandment of the Ten Commandments should therefore be read after the words: "I am the Lord your God, who brought you out of Egypt, out of the land of slavery!"

Christians are free. Our life was at a dead end. God opened up a new way through His Son. We want to serve the Lord of love in freedom. He gives us His Spirit to do just that. The Spirit guides us every day as a good guide on this path of freedom. Therefore, we can serve no one else!

Do you understand your freedom? It is a freedom to serve God and your fellow man. This is what the Ten Commandments are about!

Spirit of God, I thank You that You have set us free to serve You and those around us, in Jesus' name. Amen.

June 5

Blurred or Clear Vision?

"The eye is the lamp of the body. If your eyes are healthy, your whole body will be full of light...No one can serve two masters."
Matthew 6:22, 24 NIV

I go for regular eye tests as I get older, because it becomes more and more difficult to read. Blurred vision is a problem! Yet, blurred or double vision is a much bigger problem for Christians. Someone with double vision sees two things while he only needs to see one. Jesus says that our eyesight, our focus, is essential when we are citizens of God's kingdom.

Jesus only explains here what is already stated in the Ten Commandments. The Lord God demands undivided faithfulness and love (Exod. 20:5). If our eyesight is bad, our lives are divided between the Master and the masters of this world, between the ideals of God's kingdom and the ideals of the world. While the Lord's kingdom must be the first priority, other things fill our horizons.

Citizens of God's kingdom need to get new glasses. These glasses are to judge everything with one question: Does it serve God's kingdom or not? We are constantly tempted to lose our hearts on earthly things. It is dangerous. Why? Because earthly things perish (Matt. 6:19). If you focus only on the earthly things, your life will be very dark (6:23).

It is foolish to have a divided heart. It is foolish to have double vision, while we can see better.

Spirit of God, give me a single vision! Lord, enable me to serve You today with an undivided heart. Amen.

June 6

Where Is Your Heart?

*"For where your treasure is, there your heart will
be also...No one can serve two masters..."*
Matthew 6:21, 24 NKJV

Martin Luther said that what you ultimately trust in your life is your god. It is that person, dream or ideal, that matter or asset, that is most important to you. If there is one thing that is more important than God, it is your god.

Jesus warns therefore that double vision, a double heart, is a symptom of a sick relationship with God. We cannot have two gods in our lives. Two gods are tiring—they demand time and energy. Ultimately, we have to choose between the gods in our lives. When you make that choice, it will ultimately show in your life.

There are so many things that take over our lives: money, the search for power and popularity, dreams and ideals, positions and titles. These things often fill the horizons of our lives in such a way that God is driven out of our lives. But a life before God means judging every aspect of our lives. We need to put it on the scales. Does it weigh more than God?

Jim Elliot said, "He is no fool who gives what he cannot keep to gain what he cannot lose." What is it in your life that you want to keep, while losing what is most important? What are you willing to give up, because God has taken the most important place in your life?

Father, enable me to get my priorities in order and place everything under Your rule, in Jesus' name. Amen.

June 7

My Ultimate Concern

"Seek the Kingdom of God above all else, and live righteously, and He will give you everything you need."
Matthew 6:33 NLT

I have many friends who struggle with mental illness. As someone who has experienced episodes of depression, I understand something of their struggle. One of the symptoms is that they feel they have no purpose in life. The feeling is that their dreams are shattered and there is not much of a future. Very often they are worried and anxious about the future.

Jesus refers to birds and lilies in Matthew 6. The Lord looks after them. Birds and lilies were not created to sow and harvest (traditionally men's work) or make clothes (traditionally women's work). The birds and flowers only had to fulfill the purpose for which they were created. God made the lilies beautiful and provided food for the birds.

With this image, Jesus emphasizes that it is not our purpose to worry about our lives. We are worried about many things. What are we going to eat, drink or get dressed in tomorrow? The Lord has promised that He will take care of us. We cannot extend our lives by a single hour by worrying. We need to live for the purpose for which we were created—to do God's will and to be people who put His kingdom first. This is your purpose. This is your goal. Leave the rest to God! He will look after all the things that are beyond your control.

Lord, I commit myself to You again today, in Jesus' name.

Amen.

June 8

Part of God's Family

For this reason I kneel before the Father, from whom every family in heaven and on earth derives its name.
Ephesians 3:14-15 NIV

There are people who say they are believers but they do not need the church. Cyprian said that we cannot have God for our Father and not have the Church for our mother. The community of believers is the creation of the Father (3:14-15). The Father of Jesus Christ lives by faith and through the Spirit in our hearts (3:16-17).

Earlier in his letter, Paul emphasizes that all those who were saved by grace, through the blood and body of Jesus Christ, have free access to the Father by the Spirit (2:1-22). We talk with our Father. We are part of the body. We are part of God's family. We are part of God's building. We are no longer strangers and foreigners. We are brothers and sisters. People who call God Father, cannot avoid contact with their family members. Such an attitude reveals that the family is dysfunctional.

The church is like a mother with many children. We are part of this family of which Jesus Christ is the cornerstone. We discover His love more and more together with other family members (3:18). Can we have God as Father without being part of the church? It is a biblical impossibility.

Lord, let me love You and Your church, for Christ's sake.

Amen.

June 9

The Playing Field of Life

> Therefore, brethren, be even more diligent to make your call and election sure, for if you do these things you will never stumble; for so an entrance will be supplied to you abundantly into the everlasting kingdom of our Lord and Savior Jesus Christ.
> 2 Peter 1:10–11 NKJV

I met a doctor in Northern Ireland who had a passion for the gospel. On his deathbed, he used the opportunity to explain the gospel to his children and grandchildren for the last time.

Only those who believe will have eternal life. Those who do not believe do not have eternal life. For children, parents, grandchildren and friends who believe in Jesus Christ, death is only a temporary separation. We train ourselves for the life to come, where there will be no more separation, pain, tears and hurt. Therefore, we pray, "Spirit of God, fill us with faith, hope and love, through Jesus Christ our Lord. Amen."

Christians, waiting in hope for this new world, should aim to be the sort of people who can enter it—the expectation of the *Parousia* (return of Christ) should be a motive for Christian righteousness.

Our life here is the playing field where decisions of eternal importance are made. Without faith in Jesus Christ, there awaits only eternal separation between God and us and between those we love and us.

Spirit of God, give us faith in You, by the power of Your Spirit.

Amen.

June 10

The Book of Life

*Anyone whose name was not found written in the
book of life was thrown into the lake of fire.*
Revelation 20:15 NIV

As I get older, I sometimes calculate how many years, humanly speaking, remain for me. My life is not going to last forever. Sometimes I feel dread when I read a passage in Scripture saying that God would then hold us accountable for everything we have done. The Day of Judgment is a frightening thought for many people. This is what I have been taught since childhood.

Should Christians dread this day? No, we should look forward with joy to the day when we will meet the Lord. If it is true that the Lord has written off our sin, why should we be judged on the basis of our works?

In Revelation, there are books in which the deeds of people are recorded. However, there is also talk of a book where names are written down. The group whose deeds have been recorded are the people who will be judged on the basis of their deeds. The good news is that the Lord does not know His children according to their deeds. The Lord knows His children by their names.

The good news of the gospel is that God does not keep a record of your sins. Your name has been written down because your sin has been written off. Anyone who rejects Christ will be held accountable for what he or she has done. Therefore, trust Christ and look forward with joy to the day when you meet the Lord.

Thank You, Lord, that You know me by my name, through Jesus Christ. *Amen.*

June 11

Expensive Grace

For you know that it was not with perishable things such as silver or gold that you were redeemed from the empty way of life...
1 Peter 1:18 NIV

Cheap grace. It means that people use the church to get what they want, but do not live as followers of Jesus Christ. They look for places where grace demands nothing from them. Do we not make it too easy for people to be saved? Are we not making God's grace cheap? I think so.

Cheap grace can also refer to something else. We can make God's grace cheap by thinking we can buy it with our good works. Peter says that our money cannot buy grace. We are not born again because we have repented, believed or confessed our guilt. We, like our deeds, will wither like grass in the hot sun (1:23-24). God's grace is written in blood. The precious blood of a perfect sacrifice was shed to redeem us from our sin. Therefore, it can never be cheap. The living and eternal Word of the gospel convinced us of God's grace (1:23-25).

So today we are challenged by two extremes: Firstly, do I make God's grace cheap by just looking for a safe place where the gospel of God's grace demands nothing from me? In other words, I want God's grace, but don't ask me to follow Jesus. Secondly, do I want to buy God's grace with my piety or religious behavior? Both extremes will have the same effect—making grace cheap.

Lord Jesus, make me thankful for Your perfect sacrifice.

Amen.

June 12

Desert Times

Dear brothers and sisters, when troubles of any kind come your way, consider it an opportunity for great joy.
James 1:2 NLT

The Arabs, Egyptians and Namibians have one thing in common. They know deserts! Deserts are not really known for amazing trees and vegetation. These are the places where the sun never stops shining and everything is dry.

There's a proverb that says, "Sunshine all the time makes a desert." It is true. It is also true of the life of faith. The desert people of our society can become very dry and without much growth and life. It is those who know only sunshine in their lives. I find it difficult to approach people who only know sunshine. They often have very little need for God.

Trials, James says, should fill us with joy. It tests our faith, but also makes us grow in spiritual maturity. I feel more at home with people who have experienced hardships in life. If they embrace it as a time of growth, they have hearts of compassion and love for God. They are not as hard and unapproachable as the desert. They provide shelter when we are going through hard times, because they know hard times. They are like trees in the desert!

I pray that the Lord will use the rainy days in your life to be an oasis for others where they can find rest and refreshment.

Lord, use the trials in my life to let me grow in maturity, in Jesus' name. *Amen.*

June 13

Depression and Faith

A happy heart makes the face cheerful, but heartache crushes the spirit...All the days of the oppressed are wretched...
Proverbs 15:13, 15 NIV

According to the World Health Organization, depression is now the leading cause of ill health and disability in the world. There are more than 300 million people around the world who have been diagnosed with depression. Between 2006 and 2015, there was an 18% increase in this disease. What the causes are we will not easily understand. Yet, we need to show understanding when people struggle. We can be part of the healing plan of God in the lives of these people.

The poet knows that sad and bad news cause heartbreak instead of joy (15:13, 30). All people are sensitive to loss, but some more than others. Every piece of bad news we receive is a form of loss. It may affect our expectations and dreams. It can influence our status. It can threaten our marriage and family life. It can make us feel lonely. The poet says that those in difficult circumstances have a very difficult life.

Does faith help? In his commentary on the letter of Paul to the Philippians, Gerald Hawthorne writes that joy is an understanding of existence that encompasses both elation and depression. Joy does not mean that we smile all the time. The source of joy is "to see beyond any particular event to the sovereign Lord who stands above all events and ultimately has control over them."

Father, give those who are depressed a vision of Your presence in their circumstances, in Jesus' name. *Amen.*

June 14

Health and a Cheerful Heart

> ...for the happy heart, life is a continual feast...A cheerful look brings joy to the heart; good news makes for good health.
> Proverbs 15:15, 30 NLT

Scientists say that laughing does something to the chemicals in our brains that make us feel better. You and I can make a difference in the lives of depressed people by being bearers of hope. The poet says that people might become healthier if they see joy in their eyes and hear good news. When someone sees the joy in our eyes about the hope God brings in difficult circumstances, it can make a huge difference.

There is nothing that fills our lives with more hope and joy than the resurrection of Christ. When Peter wrote about the power of the resurrection of Christ, he referred to our assurance of eternal life and the treasure we have in heaven, amid severe hardship. Then he says, "In all this you greatly rejoice, though now for a little while you may have had to suffer grief in all kinds of trials...Though you have not seen Him, you love Him; and even though you do not see Him now, you believe in Him and are filled with an inexpressible and glorious joy" (1 Pet. 1:6, 8 NIV).

When we look beyond what we can see, we become bearers of hope. Be a bearer of this joy today, without judging those who struggle. Let them rather see the light in your eyes, brought about by your love for the Lord and for them!

Spirit of God, make me someone who will bring joy and hope in other people's lives today, because Jesus Christ lives. *Amen.*

June 15

God's Fools

> When they heard about the resurrection of
> the dead, some of them sneered, but others said,
> "We want to hear you again on this subject."
> Acts 17:32 NIV

How do we measure success as Christians? Do we say that something is successful when there are good results? If this is the way we measure success, we should think twice.

Paul was not very "successful" when he talked to the Jews, philosophers, the council of the Areopagus and the people in the city square in Athens. Some of them asked, "What is this babbler trying to say?" (17:18 NIV). The Greek word they used was also used for people removing rubbish from the market square. This was a clear insult. We also read that others sneered. People shook their heads and made fun of God's fool. This is what the Athenians did to Paul when he explained the essence of the gospel, namely the resurrection of Jesus.

Yes, we are God's fools in the eyes of the world. This should not silence us. It is better to be God's fool than to remain silent. Sometimes it feels as if sharing the gospel with our friends, family and colleagues is falling on deaf ears. Continue to do your part. The Lord will take care of the harvest. He did the same in this case. We read that some people became believers—even a member of the Areopagus! Some sneered, but some kept the door open, saying, "We want to hear you again on this subject."

Do not underestimate the power of the Lord!

Lord, I trust You, even when nobody seems to listen. Amen.

June 16

His Gracious Choice

All praise to God, the Father of our Lord Jesus Christ, who has blessed us with every spiritual blessing in the heavenly realms because we are united with Christ. Even before He made the world, God loved us and chose us in Christ to be holy and without fault in His eyes.
Ephesians 1:3-4 NLT

To play for your country in an international tournament in any sport is the dream of most sportspersons. You have to work hard, spend hours every day in training, and eat, drink, sleep and dream it. And even then, it is sometimes not good enough. Sometimes selectors like one player more than another.

Fortunately, God chooses us by His grace only. There is no competition for a place in His kingdom. God has chosen Jesus to be the Savior of the world. In Him, God's whole plan of salvation became clear (1:3-14). The Son of God shares His chosenness with us. In the kingdom of God, each person is precious and unique. God's choice is not based on competition, but on compassion and grace!

Everyone who trusts in Jesus is now God's most precious child. What do you think about yourself? Do you believe that God has chosen you by His grace? You don't have to work hard for it; it is God's gift to you through Jesus. May God give you the eyes to see this!

Lord, thank You that You have chosen me by Your grace, through Jesus our Lord. Amen.

June 17

The Stability of God's Faithfulness

*I lift up my eyes to the mountains—where does my help come from?
My help comes from the LORD, the Maker of heaven and earth.*
Psalm 121:1–2 NIV

A theology student visited an elderly woman as part of his practical work. As he was about to leave, he said that he wanted to give her a promise from God's Word, namely that the Lord is always with us. The woman said, "Son, it is not a promise. It is a fact."

What facts are you working with in life? That the economy will improve? That you will keep your job? That you are healthy and will be able to work? That you will keep your house?

Our help is from the Lord, Maker of heaven and earth—only from Him. We hear from the Bible, "'I am the Alpha and the Omega,' says the Lord God, 'who is, and who was, and who is to come, the Almighty'...'Do not be afraid. I am the First and the Last. I am the Living One; I was dead, and now look, I am alive for ever and ever'" (Rev. 1:8, 17–18 NIV).

God is not an emergency measure. Blaise Pascal wrote: "It is impossible that God should ever be the end if He is not the beginning. We lift our eyes on high, but lean upon the sand..."

Who is your help? Our help is from the Lord—immovable in faithfulness!

Lord, You are everything to me. I place my trust in You alone, through Your grace. Amen.

June 18

Integrity

"Our Father in heaven..."
Matthew 6:9 NIV

In a short prayer, John Keble prays: "Help us, this and every day, to live more nearly as we pray." There is an old rule in Christianity expressed in Latin: *"lex orandi, lex credendi, lex vivendi."* In simple terms it means: What we pray is what we believe and is the way we live. There can be no separation between these aspects of our lives.

Prayer can easily be seen as an armchair life. You surrender everything to God, but do not move a finger to work together with God to accomplish what you have asked for. There is a proverb that says, "Pray to God, but row towards shore."

When we pray the prayer that Jesus taught us, we become part of it. When we ask that His name be sanctified, that His kingdom come, that His will be done, that we receive daily bread, that our guilt be forgiven, and that we be delivered from evil, we become partners with God to do this. We do everything to sanctify God's name, do His will, seek His kingdom, give bread to people, fight against evil and to forgive others their sins.

Matthew adds a note at the end of the prayer: If you do not forgive others, God will not forgive you! Can it be said more clearly that our responsibility is incorporated into our prayers?

Spirit of God, make me active when I pray, in Jesus' name.

Amen.

June 19

Our Status Before God

> Believers in humble circumstances ought to take pride in their high position...the rich will fade away even while they go about their business.
>
> James 1:9, 11 NIV

The Bible is very clear that our possessions and money can prevent us from following Jesus wholeheartedly.

James often equates rich people with unbelievers (2:6; 5:1). It is clear that there was an issue between the rich and poor in the faith community. Rich people were treated well (James 2). Poor people were exploited by the rich. They gathered wealth and possessions and did not pay the daily wages of the poorest people (5:1–6). Their wealth and social injustice went hand in hand.

Listening to what James is saying, reminds us of the parable of the rich fool (Luke 12:13–21). He and the rich in James's time did not consider the fact that their lives were like a wildflower that perished when plucked (James 1:10–11).

Therefore, rich believers should rethink their status before God. Their wealth did not give them an advantage before God. They are equal with the poor before God. On the contrary, a poor believer has a better position before God than a rich person who does not respect God and the poor.

James makes it clear: It does not matter what your status in society is, the primary consideration is if God takes center stage in your life. Our greatest gift is not money and possessions, but that we have received the Kingdom as a gift (2:5).

What gives you status? God or your position or possessions?

Lord, let me use my possessions to honor You, in Jesus' name.

Amen.

June 20

Let the Word Control You

So get rid of all the filth and evil in your lives, and humbly accept the word God has planted in your hearts, for it has the power to save your souls.
James 1:21 NLT

People today certainly do not think the same about issues as a few decades ago. Think about the changes in viewpoints on some ethical issues, like abortion, divorce, euthanasia and human sexuality. There are so many changes in society.

We need discernment. We must admit that our "openness" to change has also contributed to the moral decay in our society. The borders between right and wrong have become blurred.

James says that people who have God's Word in their lives should always be controlled by it. This Word is not subject to the changes of this world. We should do what it says (1:22). This Word enables us to resist the moral decay in our society, not to give in to the suction power of this world, and to become involved with those who are broken people because of a broken world (1:21, 27).

Lord, plant Your Word in us, so that our viewpoints will be consistent with Your point of view, in Jesus' name. *Amen.*

June 21

With God in My Crisis

*Better is a little with the fear of the LORD,
than great treasure with trouble.*
Proverbs 15:16 NKJV

Many of us needlessly complain about our quality of life. Most of us reading this have a roof over our heads and something to eat. Yet we often toss and turn at night and worry about tomorrow. Why are you worried now? Maybe it bothers you that you no longer have the same status as in the past. Perhaps you do not have as many possessions as always. Maybe you are afraid because your job is uncertain. Maybe you worry about your investments.

Hans Walter Wolff, a German theologian, once said that he would rather be with God in his crisis than without Him in his prosperity. To experience God's presence when you are not rich, not happy and have almost nothing is only possible when you sit at the feet of the Lord. There one discovers that even the biggest crisis cannot withhold us from His presence.

The author of Hebrews says, "Don't love money; be satisfied with what you have. For God has said, 'I will never fail you. I will never abandon you.' So we can say with confidence, 'The LORD is my helper, so I will have no fear'" (Heb. 13:5-6 NLT).

God is with you today. It does not matter how insecure your future is.

Lord, we thank You for the wealth of Your presence. Amen.

June 22

Worship Every Day

> The LORD detests the thoughts of the wicked, but gracious words are pure in His sight. The greedy bring ruin to their households, but the one who hates bribes will live.
> Proverbs 15:26-27 NIV

Wisdom is worship in everyday life. How do we worship every day? When our relationship with God is inseparable from our relationship with those around us. A soft answer (15:1) and calming words (15:4) build the relationships between people. Refusing bribes gives you a meaningful life (15:27). It shows wisdom. This wisdom is the gift of God (15:33). God approves of such a life (15:9).

When we hurt each other, become wealthy at the expense of another person and live independently from God, we are fools. God does not accept the sacrifice of such people (15:8). He hates such a way of life (15:9).

Worship in your daily life is when your relationship with God determines your relationship with your neighbor. John makes this clear in his first letter. Everyone who understands the love of Christ will care with love for his or her fellow human beings, "Dear friends, since God loved us that much, we surely ought to love each other. No one has ever seen God. But if we love each other, God lives in us, and His love is brought to full expression in us" (1 John 4:11-12 NLT).

G. K. Chesterton said that we make our friends and we make our enemies, but God makes our next-door neighbor. Let your worship begin!

Father, teach me to be like You, full of love and mercy, by the power of Your Spirit. Amen.

June 23

Logical Faith?

"And though the city will be given into the hands of the Babylonians, You, Sovereign LORD, say to me, 'Buy the field with silver and have the transaction witnessed.'"
Jeremiah 32:25 NIV

There is a Greek proverb that says, "A society grows great when old men plant trees in whose shade they shall never sit." This is an act of hope. We care for the place we live, even when it is not always a positive and good place.

Jeremiah is acting in a very specific historical situation. The enemy will occupy the place. Their faith will be under pressure. Yet, he is commanded to stay there, to blossom where God has placed him at this stage.

There is a lot of negativity around. Constant worries about recessions, unstable money and property markets, food and fuel prices, corruption, and the undermining of God's values. Pessimism rather than optimism threatens to overcome us. The financial advisory services of Jerusalem would probably rather advise Jeremiah to invest in the emerging market of the world power, Babylon. Yet he buys a piece of land where he will probably never plant a tree, prune vineyards or build a house.

Hope does not lie in our historical circumstances but in God. Hope is born when one sees God and His plans and then looks at the circumstances anew. We see that God is at work, even in troubled and threatening circumstances. The challenge is to attentively listen to the voice of God in these circumstances and to do what He calls us to do.

Father, make me attentive to Your voice, in Jesus' name.

Amen.

June 24

Will Our Children Have Faith?

...we will tell the next generation about the glorious deeds
of the LORD, about His power and His mighty wonders.
Psalm 78:4 NLT

While driving with my grandson, he asked me if a certain relative of ours had a husband. I told him that she had a good friend. The first thing he then asked was: Does he believe in the Lord? The first thing that he had in mind was faith in God.

Psalm 78 can be seen as an "educational" poem. The poet refers to lessons from the history of Israel. God rescued them from Egypt and led them into the Promised Land after experiencing His care in the wilderness. The rest of the psalm is reciting this great act of salvation.

What is the purpose of reciting it? The basic theme of the first eight verses is that future generations should learn how to live. The present generation has heard it from their fathers (78:3). The present generation must pass it onto their children (78:4). The generation after this must pass it onto their children again. There should be an unbroken chain of remembrance and teaching between the generations. This will help people to trust in the Lord alone from generation to generation (78:7). If they keep on doing this, it will keep them from living a disobedient life. It will guarantee a generation believing in God.

My grandson had it right: The most important thing in our lives is faith in God. We should be a channel of this message while we can.

Lord, make me a channel of Your message of salvation, in Jesus' name. Amen.

June 25

Faith Is Not Religion

> "It is not the healthy who need a doctor,
> but the sick. But go and learn what this means:
> 'I desire mercy, not sacrifice.' For I have not
> come to call the righteous, but sinners."
> Matthew 9:12–13 NIV

Jesus speaks out against the attitude of religious people in Matthew 9. They could not understand why Jesus identifies with sinful people, traitors of the nation and collaborators with the political oppressors (9:11). To eat with these people was to associate with them, accept them and see them as friends. This was unacceptable for any good religious Jew.

The problem in this passage is religious pride. These religious people believed that they were better than the sinners and tax collectors. They missed the point of Jesus' mission. He is the healer of broken people, not their judge. He came for those who needed Him, not for those who believed that they were good and religious enough, the spiritually superior.

Christianity is not a religion but a relationship with a Person, Jesus Christ. As Christians, we show mercy to all who need Jesus, just like God. Christ's love should shine through us.

Father, let me not judge, but rather be merciful like You, in Jesus' name. Amen.

June 26

Thanksgiving

Those who sacrifice thank offerings honor Me...
Psalm 50:23 NIV

In many churches, it is the custom to sing songs of praise and worship at the beginning of the service. Sometimes it includes the repetition of words and choruses. In itself this can be a very blessed experience. Imagine sitting in such a service of worship. People are intensely aware of the presence of God. Suddenly the place is filled with a sharp light and smoke. We hear a voice saying: "Listen to Me...it is not because you do not praise or because you do not make a contribution to the church that I have a case with you. I am interrupting your praise because it means nothing. They are just empty words."

This is what happened here. Israel's temple worship is "interrupted" by a sudden appearance of God. He accuses them because their life before Him goes directly against His will. How can this be? How can we praise God and worship Him and then be against His will? God gives the reason. They were acting against God's will because they believed that outward worship could replace their relationship with their fellow human beings. They trample on their fellow human beings (50:16-20). They basically ignored six of the Ten Commandments.

Praise is not something we bring with our mouths. The praise with the mouth is only the "overflow" of what happens in our lives before God. Life before God is to live in peace and harmony with our fellow human beings. This is thanksgiving!

Father, fill me with Your Spirit so that I can bring offerings of thanksgiving. Amen.

June 27

Beware of Temptation

Let no one say when he is tempted, "I am tempted by God"; for God cannot be tempted by evil, nor does He Himself tempt anyone. But each one is tempted when he is drawn away by his own desires and enticed. Then, when desire has conceived, it gives birth to sin; and sin, when it is full-grown, brings forth death.
James 1:13–15 NKJV

Someone wrote that opportunity might knock once, but that temptation bangs on our front door forever. We should not blame God for it. He does not tempt anybody (1:13).

Temptation is not a problem. In many cases, we are able to avoid or exclude some temptations in our lives by avoiding some situations. The problem is our reaction to temptation. Evil thoughts and our own desires make us give in to temptations. John Owen wrote that temptations and occasions put nothing into us, but only draw out what was in us before.

Sometimes we want to give in to temptations because we lost our way. It starts with a "meaningless" act of unfaithfulness to God, but it becomes bigger as our hearts become less sensitive to God.

There is just one answer to temptations: Return to the Lord. This return begins with a prayer of total dependence on the Lord: "And do not lead us into temptation, but deliver us from the evil one" (Matt. 6:13).

Lord, keep us close to You in temptations and give us victory, through Jesus Christ our Lord. Amen.

June 28

God Willing

*In their hearts humans plan their course,
but the LORD establishes their steps.*
Proverbs 16:9 NIV

Deo volente—God willing. My mother liked to say that we would do something, "God willing!" Do we still live according to this principle? Of course, it is right that one plan. All organizations and individuals should do so. One must determine one's course and walk the path (4:26).

What if our planning does not work out the way we thought it would? There is always the danger that we can live independently of God and ask the Lord to put a stamp of approval on our own plans. Then we are trying to take control of our own future.

The poet comforts us. The Lord is the one who takes our path of life in His hands and makes the best of it. Of course, it does not mean that He determines all our movements and makes our decisions for us. We are not pawns on a chessboard. My mother often said, "God willing and if I remain healthy." She wanted to say that we are working hard, that we plan and make decisions when we are healthy. We are responsible for our decisions. Ultimately, however, our decisions and planning must fit into God's will.

Richard C. Halverson wrote, "God has a time for everything, a perfect schedule. He is never too soon, never too late. The when of His will is as important as the what and the how."

Father, thank You that You are always on time in spite of our failures and bad decisions. *Amen.*

June 29

Total Dependence

*Commit to the LORD whatever you do,
and He will establish your plans.*
Proverbs 16:3 NIV

Sometimes we fail in our decisions and it has disastrous effects. The comfort is that in God's almighty hand, He also takes our failures and wrong decisions and turns our minuses into pluses. Therefore, one can leave what one does to the Lord. He will take care of the right outcome. It is the same idea expressed in Proverbs 3:5-6 (NIV): "Trust in the LORD with all your heart and lean not on your own understanding; in all your ways submit to Him, and He will make your paths straight."

Yes, it is a comfort. We know that He will take our decisions and plans made in dependence upon Him and make the best of it. Even when we do not understand correctly, we are not left at the mercy of our decisions. We plan, but God knows the future. He is sovereign!

It is a challenge to live in this comfort. It is a challenge to do all your planning in dependence upon God. However, we must trust the Lord in all of this (16:20). James says that we should not plan as if God is not part of it (James 4:13-17).

We should learn to say, *Deo volente*. Let us, however, learn to plan and live with the principle, "God willing". He knows the best. Paul says that God makes everything work for the good for those who are His children (Rom. 8:28).

Father, I am totally dependent on You. Let me plan everything while I keep my eyes on You, in Jesus' name. Amen.

June 30

Pray for Justice

*A king detests wrongdoing, for his rule is built on justice.
The king is pleased with words from righteous lips...*
Proverbs 16:12-13 NLT

Israel's kings had many rights and duties (1 Sam. 8:1-22). One of the most important rights the king had was that people had to respect him as God's anointed. Several psalms speak about the king of Israel as God's institution (Ps. 2; 72). However, the king would only be respected if he maintained God's justice. He had to rule in such a way that God's people were treated with justice. He had to ensure that the widows, orphans and other disadvantaged people would be treated well. The favor of a king is like a cloud bringing spring rains (Prov. 16:15). Likewise, the king exercising justice and righteousness is like rain for plants (Ps. 72:3-7).

Where should the king learn these norms? God is the prime example of fairness and justice (Prov. 16:11). We no longer live in a so-called theocratic community. God does not rule in our secular state by His Word. Although we all want it to be like that, secular states are no longer interested in God's Word. The governments of the day (and past governments) do not (and did not) necessarily take God into account when they made laws.

Let us pray today that God will bring forth His justice and righteousness—by us and also through the government of the day. His Spirit has the ability to do more than we can ever pray or imagine.

God of grace, let Your justice and righteousness be promoted by those who govern, by the power of Your Spirit. Amen.

July

July 1

Pray for Authority

> I urge, then, first of all, that petitions, prayers, intercession
> and thanksgiving be made for all people—for kings
> and all those in authority, that we may live peaceful
> and quiet lives in all godliness and holiness.
> 1 Timothy 2:1-2 NIV

Praying for governments and leaders can be a challenge. How do you pray for leaders who actively reject God? How do you intercede for governments that start wars or commit atrocities, oppress people and put people in prison?

Paul often experienced severe punishments from authorities. Yet, he never commanded his readers to stand up and fight against these authorities. He challenged the believers to use a different "weapon". Pray and intercede for them! Paul gives a very good reason why we should do this: so that we can lead a peaceful and quiet life and remain dedicated to God.

Prayer for authorities is part of our life before God. Paul goes further. He says that this prayer can also contribute to the salvation of all people. He immediately crossed the line to Gentile nations for which he was appointed preacher, teacher and apostle (2:7). Intercession for authorities must serve the proclamation of the gospel to those who do not know the Lord.

We must pray for the authorities in countries where the gospel is difficult to preach. Pray that the Lord will create an atmosphere of tolerance there. Pray that the Lord will open the doors for the proclamation of the gospel. In this way, we contribute to the spread of the gospel message.

Lord, let Your kingdom come, even where You and Your laws are rejected by authorities, in Jesus' name. Amen.

July 2

No Favoritism

> But if you show favoritism, you sin and are
> convicted by the law as lawbreakers.
> James 2:9 NIV

Sometimes it is difficult to treat everyone equally. When someone has a specific appearance or social status we favor them. When others do not reach those standards, we exclude them from our love, care and friendship. We put labels of prejudice on them. When they are in our category of "good people", we show favoritism. Otherwise, we exclude them.

Christians can never be like this—it is a sin. James writes to his fellow believers about this sin. They showed favoritism. When rich and important people entered the place of worship, they were treated with respect. The poor had to sit somewhere else. James, the brother of Jesus, says that when we judge people based on their outward appearance, God's law condemns us as transgressors.

These are harsh words, but we need to hear it. The love of Christians knows no labels or boundaries. We fulfill the law by loving as God does—without favoritism.

Spirit of God, change my thinking about my fellow human beings, in Jesus' name. Amen.

July 3

All or Nothing

> For the person who keeps all of the laws except one is as guilty as a person who has broken all of God's laws.
> James 2:10 NLT

The following joke was published in a student magazine: "You will write exams. The questions will not be a problem. The answers will be the problem!" Nobody likes exams. It is all about performance. Will I pass or fail? Some people think that God also sees if we pass or fail. My grandmother firmly believed that she would go to heaven because she did not dance, smoke or sleep with a man other than her own. Many of us grew up with this notion. If you at least get above 50% for the Ten Commandments, you stand a good chance of getting into heaven.

James clearly differs from this. The law is the law of God. Every part of God's law is of equal value. Whoever breaks one of the Ten Commandments is guilty before God (James 2:8-10). So, whoever relies on the law to be saved is in a dead end.

James spells out in his letter that faith in Christ includes a life of good deeds. The law is not the way to heaven, but Jesus is the way to the Father. He was perfectly obedient to God. Those who believe in Him are also considered by God to be perfectly obedient.

Are you going to keep trying to save yourself? Or are you going to rest in the salvation that has already been wrought for you? Rest in Jesus' merits today!

Lord Jesus, thank You that Your obedience covered my disobedience. Amen.

July 4

I've Got to Tell Somebody!

...that you may declare the praises of Him who called
you out of darkness into His wonderful light.
1 Peter 2:9 NIV

Psychologists tell us that finding one's identity is one of the most important elements in our lives. Sometimes we struggle with our identity because of a parent or a pastor or someone else telling us that we are failures and not worthy of grace. We are not loveable. We are not worthy of anything.

But this is not how we who are Christians should think about ourselves. We are children of God. This is our identity. Peter explains this identity by using beautiful titles we have received from God: "...a chosen people, a royal priesthood, a holy nation, God's special possession...you are the people of God...you have received mercy" (2:9-10 NIV). We are chosen, kings, holy! God poured out His love and mercy upon us. It is nice to know that we belong to the Lord. It warms our hearts. We have a beautiful identity.

What happens when we discover this identity? It changes the way that we live and love. It makes us passionate witnesses. Other people should discover who they are in Christ as well. God saved us so that we can go and tell them about it!

How will others be saved if we remain silent? How will others be able to see the light if we are not light bearers in a lost world?

Lord, make me what I should be because I am Your child, a witness of Your salvation, in Jesus' name. *Amen.*

July 5

Enjoy Life

Even so, I have noticed one thing, at least, that is good. It is good for people to eat, drink, and enjoy their work under the sun during the short life God has given them, and to accept their lot in life.
Ecclesiastes 5:18 NLT

Sometimes people do not see any joy in Christians. We are like horses with long faces. Pleasure is not always part of our Christian tradition. We often hear the expression: This is so much fun; it must be sin.

A Scottish pastor had to ski to church on a Sunday due to a snowstorm. His church council was very upset. After an explanation, they said it was okay—as long as he just did not enjoy it!

Pleasure and enjoyment are essential parts of our life of faith. We hear the call to enjoy life time and again in Ecclesiastes, this pessimistic book of the Bible. God gives us so much. The intention is not that we should enjoy it half-heartedly but that we should use it!

Not enjoying life and its gifts with boldness is a slap in the face of the Giver. Therefore, enjoy every moment of life. Enjoy every gift from His hand. He is happy if you are happy, too.

Lord, let me enjoy the gifts You gave me, in Jesus' name.

Amen.

July 6

Praise Him Now!

You turned my wailing into dancing; You removed my sackcloth and clothed me with joy, that my heart may sing Your praises and not be silent.
Psalm 30:11-12 NIV

When someone does something to help us in difficult times, it is only natural to say thank you. Have you thanked God today for what you have? For food, clothes and His forgiveness?

At the dedication of the temple, the people sang this psalm because they, along with David, could testify that the Lord had not let them down. He was very close to the grave (30:3). He was probably seriously ill. He thought that his time to communicate with God in this life was coming to an end (30:9). His experience of suffering was deepened when he felt that God had left him (30:7). His enemies probably also began to mock him (30:1).

Yet, things changed radically when God healed him. First there was mourning, sickness and death, but now there is health, strength and joy (30:2-3, 11). Therefore, God must be praised (30:1, 4, 12). He gave meaning to life again. Life is the place where God is praised.

How much more should Christians be grateful? After all, death has been overcome and our praise will last forever! Let us start today to say thank you for the free gift of God's care and grace.

Lord, my heart will sing Your praises and will not be silent, in Jesus' name. Amen.

July 7

Laws or Conscience

> With narrowed eyes, people plot evil;
> with a smirk, they plan their mischief.
> Proverbs 16:30 NLT

We can complain because the laws of the country are not stricter about certain crimes. We can complain about corruption in government circles. We can condemn the injustice committed in the name of the Lord under previous governments.

Unfortunately, justice and righteousness are not necessarily determined by laws. We should make sure that we live with fairness. If we cannot be honest, no law can change our hearts. This is why proverb after proverb speaks out against injustice between people. People who only want to do evil (16:27), lie and gossip (16:28), and deceive their fellow human beings (16:29) do not comply with the most basic aspects of fairness and justice.

Someone once remarked that when we abandon ethics, we cease to make sense. Another philosopher noted that many laws in a country are like a lot of doctors—it is a sign of weakness and illness. If we need a law for everything, it is clear that we cannot control ourselves.

The Lord God writes the law on our hearts through His Spirit. He fills us with His fruit. Then we become people of love (Gal. 5:22-23).

Spirit of grace, grant me integrity, honesty and sincerity, through the power of Your Spirit. Amen.

July 8

Reconciliation

Whoever would foster love covers over an offense, but whoever repeats the matter separates close friends.
Proverbs 17:9 NIV

How can we forget if someone deliberately steals our future, our security, our marriage, our family or our dignity? It touches us deeply and hurts us terribly.

Yes, there are people who are always looking to harm others. They like to listen to stories that hurt you and cast a shadow over your integrity; they take great pleasure when they see another's misfortune and they seek to destroy relationships between people (17:4-5, 19). They will even ignore your good attitude and hurt you (17:13). Evil is always present—at all times and in ourselves. You do not have to go searching to find it. Unfortunately, we often choose the path of malicious people.

Yet, the poet prefers the path of reconciliation. We will keep good relationships if we ignore the evil things done to us (17:9). Peace is more important than a prosperous life (17:1). Scripture says that we should not repay evil with evil (Rom. 12:17-21). We should treat our enemies with kindness. We should concentrate on what is helpful and build others up (Eph. 4:29). There is a proverb that says, "Write the bad things that are done to you in sand, but write the good things that happen to you on a piece of marble."

Spirit of love, teach me Your love. Let it overcome my limited love and desire for retribution, for the sake of Jesus. Amen.

July 9

Justified Sinners

You see, at just the right time, when we were still powerless, Christ died for the ungodly.
Romans 5:6 NIV

A minister preached passionately about sin. He said that all people were sinners. If there was anybody in the church who could claim that they have not sinned, they should get up and say it. An old man raised his hand. "Do you want to tell me that you have no sin?" the minister asked. The old man answered, "No, I just speak on behalf of my wife's first husband. Apparently, he had no sin!"

The so-called "saints", the people we remember for the example they set by being faithful to God, used to be sinners. They were not better people than we are. They received a future when Jesus came to give them a future through His death. By receiving this future through faith, they have embarked on the path forward in trust because God was merciful to them.

This is the basis for our life of faith. Every sinner has a future. Jesus died for the powerless, sinners and the wicked (Rom. 5:6-10). He did not look at us as saints and then decide that we were worthy of His love. He gave His life in spite of our unholiness!

The worst among us is given a fresh start—even you. What are you going to do with it?

Father, thank You for the future You gave me, in spite of my sin, in Jesus' name. *Amen.*

July 10

Apathy or Love?

For as the body without the spirit is dead,
so faith without works is dead also.
James 2:26 NKJV

James is writing about apathy. We see the need, but it does not have any effect on us. Affection is missing! Some are hungry and we do nothing about it. Someone is without clothes and it does not move our hearts. We send them away to look after themselves.

Do you believe in God? If you do, James says, do not think that this is the ultimate question in life. He says that even the demons would agree with the basic confession of our faith, namely that there is only one God (Deut. 6:4). What is the ultimate test of real faith in God? When the demons say that God is one, they shudder. There is a response! If we, who say that we believe in God, do nothing, we are worse than the demons.

The ultimate test for real faith in God is acts of love and compassion. Otherwise, our faith is dead! Faith and deeds belong together. If you confess that there is only one God, it moves you if someone does not have food or clothes or proper housing. You do not ask about the merits of the case before deciding in your wisdom whether you are willing to contribute. You help, because faith does this.

Father, give me compassion for those in need, in Jesus' name.

Amen.

July 11

At Our Own Cost

What good is it, my brothers and sisters, if someone claims to have faith but has no deeds? Can such faith save them?...As the body without the spirit is dead, so faith without deeds is dead.
James 2:14, 26 NIV

Someone said that we should set some conditions to the help we provide. We will only help if someone is willing to do what we want them to do. Is this biblical? Is this God's compassion? Phillips Brooks wrote in one of his sermons that we should not allow the seeming worthlessness of sympathy to keep us from showing it. When people are suffering, we should show it without asking if it is worth the while. God's compassion sends us to His needy children.

Faith is to act. Without deeds faith is dead. Our deeds come from God's heart of love. We must try to reveal Jesus in our dealings with others. It is no good to just say that we will pray for someone who is hungry, thirsty or sick and leave it at that. We need to take action. We need to show the love of Jesus in our deeds. It must cost us something.

Lord, teach us what faith is, by the power of Your Spirit.

Amen.

July 12

By Your Grace

Restore us, O LORD, and bring us back to You again!
Lamentations 5:21 NLT

When someone asked the Dutch minister Herman Kohlbrugge if he had an exact date when he was converted, he immediately said that he had. He was converted 2,000 years ago at Calvary. Some people were annoyed with what he said, because they wanted him to give a date in his lifetime. But Kohlbrugge wanted to emphasize something else. He wanted to say that Jesus' death on the cross is the only fixed date on which we can build our salvation. Our emotions vary and our sin does not necessarily get less.

One of the most dangerous things that can happen is when people make their experience of conversion the norm for other people. So, if you have not been converted in your own way, you are not yet a "true" Christian. No, we should not build our certainty on our repentance, but on God's grace.

In high school the Gideons gave us a Bible. There was a place where one could write one's date of conversion. I had many dates, because every time I sinned, I felt that my sin made the previous date invalid. I was mistaken. God works repentance by His grace (Jer. 31:18). His grace is enough.

> Lord, thank You that our salvation is based on Your grace and not on my emotions and experience, in Jesus' name. *Amen.*

July 13

Unity

> "I in them, and You in Me; that they may be made perfect in one, and that the world may know that You have sent Me, and have loved them as You have loved Me."
>
> John 17:23 NKJV

I lived in a country that started a military operation in a neighboring country. Apart from the terrible loss of life in both countries, there was another tragic result. One of the pastors from the country where the conflict erupted was a student of ours. He said that pastors in that country started to preach the message of revenge. Some of them broke off all contact with their colleagues in the other country. In short, the church of Jesus Christ was torn apart.

Jesus is on His knees in John 17. He is interceding with God for His disciples and the people who would become part of the faith community through their testimony. Jesus prays in our passage for the unity between believers.

Why is this unity so important? Unity among believers is a powerful testimony. It should convince the world that Jesus was the Messenger of God (17:21, 23). Where Christians are divided among themselves, the world will have a hard time believing that Jesus is the Son of God. Paul writes that we must maintain unity among ourselves because unity is the work of the Spirit of God (Eph. 4:1-2).

Unity among believers is not an option. It should be a visible unity, otherwise the world will not believe that we are serious about God. We should be the answer to this prayer of Jesus.

Father, make us one, by the power of Your Spirit. Amen.

July 14

Glass Houses

> "I am the light of the world. Whoever follows Me will never walk in darkness, but will have the light of life."
> John 8:12 NIV

We easily throw stones while we live in glass houses. We should know the difference between right or wrong, but we should not use God's Word to condemn one kind of sin above others.

This is what happens in John 8:1-11. The story of the woman who was caught sleeping around is probably one of the most moving stories in the Bible. She was guilty. In terms of Jewish laws, she had to be stoned. The religious leaders were quick to respond to her dark life. Yet, their hearts were filled with evil intent, trying to trap Jesus Christ.

Jesus uses the situation to do something beautiful. A woman of the night experiences how the Lord brings light into one's life. God's love is not limited by laws. He knows we all have our faults. When we come to a dead end—even if it is our own fault—the Lord gives light. He forgives this woman unconditionally and calls her to a new life of obedience.

Sometimes God uses a dark place to prove that He is the light—even if we have placed ourselves in the dark.

Thank You, Lord, that You used the darkness in my life so that I could see Your light, in Jesus' name. Amen.

July 15

Lighting Up God's World

"I am the light of the world."
John 8:12 NIV

Power outages are terrible. When it happens, it is a crisis. Life almost stops. With Jesus it is different. He is the light in darkness. There is no power outage! God is our light and salvation, says the psalmist. Jesus applies this reality to Himself, because He is God Himself. His words here follow a story of an adulterous woman who was brought before Him. The religious people wanted Jesus to make a judgment about this situation. Obviously, they wanted to set a trap for Him.

Jesus shames them by asking them to throw the first stone if they are without sin. On the other hand, this adulterous woman discovers the light of Jesus. He does not pronounce judgment on her but gives her a fresh start. Through His forgiving love, she discovers that her life in darkness is not the only option. Jesus opens up a new life for her.

When God's light breaks through, darkness disappears. Everyone who encounters Jesus discovers new meaning in life. Everywhere Jesus is sharing God's creative light.

On the Irish coast there are two lighthouses about 500 meters apart. At a distance, the lights of both lighthouses seem to be shining. In fact, one only reflects the other's light. Like the lighthouse on the Irish coast, we should reflect God's light of grace in this world today.

Lord, let Your light shine through me today, so that even the most hopeless person can have hope, in Jesus' name. Amen.

July 16

The Wealth of Family Life

> Better a dry crust with peace and quiet
> than a house full of feasting, with strife.
> Proverbs 17:1 NIV

Few things come close to a loving family. A family where mom and dad love each other, support their children and truly live in peace. This love forms the foundation of our existence and determines how we will interact with other people in future. Having loving parents can change your life.

Faith is the key to a healthy family life. Ephesians 6:1-4 (NIV) tells us: "Children, obey your parents in the Lord, for this is right. 'Honor your father and mother'—which is the first commandment with a promise— 'so that it may go well with you and that you may enjoy long life on the earth.' Fathers, do not exasperate your children; instead, bring them up in the training and instruction of the Lord."

The wealth of family life is that we serve and love the Lord. If this is not the case, children are no longer proud of parents and grandparents. We are no longer people for whom one can have respect.

Remember what Francis Bacon once said, "He that gives good counsel and example, builds with both; but he that gives good admonition and bad example, builds with one hand and pulls down with the other."

Lord God, make us faithful to You so that we do not become embarrassed by our foolishness, through the power of Your Spirit.

Amen.

July 17

Embarrassment for Our Children

Children's children are the crown of old men,
and the glory of children is their father.
Proverbs 17:6 NKJV

A friend once told me how wonderful it was to be a granddad. Nothing could be better than this. Now I understand why he said this, because I am now a grandfather of many!

Grandchildren are the pride of the elderly! The relationship between parents and children is mentioned often in Proverbs. It is especially the importance of a good education that is brought to the attention of children time after time. We have already addressed the stability that parents' relationship with the Lord gives to children.

There are, of course, other sides to the relationship between parents and children. Something not often mentioned is that parents can sometimes be a terrible embarrassment to their children. For the people of the Ancient Near East, a father figure was very important. He had to be dignified and wise. An older person acted in a way that would bring about respect. Children looked up to them. Therefore, the poet says that fathers are the pride of their sons. A father is almost like the crown on someone's head.

If, however, the father is not wise, if he walks his own path, despises God and rejects wisdom, he is an embarrassment. Just as children can be a huge embarrassment and can bring a lot of sadness to their parents when they go their own way (17:21, 25), parents who act foolishly are a huge disappointment to children.

Father, enable us to be good parents and grandparents, in Jesus' name. Amen.

July 18

Boasting about Tomorrow

> Instead, you ought to say, "If it is the Lord's will,
> we will live and do this or that."
> James 4:15 NIV

My grandparents lived in a small fishermen's village where there was a harbor. Sometimes a car would plunge into the water because it came too close to the edge of the harbor. I was always terrified when someone drove too close to the edge.

Harbors should not be dangerous places. Martin Luther said that our life is like a voyage to a safe haven. In the harbor there is real safety after we come from the stormy sea. Our ship cannot withstand stormy waters for too long. Therefore, we need a capable captain to steer the boat of our lives to the safety of the harbor. This captain, Luther said, is God. Whoever throws Him overboard in times of storms must know that the ship will sink. Then it is not the Captain's fault. This is because we want to steer our ship ourselves.

James warns against an attitude in which we plan without taking into account that our life is a gift from God. We do not own our lives. The Lord gives it to us every day. Therefore, He also wants us to give Him the glory for what we achieve. Boasting is associated with an attitude of being too sure of yourself (4:16). He who knows that he cannot live without God remains humble. We say, "If it is God's will and we live…"

Who's the captain of your ship? Give your life anew to the best Captain!

Lord, today I acknowledge that You are the captain of my life, in Jesus' name. Amen.

July 19

Ready for His Return

"I tell you the truth, when you did it to one of the least of these My brothers and sisters, you were doing it to Me!"
Matthew 25:40 NLT

As a child, I watched a very scary movie about the return of Christ. I was terrified the night I watched it and could not sleep. Yet, for Christians the return of Christ is good news! It will bring an end to all the sadness and suffering in the world.

So, shall we just wait until all of this will change? The prophetic speech of Jesus (Matt. 24-25) contains one parable after another in which it is said that we must be ready for the return of the Lord every moment. In none of the preceding parables is it said *how* the church should be ready.

The last parable shows how ready people are active when they await the return of Christ. We do not just wait. We are actively involved in alleviating the pain in this world. We are feeding hungry people, visiting people in prison, providing shelter for the homeless and giving clothes to people who do not have clothes. This is how we wait. This is how we are ready for His return.

Did you know that Jesus is coming today? No, it may not be His final coming, but He is going to come to us in the hunger and thirst of people who cross our paths today. When we help them, we are in fact helping Jesus Himself. Jesus comes to us disguised in the needs of others.

Lord, make me an instrument of Your love and care today, in Jesus' name. Amen.

July 20

God Is Our Home

> When anxiety was great within me,
> Your consolation brought me joy.
> Psalm 94:19 NIV

Many people turn their backs on God because of the injustice in the world. In a sociological study some years ago, the researchers identified this as the number one reason people leave the church and eventually stop believing.

Psalm 94 speaks about terrible injustice. Widows and orphans, the marginalized and defenseless of society are oppressed by arrogant people (94:3-6). The individual who is speaking here also endured this injustice: "Who will rise up for me against the wicked? Who will take a stand for me against evildoers?" (94:16 NIV). These arrogant people believed that the Lord did not see what they were doing: "The LORD does not see; the God of Jacob takes no notice" (94:7 NIV).

Is the Lord absent amid so much injustice? No, says the psalmist. "The LORD knows all human plans; He knows that they are futile" (94:11, NIV). He has an ear that hears and an eye that sees and will punish those who cause pain.

We cannot always change the world, but *we* can change. How can we keep on standing in these circumstances? We trust in God. If we have nowhere to hide, we will be blown away. The eternal God is a home.

Take refuge in God (94:12-15). When we think we are going to fall, the love of the Lord keeps us upright. Only this dispels the unrest in our hearts (94:18-19).

Lord, You are my hope. I take refuge in You. *Amen.*

July 21

Witnesses

*"But you will receive power when the Holy Spirit
comes on you; and you will be My witnesses."*
Acts 1:8 NIV

As Christians we are in God's service. Firstly, being a witness is not really an option. Spirit-filled people are witnesses. Jesus said that when we receive the power of God's Spirit, we become witnesses. There is no choice.

Secondly, we do not have a choice where we want to be a witness. The whole world is our calling. The disciples did not properly understand the meaning of Jesus' resurrection from the dead and what it meant to be Spirit-filled witnesses. With a Leader who could overcome even death, they thought they could certainly restore the lost glory of Israel.

We are witnesses to the world. Jesus did not call the disciples to be witnesses only in Jerusalem. He called them to witness in Jerusalem as well as in the other places.

You have received the Spirit! Therefore, the world that does not know Christ is on your agenda. Start with that today. It is your calling!

Lord, thank You that we may be witnesses of Your goodness, by the power of Your Spirit. Amen.

July 22

Ever Changing

And we all...are being transformed into His image with ever-increasing glory, which comes from the Lord, who is the Spirit.
2 Corinthians 3:18 NIV

How does your diary look today? Yes, our competitive world demands that we should work hard, have appointments and attend meetings. Sometimes we find little time for the people and things we really love. Sometimes we are not only victims of our competitive world, but we play along and make life difficult for ourselves. We want more and more, to climb the ladder of success and to be independent from everything and everyone. It makes us very busy people.

Let us just stop for a moment and ask where we are heading with our lives. Where does God fit into our daily lives? I am not talking about a kind of a life in which we need to say how many hours we pray or do Bible study. The issue is rather this: Are our lifestyles and the way we work and plan places where we allow the Spirit of God to fill us and change us? After all, the Spirit is a Creator of something beautiful in us.

Paul says the Spirit is creating the image of Christ in us. His primary purpose in our lives is not to make us successful, but that Christ can be shown through our lives to others.

Spirit, change me so that I can reflect Your glory in this world, in Jesus' name. Amen.

July 23

Old and New Ways

Though I am free and belong to no one, I have made myself a slave to everyone, to win as many as possible....I have become all things to all people so that by all possible means I might save some.
1 Corinthians 9:19, 22 NIV

A minister remarked to me that some of the churches in his area need help understanding that we are in the 21st century! Let us be honest with ourselves. The old ways do not always appeal to the people who are on the fringes of the church—people who have still not made up their mind about the church.

To be a church in new circumstances, and in an emerging new culture with changing world views, is one of the greatest challenges for the church today. We must not compromise on biblical truth and accuracy but we still need to reach others with the message of salvation.

Paul says that he often had to adjust to win as many as possible. This is the test—the salvation of others. How much do we care about those on the outside? The more we care about them and their salvation, the more we will pursue ways to be a church where these people will also experience fulfilment. If the salvation of all people is not our passion, we will expect them to adapt to us.

Spirit of God, give us the wisdom to be Your church in a changing world to win more people for You, in Jesus' name. Amen.

July 24

Beautiful Grace

"The LORD did not set His heart on you and choose you because you were more numerous than other nations, for you were the smallest of all nations!"
Deuteronomy 7:7 NLT

People tell the most incredible stories of how God saved them from a life that was heading for an eternity without God. I am always grateful to hear how God works and changes people through His grace. The Lord is alive and active. It is always a miracle!

Although these stories are great, it should never be the primary focus. Someone said that the devil changes tactics when someone is converted. At first, he tries to stop it, but when God's love becomes too strong for us and we repent, the devil likes to make us proud!

We should always listen to the heart of the biblical message about the changes in our lives. Israel was reminded of this numerous times. God's grace was not given because of their qualities. It was bestowed upon them despite their weakness and stubbornness (Deut. 7:7; 9:6).

Thank God for the beautiful stories of God's grace in your life, but don't become proud of it. If you do not have such a story, ask again that He should turn your heart to Him. He loved us before we could change, believe or repent. He gave Himself on a cross to die for stubborn people like us. May God change you so that you can love Him back!

All glory to You, Lord God, for the love You showed to me.

Amen.

July 25

Holiness Received, Not Achieved

*Rebuke is more effective for a wise man
than a hundred blows on a fool.*
Proverbs 17:10 NKJV

To learn wisdom requires that you use the relationship that God created with you. He came to live in you through Christ and through His Spirit. In love, He gave His best to you.

Still, we do not really learn wisdom. Do you sometimes feel that you are not touched by the Spirit of the Lord as you should be? Do you also sometimes feel that your commitment as a Christian does not really make a big difference to your lifestyle? Perhaps you started on fire, but the flame now burns low.

It is necessary that we discover the foolishness in ourselves all the time. We are often like the fool who will not change with a hundred lashes (17:10). We are sometimes worse than a bear robbed of her cubs, because we do not live from the relationship that God has with us (17:12).

When the poet speaks about wisdom, he does not say that wise people are sinless. He sketches the ideal wisdom. He shows the direction in which we should grow. Therefore, our Christian life and growth are never completed.

It is said that holiness is something we receive, not achieve! We are always on a journey. We always seek greater wisdom, always want to understand more and more how broken we are and live daily in the expectation and dependence that God will make our lives new through His Spirit.

Spirit of God, keep on educating me that Your name may be glorified. Amen.

July 26

Cover It!

Whoever would foster love covers over an offense,
but whoever repeats the matter separates close friends.
Proverbs 17:9 NIV

God forgives and does not remember our sins (Isa. 43:25; Heb. 10:17). Forgiveness is so radical that we never have to think about our past sins. We receive a clean slate, a new beginning.

It is so strange that we remind each other so much about the past. Parents do it with their children. Children also easily blame parents for their failures that had a severe negative impact on their lives. Spouses do it to one another. We will forgive, but not forget.

We find this behavior in the most beautiful religious communities. They just cannot forget the past. They love controversy and arguments—something that is rejected by the poet (Prov. 17:14). He says that people who are false and unjust eagerly listen to gossip (17:4). It shows the old human nature still controlled by our sinful nature (Titus 3:2-3; Gal. 5:20). This behavior is typical of humans, but is not Christian.

Put the shoe on the other foot. What would you want most if you caused hurt? How would you feel if people were gossiping about it, constantly bringing it up or reminding you of it, despite the fact that you confessed your sins to them and God?

Reconciliation is one of the hardest and rockiest roads on our journey of faith, but it must be travelled. It is the only option if we want to be healed and want to grow to greater maturity spiritually and emotionally.

Forgiving God, enable us by the power of Your Spirit to reconcile with those who have hurt us. Amen.

July 27

Intelligent Fools

> Fools find no pleasure in understanding
> but delight in airing their own opinions.
> Proverbs 18:2 NIV

A foolish person is not unintelligent. There are extremely intelligent fools. This is sometimes the problem. Many smart people are so clever in their own eyes and need nothing and no one.

A foolish person is very lonely. A fool even says, sometimes unknowingly, that there is no God. Trusting in yourself is a motion of no confidence in God. Therefore, a foolish person must do everything himself (18:2). And this is loneliness. Foolishness, somebody said, is even worse than wickedness. A godless person consciously lives without God. A fool does not even realize it.

Are your opinions most important? Do you think that you don't need anything or anyone? Beware, we must understand that self-reliance and pride often precede our fall (18:12).

Do you prefer to find your strength in humility in the name of the Lord (18:10)? Only He is the source of true security. Therefore, Peter says to the foolish religious leaders who want to silence him, "Salvation is found in no one else, for there is no other name under heaven given to mankind by which we must be saved" (Acts 4:12 NIV). The reaction of the leaders is interesting, "When they saw the courage of Peter and John and realized that they were unschooled, ordinary men, they were astonished and they took note that these men had been with Jesus" (4:13 NIV).

Father, make me a humble person so that I will learn from You and grow in wisdom, in Jesus' name. Amen.

July 28

Rich and Poor

> Now listen, you rich people, weep and wail
> because of the misery that is coming on you.
> James 5:1 NIV

The gap between rich and poor is not getting any smaller. The rich become richer and the poor poorer. Very often, in situations like this, the poor are exploited. They work harder and longer for less wages. The rich are in the driving seat and determine the payment.

The judgment of the rich in James 5 is related to this. They make people work hard. Hard work is fine. The problem is the treatment of their workers. It borders on murder (5:6). The poor people depended on their daily wages. These wages were a matter of life and death. The rich held it back (5:4).

Meanwhile, the wealth of the unjust rich accumulated. Clothes not used are eaten up by moths. Money not used is corroded (5:2-3). They have everything, but they do not use it to serve the poor. They gather and live in luxury without realizing that their time is running out (5:3, 5).

James comforts the poor. God heard their prayers (5:4). The wealth of the rich will come to nothing. The Lord is the Judge standing at the door (5:9). Their judgment is immanent.

God is in control. The prophets were often treated unfairly, but they persevered in their task. Job had nothing, but he persevered. In all of this, God knows and loves us—even when we suffer at the hands of unjust people (5:11). Therefore, we can patiently continue with our work (5:7).

Lord, help me to trust that You will not let us down, in Jesus' name. *Amen.*

July 29

Powerful Prayer

> The earnest prayer of a righteous person
> has great power and produces wonderful results.
> James 5:16 NLT

Two men landed on a barren island after a shipwreck. They divided the island and decided to pray for the same things to see whose prayers would be answered. One man received everything. The other person received nothing. Eventually the man who received everything was saved. When he left, God asked him why he left his friend behind. He said that he deserved the rescue, because God favored his prayers. Then God said that the man who received nothing had only one prayer: that the other person's prayers should be answered!

Our prayers are often very self-centered. Yes, God answers our prayers. Very often, however, the blessings we experience in life are the result of the prayers of our parents, children and friends who pray for God's blessings and healing in our lives.

To pray for others is to share in God's work. When we bring people before God, we expose them to the love of God. The walls and distance that separate us fall down. We are bound together as one big, intimate family. There is no greater intimacy than when I pray for someone.

It is such a blessing that I can pray for my children and grandchildren, my friends and other Christians while I am thousands of miles away from them. We are bound together in an intimate family when we pray together.

Lord, thank You for those who pray for me. I bring them before You today with thanksgiving. Amen.

July 30

Ready to Bless

"I am the LORD your God, who brought you out of the land of Egypt; open your mouth wide, and I will fill it."
Psalm 81:10 NKJV

Lost chances. I am sure you had some of those. Sometimes we regret that we have not taken a specific road in our lives and then we wonder for a long time what could have been! How would our life's story have been if we moved from one town to another, but did not. How would our life's story have been if we chose a specific profession, but did not.

In this psalm, the people were probably called to a feast to reflect on God and on themselves. What did they need to hear from God again? The words of Psalm 81:10 are literally the same as the preface to the Ten Commandments. They heard that they were truly set free. There was a time when they were slaves, but the Lord took that burden off their shoulders (81:6–7).

Yet, the psalm also contains the thought of "if only". Their ancestors did not respect God for what He did for them (81:11–14). He gave them over to their stubbornness and own desires. What a tragedy! If they had only listened, things could be so different: "how quickly I would subdue their enemies and turn My hand against their foes" (81:14 NIV).

The Lord's deliverance brings freedom. Freedom is not following your own desires; it is to love God who liberated us. The God who liberates blesses people who love Him!

Lord, I love You, by Your grace. *Amen.*

July 31

Freedom!

> It is for freedom that Christ has set us free. Stand firm, then, and do not let yourselves be burdened again by a yoke of slavery...You, my brothers and sisters, were called to be free. But do not use your freedom to indulge the flesh; rather, serve one another humbly in love.
> Galatians 5:1, 13 NIV

Freedom! People fight for freedom. Some divorce to obtain freedom. People do not want to be tied down by anything. They do not want to be controlled. "I want to be free. I am in the center of my life". This kind of freedom is sin. It hurts. It destroys families.

Martin Luther says a Christian is the freest lord of all, and subject to none. It is true. Christ truly liberated us. He made us free from Satan and sin. Christ bought our freedom with His blood. However, Luther immediately adds: A Christian is the most dutiful servant of all, and subject to everyone. As free people we also are subdued to everything and everybody. As free people, we serve others.

Christian freedom is service. It is love. It is a sacrifice. The needs of others become more important than our own. It promotes the interests and freedom of other people.

Oh, may our freedom not lead to atrocities and hurt. May it make the world a better place.

Lord, teach us the freedom to love each other as You have loved us, in Jesus' name. Amen.

August

August 1

Representatives

*God saw all that He had made, and it was very good.
And there was evening, and there was morning—the sixth day.*
Genesis 1:31 NIV

War, viruses, murder, theft, broken relationships, poverty, child abuse and animal cruelty are on the news every day. God's intention was completely different. After each day's work, He said that everything was good. It was very good. God created a world of light, water, life, breath, and people from nothing. He spoke, and it happened.

The chaos in the world is our fault, but God does not give up on us. John Calvin wrote that everybody who seriously believes the universe was made by God will be persuaded that He takes care of His works. Jesus came into the world as God's Word. By His word, He drove away the darkness—disease, suffering, and ultimately death. God loves this world. God has a new heaven and earth in mind. You may believe it because the Spirit is God's guarantee that it will happen (Eph. 1:13-14).

Therefore, we may not give up the world as a lost cause. If God loves the world (John 3:16), we should also love the world. Indeed, we are God's representatives (Gen. 1:26-28). Come on, God's ambassador! Let us go into the world with the Message of hope. Let us do something about the distress in which this world finds itself.

Lord, make me a representative of Your care and love for the world, in Jesus' name. *Amen.*

August 2

Take Care of the Earth

> Then God said, "Let Us make man in
> Our image, according to Our likeness."
> Genesis 1:26 NKJV

I have the privilege of going to different places in the world because of my work. The different cultures and lifestyles are fascinating. Then I see the people. When I walk in the streets, see people going to work or begging, I am often very sad, because we have lost sight of the fact that we are God's image, God's representatives.

On the one hand, we see the brokenness of our fellow human beings. So many people are lost and do not know and serve God. It was God's intention that we should reflect His image. On the other hand, I am sad because I am not sure if those who do not know God experience something of God through the way I live. Does creation experience God's touch when I walk on earth? To be an image of God especially means that God made us in relation to Him, our fellow human beings, and creation.

We also have a responsibility to people and creation. We must take care of them. We should reflect God's love. We should manage God's creation as God's creation, not our property. This earth gives us the space to live and earn a living, but we pollute the air, rivers and sea, waste water, and destroy vital vegetation.

Being God's people in God's world requires greater responsibility from all of us.

Father, let Your likeness shine through my life, by the power of Your Spirit. Amen.

August 3

True Friends

*One who has unreliable friends soon comes to ruin,
but there is a friend who sticks closer than a brother.*
Proverbs 18:24 NIV

C. S. Lewis wrote that "Friendship…is born at the moment when one man says to another 'What! You too? I thought that no one but myself…'" Shared experiences, joys and pain bind people together.

Jesus calls us His friends (John 15:5). His friendship bears fruits of love (John 15:15–16). His friendship led Him to the cross. When we come to know Him, our Brother who became like us even until death (Heb. 2:17), it changes our friendships. Then our friendships are not about us. We become closer to one another than to our own families because we become one family in Him (Eph. 2:19).

True friends accept one another despite all the flaws we have. It should never bring separation. Our friendship is built on the friendship of the One we accept as a brother. His forgiveness and compassion are unlimited. Yes, "what a friend we have in Jesus, all our sins and griefs to bear!" It transforms our friendships!

Lord, thank You for friends that understand and love me despite all my flaws, for the sake of Jesus Christ. Amen.

August 4

The Gift of a Good Spouse

> Houses and wealth are inherited from parents,
> but a prudent wife is from the LORD.
> Proverbs 19:14 NIV

On the one hand, the poet speaks very negatively about a bad woman. He knows that the temptation of a woman's seduction is almost irresistible to men.

On the other hand, the poet emphasizes the greatness of a good woman. A good wife is a sign of the kindness and goodness of God (18:22). She brings happiness to our lives. In Proverbs 31, the perfect woman is described as the ultimate wisdom.

Where do you get such a good wife? Who knows if the woman with whom I want to share my life will stay with me? It is a gift from the Lord when we get such a wife (19:14). She is not inherited or possessed. She belongs to God and is a gift from Him.

If it is true that the Lord gives us our spouse who is wise, then we must of course also deal with this gift of God in a loving and responsible way. He or she remains God's gift to me.

How do you treat your gift from God? Martin Luther said that marriage is not a natural matter, but a gift from God. It is an extremely sweet life.

Lord, thank You for the gift of good marriage partners, in Jesus' name. Amen.

August 5

A Godly Family

And what does the one God seek? Godly offspring.
Malachi 2:15 NIV

Broken homes and fatherless children are part and parcel of our contemporary society. So many children suffer because of the absence of parents or abuse at home. Nothing can replace a good and stable family life in the upbringing of our children.

This was also an issue in Malachi's time. Yet, the issue about divorce was on a slightly different level. God's people did not understand that marriages with people of other religions touched the core of the faith community. They divorced to marry women of other religions.

By doing this, faith in the one true God was compromised. This was of central importance to God's people. What would the children believe? Malachi says that divorce from a person of the same faith could lead to the loss of offspring who serve the Lord. The primary point Malachi wants to make is that faith in the true God outweighs everything!

Although our context differs, it still remains true that the healthy unity of a family provides a safe space within which children can learn the wonder of God's grace. A healthy marriage in which parents are committed to Jesus Christ, forms and nurtures the faith of the children. Therefore, we must try to maintain the unity of families at all costs. God wants offspring that serve Him.

Father, grant that our marital relationship will lead our children to worship You alone, in Jesus' name. Amen.

August 6

Boring Churches?

> How lovely is Your dwelling place, O LORD of Heaven's Armies.
> I long, yes, I faint with longing to enter the courts
> of the LORD. With my whole being, body and
> soul, I will shout joyfully to the living God.
> Psalm 84:1-2 NLT

In one of the busiest streets in Birmingham, England, a church's notice board said that anyone who thinks Christianity is "boring", should come and visit them on Sundays. I never went there, but I thought a lot about this bold statement. What does it mean? Do they entertain people? Is the preaching exciting?

Is the church boring? This is the wrong question. The fault in nine out of ten cases does not lie with the church as an institute, with the music in the church, or with the preacher. The fault lies with my expectations. Along with the pilgrim songs (Ps. 120-134) and Psalm 42 and 43, Psalm 84 is surely one of the psalms that expresses the purest longing for God's presence. We don't go to temples anymore, but we certainly need God's presence. To the poet, God's presence is like coming home (84:4), like rain after drought (84:6), like a surge of new strength (84:7).

When we discover that God is the Source of our lives, that He is the living, life-giving God, the Protector of people, it makes a difference. There will be a zeal and strong desire to continually long for moments with God.

Lord, give me more longing for You, in Jesus' name. *Amen.*

August 7

Rooted in Love

> I pray that…Christ will make His home in your hearts
> as you trust in Him. Your roots will grow down
> into God's love and keep you strong.
> Ephesians 3:16-17 NLT

The goal of our fellowship with each other, which goes beyond natural and confessional boundaries, will always be the discovery of Christ's love (3:19). We do not meet to become better people or to create a new culture, but so that we can be rooted and established more and more in this love (3:17). There can be no other Source for the Christian community. We are not established in the community, but in Christ.

When this foundation is solid, it will lead to a sincere Christian love, unity and service to each other and the world around us (4:1-2). It will lead to a new song of praise about the unlimited power of God, which will never end, "Now to Him who is able to do exceedingly abundantly above all that we ask or think, according to the power that works in us, to Him be glory in the church by Christ Jesus to all generations, forever and ever. Amen" (3:20-21 NKJV).

Our struggle is not to do good or to be good. The Christian faith is an encounter with Christ, of which morality and ethical living are by-products.

> Lord, lead us to a daily encounter with You so that our lives will bring constant praise to You, in Jesus' name. *Amen.*

August 8

Sent in the Power of His Spirit

> So Jesus said to them again, "Peace to you! As the Father
> has sent Me, I also send you." And when He had
> said this, He breathed on them, and said
> to them, "Receive the Holy Spirit."
> John 20:21-22 NKJV

In the 1960s, the hippie movement wanted peace. One of the slogans was: Make love, not war! Love and peace should govern, not the imperialistic and power-hungry governments. This message was "proclaimed" throughout the western world.

"Peace be with you!" These are the words of Jesus. It has a totally different meaning from what modern peace movements work for. This peace comes from death! Jesus was raised from the dead. He overcame all hostility. This is not the peace of the cemetery, but the peace of God—unlike the world's (14:27).

All four gospels record that the disciples were afraid (20:19), full of doubt (Matt. 28:17), unbelieving (Mark 16:11) and even terrified (Luke 24:37) after Jesus' resurrection. They all ran away when Jesus was taken prisoner. Then Jesus suddenly stands among them. He announces His peace, which restores relationships.

Jesus gives this life-giving, inspiring and empowering gift. Like God breathed life into the first person (Gen. 2:7), Jesus breathes on them and gives them the Holy Spirit.

Your fear and failures do not determine your life. God gave you His peace and restored your relationship with Him. He will equip you by His Holy Spirit to do His work of love and peace today.

Lord, use me in Your service, by the power of Your Spirit.

Amen.

August 9

Dying with Christ

> Slaves, in reverent fear of God submit yourselves to your masters, not only to those who are good and considerate, but also to those who are harsh.
> 1 Peter 2:18 NIV

Peter's readers experienced difficult circumstances at work. Apart from being marginalized in society because they were Christians, they were sometimes treated unfairly by their bosses.

Remember that slaves belonged to their masters in those days. Some of these owners treated them well, but others were harsh. They had very few other options. Yet Peter calls on them to show the necessary respect to their employers. It costs more than perseverance to stay calm in an unfair work situation where you are insulted and falsely accused.

How is it humanly possible to persevere in these circumstances? It is not humanly possible. It is only possible through Jesus. He died so that we could die to our old lives (2:24). We do not do things in the old way. We do not insult others if they insult us. We do not back down from our Christian principles when someone humiliates us. Our life becomes a witness. We live in obedience to God's will. This is how we do what Jesus did when He was falsely accused and insulted.

Do not act like an unbeliever in your work situation. We are called to follow Jesus' example (2:21).

> Lord Jesus, thank You for allowing me to follow Your example because You set me free to do so. *Amen.*

August 10

Faith and Conduct

The earth is the LORD's, and everything in it.
The world and all its people belong to Him.
Psalm 24:1 NLT

Some people believe that ethics give meaning to our lives. If we abandon our ethics, we cease to make sense regardless of our professional degrees and licenses. What does this have to do with Psalm 24? The psalm begins with the confession that the Lord made everything. Jerusalem was the city of God, the mighty King. Within the gates of Jerusalem, they were reminded of all that the Lord had done for centuries to make them His people.

This, however, was not all that they learned there. Here their ethics determined if they could come into God's presence. Only those with "clean hands and a pure heart, who does not trust in an idol or swear by a false god" (24:4 NIV) could stand in the presence of God.

Ethics are not an option. It shows that we are serious about God. When we confess that the Lord made everything and everyone, that He saved people through the ages and saved us, we will also take care of His earth, His people, His animals, His plants.

We will live with integrity as He wills it—with clean hands and a heart focused on Him. His will is our joy! We only really do this when the world of God and His people is as important to us as it is to Him.

Lord, let me live with integrity before You and others, in Jesus' name. Amen.

August 11

Google Cannot Help!

*Then Jesus declared, "I am the bread of life.
Whoever comes to Me will never go hungry,
and whoever believes in Me will never be thirsty."*
John 6:35 NIV

Very often, we will see a notice board outside a church building with a striking message on it. One of these messages I've seen read: "Not all questions are answered by Google."

I asked a group of young people if they could think of some questions that cannot be answered by Google. One said, "Who am I?" Another said, "Who are my parents?" Yet another said, "What is the meaning of life?"

What is the meaning of life? Maybe you are searching for direction, truth and meaning in life. Google really cannot help you. But God can. Jesus stands before us as God's answer to our questions. He is the way that gives direction, the truth in which we discover the heart of God's love, and the life of compassion and love that will never end, because He is the Bread of Life (6:35; 14:6). He quenches our thirst and stills our hunger. Why search on Google for answers?

As someone said, the purpose of life is a life of purpose. We do this by loving God above everything, and by giving meaning to the lives of people around us and pointing them to the Bread of Life!

Lord, I accept You once again today as the meaning of my life, by the power of Your Spirit. Amen.

August 12

God's Grace When We Are Foolish

> A person's own folly leads to their ruin,
> yet their heart rages against the LORD.
> Proverbs 19:3 NIV

We all feel pain at one time or another. Pain takes on different forms. It can be physical pain, but more often it is emotional pain. Sometimes we lie and cause pain in our lives (19:5, 9). Sometimes we do not control our temper and others must help us to get out of the mess (19:11, 19).

Sometimes I am angry with the Lord about what happens to me. Could He not have stopped it? Could He not have prevented me from making senseless decisions? The poet says that we are often angry with the Lord about the decisions we have made (19:3).

We are not pawns. He does not move us as He decides. He gives us freedom. Sometimes we make wrong decisions and sometimes we make good decisions. In all circumstances, we are responsible before God for the choices we make. Yet, He is the loving Lord who overwhelms us with His love. When we then make wrong choices, we do not blame the Lord, but bow in confession before Him. We know that this Lord knows our weakness and forgives us. He does this because Christ paid for our wrong choices.

> God of grace, thank You that we can confess our weakness and folly before You, knowing that it was forgiven for the sake of Christ. *Amen.*

August 13

Loan to the Poor

*If you help the poor, you are lending
to the LORD—and He will repay you!*
Proverbs 19:17 NLT

Proverbs 19 contrasts rich and poor. People with money and power are honored (19:4, 6). In the church or the world, it seems that influential people have many friends, while people who do not have money or position do not actually form part of our circle of friends (19:7).

To help a poor person is like giving a loan to the Lord (19:17). The Lord blesses those who care. It does not mean that we should give something to the poor so that we can receive something back from the Lord or be blessed by Him. We help people in need because we have received so much love from God.

Paul asks for contributions to the poor in Jerusalem, and says, "For you know the grace of our Lord Jesus Christ, that though He was rich, yet for your sakes He became poor, that you through His poverty might become rich" (2 Cor. 8:9 NKJV).

Someone once wrote that the poor are given to the Church so that the Church as the body of Christ can be and remain a place of mutual concern, love, and peace.

*Thank You, Lord Jesus, that You made us rich by Your grace.
Enable me to make others rich through the gifts You gave me.*

Amen.

August 14

Travelers or Settlers

"This is what I'll do. I will tear down my barns and build bigger ones, and there I will store my surplus grain."
Luke 12:18 NIV

Believers often forget so easily that we are travelers in this world. We have tents but not houses of bricks. We are supposed to be pilgrims and not settlers. We became settlers instead of pilgrims.

What happens when we become settlers? What happens when we no longer see our life as a loan that God has granted us? We become masters of our own goods. We see this clearly in Luke 12:17-19 (NKJV), which says, "And he thought within himself, saying, 'What shall I do, since I have no room to store my crops?' So he said, 'I will do this: I will pull down my barns and build greater, and there I will store all my crops and my goods. And I will say to my soul, "Soul, you have many goods laid up for many years; take your ease; eat, drink, and be merry."'"

He becomes the decision maker, managing director of his own property, without being accountable to the board. What does the rich fool say? "The stuff I have is mine. I have decision-making power over it. I decide how I spend it. It's my money, my possessions, my opportunities, yes...I am lord over my life!" No recognition is given to the God who made him rich and who made the wheat grow.

Are you a boss or manager of God's gifts to you?

Lord, keep me from thinking that I am in control of my possessions, in Jesus' name. *Amen.*

August 15

Guard Against Greed

*"Watch out! Be on your guard against all kinds of greed;
life does not consist in an abundance of possessions."*
Luke 12:15 NIV

Our earthly goods are given to us to be used, not to be collected. Our hearts cling to collected treasure. Stored-up possessions get between God and us. Where my treasure is, there is my trust, my security, my comfort, my god. Treasure means idolatry.

Wealth, money and possessions have the potential to change our focus, making us put our trust in them rather than in God. The Gospel of Luke shows how wealth and possessions stood in the way of people following Jesus Christ (Luke 18:18-25; 14:25-33; 14:18-19).

Our problem, Jesus says, is not planning, but greed. This is also the problem that the brothers are arguing about in Luke 12:13. The Lord does not treat symptoms. Our real need is not that we do not get what we should. Our real need is that because of our greedy hearts, we do not give to others what they should have.

Ecclesiastes 5:10 (NIV) says, "Whoever loves money never has enough; whoever loves wealth is never satisfied with their income." The person whose job is everything never gets enough of their job. The man whose house is everything never has a grand enough house. The man whose car is everything never has a fancy enough car. So, we can go on.

Lord, free me from my tendency of wanting more, in Jesus' name. *Amen.*

August 16

Perishing like Beasts

*"You fool! You will die this very night. Then who
will get everything you worked for?"*
Luke 12:20 NLT

Sin is in our nature. We see this in Luke 12. In Luke 12:20, we find one of the most tragic verses in the Bible. Apparently, Jesus is saying that we are in debt with God. Our life is a loan from God and at some point, He will claim this loan back. We discover ourselves in the rich man who is called to account. We have to answer the question: What happens to all the things we worked day and night for, that we spent so many hours in front of our computer for? What happens to everything we have planned? What happens to everything on which we have placed our hope? What about our insurance policies and holiday homes, cars and furniture? The verse is so tragic because the rich man could not really give an answer.

But God gave an answer: The man was poor and impoverished, because he did not take God into account when he made all his plans. The psalmist was right: People who have wealth but lack understanding are like the beasts that perish (Ps. 49:19-20).

> Father, I realize that my life is a loan. Let me not place my hope on my possessions, for Christ's sake. *Amen.*

August 17

Christ, Our Hope!

"They will place their hope on Him."
Romans 15:12 NLT

Does God love me? Some people would say "maybe". Others would say, "No, not after what I have done." Yet others would say, "Yes, definitely!" The simple truth is, God loves the world. God loves all people. This is the point Paul is making. He explains that God keeps His promises. Jesus, the epitome of God's love and faithfulness, shows that God loves the Jews.

As a Jew, Paul could surely stop here. After all, the people received God's promises. However, Paul knows that God's love for Israel also had another purpose. Jesus' coming into the world was the fulfilment of the promise that God would reach all the nations through Abraham. Therefore, Paul quotes a few passages from the Old Testament to prove that God's heart is open to the nations.

We are part of these nations! We benefited from Jesus' coming into the world. We also praise the Lord now because people have preached this gospel to us. How privileged we are! Carry on this blessing today!

Father, thank You for Your faithfulness, in Jesus' name.

Amen.

August 18

Grant Me Serenity

*I do not concern myself with great matters
or things too wonderful for me.*
Psalm 131:1 NIV

I am always amazed when I see how people know everything about a subject or about the reasons why things happen. They know what the facts are and what the truth is! Also, they know how things will be fixed!

You have surely heard the prayer attributed to Reinhold Niebuhr: "God grant me the serenity to accept the things I cannot change, the courage to change the things I can, and the wisdom to know the difference." We need this prayer today. We need to say with the psalmist that there are things we just do not understand.

In our lives, there are things we do not like and cannot change. Sometimes it is our appearance. Sometimes it is something in our personality. Sometimes our circumstances are such that we would like to change them.

The psalmist of Psalm 131 began to understand this. He came to rest with the Lord because he knew that there were certain things that were beyond his understanding. Only the Lord knows the solution. If he worried about it, he would just be wasting his energy. This is why he sits, as it were, on God's lap, as on his mother's lap and feels at rest.

Wisdom is to distinguish between what you can change and what not.

Lord, give me discernment, in Jesus' name. *Amen.*

August 19

God Makes a Minus a Plus

*"You intended to harm me, but God intended it all
for good. He brought me to this position so
I could save the lives of many people."*
Genesis 50:20 NLT

What is the meaning of suffering? Everyone goes through personal episodes of suffering. It is up to us to discover the meaning in our suffering. Some people never find the meaning in their suffering. Yet, there are stories in the Bible in which we hear how believers found meaning in suffering. The story of Joseph is one. His brothers felt that their father had a favorite son. They also felt that he was a bit arrogant. They decided to get rid of him because of their hatred and evil thoughts.

Yet, when he looks back at what happened, he finds meaning in all of it. If Joseph were bitter and focused on his brothers' wickedness, their evil thoughts and actions, he probably would not have been able to see what God was doing. But knowing the Lord, he sees that God used the wickedness of his brothers to accomplish His purposes. That is why Joseph says that God managed the process—not his brothers (Gen. 45:5-8). God was able to get right what no human could. He reversed the process of wickedness and saved an entire nation.

Maybe Joseph's story will help you to remember that good can come from evil by God's grace.

Father, in times of suffering, let me keep my eyes on You, in Jesus' name. Amen.

August 20

Living with a Purpose

GOD is in charge of human life.
Proverbs 20:27 MSG

Most people take life for granted. Abraham Heschel said that just to *be* is a blessing and just to *live* is holy.

When we realize that life is a gift from God we also have a specific perspective: Life is precious. Such people fight anything that can endanger life or make life more difficult than God intended it to be. Therefore, such people do not give their life over to substance abuse (20:1), do not quarrel (20:3) and do not repay evil with evil (20:22). They are hardworking (20:13) and do not profit at the expense of their fellow human beings (20:10, 17, 23). They respect their parents and the authorities (20:2, 20). We also understand our own unreliability and sin (20:6, 9). Who can say that he or she is without sin (20:9)?

We rejoice in the forgiveness of sin through Jesus our Lord. Because we have received new life and eternal life from God's hand, we live with purpose. We do not live to be saved but to thank God for this undeserved salvation. Therefore, "whatever you do, whether in word or deed, do it all in the name of the Lord Jesus, giving thanks to God the Father through Him" (Col. 3:17 NIV).

Lord Jesus, thank You for the wonderful love You showed us.
Enable me to glorify You, through the power of Your Spirit.

Amen.

August 21

Pray for Faithful Leaders

*Love and faithfulness keep a king safe;
through love His throne is made secure.*
Proverbs 20:28 NIV

When a king ruled in Israel, he was a representative of God. God was actually in charge. This is why the prophets spoke so directly to kings who did not meet God's standards. The king had to maintain God's justice and righteousness.

According to this proverb, a king could only be certain of his kingdom if he acted with love and faithfulness. Love and faithfulness are often named as attributes of God. If the king adheres to it, God will care for him. It meant that the king had to remove the wrong among the people (20:8, 26).

The rulers of today do not have the same dispensation as in Israel. Some do not even know God. Yet, it does not relieve us of the responsibility to pray for them. Paul says that a stable government will promote our dedication to God: "I urge you, first of all, to pray for all people. Ask God to help them; intercede on their behalf, and give thanks for them. Pray this way for kings and all who are in authority so that we can live peaceful and quiet lives marked by godliness and dignity. This is good and pleases God our Savior, who wants everyone to be saved and to understand the truth" (1 Tim. 2:1-4 NLT).

Father, today I pray for faithfulness, justice and righteousness so that Your kingdom can be promoted through the work of Your Holy Spirit. Amen.

August 22

Constant Forgiveness

"Even if that person wrongs you seven times a day and each time turns again and asks forgiveness, you must forgive."
Luke 17:4 NLT

I sometimes doubt the sincerity of people who constantly do hurtful things and then ask for forgiveness. But God does not keep count. He allows us to return every time after we have sinned and accepts us without revenge.

It is one thing to say I will forgive someone, it is something totally different to actually forgive the person. It is hard. Yet, Jesus says that it is inevitable that things will cause people to stumble. We all stumble. We have all caused some hurt in someone's life. It is almost certain that someone said to us: "I will never forgive them." Are we then in a position to say that we do not need forgiveness?

No other Christian value cuts as deep as forgiveness. It requires total self-sacrifice. It is to put myself and my own hurt aside and forgive the person who has caused it. Forgiveness means giving someone a fresh start. It means that we clean the slate, just as God gives us a clean slate every time we come before Him with our sin.

God is giving us a new beginning every day. Therefore, we should give those who have hurt us a new beginning. This is also the heart of the gospel.

Spirit of God, teach me to forgive unconditionally, like You do, in Jesus' name. *Amen.*

August 23

We Need Workers

> "The harvest is plentiful but the workers are few. Ask the Lord of the harvest, therefore, to send out workers into His harvest field."
> Matthew 9:37-38 NIV

What is your passion in life? What motivates you to get up in the morning? When Jesus looked at the people around Him, He saw people who were like sheep without a shepherd. They needed someone to care for them. They were like a harvest that was ready to be brought in. He says that we should pray that there will be people who would have this passion to bring in God's harvest.

John Wesley wrote: "I look upon all the world as my parish; thus far I mean, that, in whatever part of it I am, I judge it meet, right, and my bounden duty to declare unto all that are willing to hear, the glad tidings of salvation...as such, am employed according to the plain direction of His Word, 'As I have opportunity, doing good unto all men'."

When you look at the people around you, what do you see? Just another person, or someone who needs God's grace? There are many people like this in our society. They need you. The harvest is great, says Jesus, but the laborers are few. If we are not willing to go, no money, media or other means will help. Pray that the Lord would send people to the ends of the earth. But remember, if you pray, you may be the answer to that prayer!

Lord, we pray for laborers so that Your harvest may be gathered. Use me, in Jesus' name. Amen.

August 24

Different Vision

In the morning, LORD, You hear my voice; in the morning
I lay my requests before You and wait expectantly.
Psalm 5:3 NIV

When David closes his eyes in Psalm 5, he sees a listening Lord (5:3). David suffers under the pressure of enemies (5:9–10). His prayer against his enemies makes us feel a bit uncomfortable, because as Christians we do not pray for the destruction of our enemies anymore. The Lord will judge, not us.

However, David's psalm teaches us to pray for something that is also very close to our hearts. This is that justice and righteousness might prevail and that the injustice in the world might end (5:4–6). With Isaiah, we dream about God who will establish and uphold His kingdom with justice and righteousness (Isa. 9:7).

This dream also makes us think about our own ways. Amid the injustice, David prays, "Lead me, O LORD, in Your righteousness; make Your way straight before my face" (Ps. 5:8 NKJV). Yes, close your eyes and you will see a listening Lord. When you are in trouble, He listens. You may dream with Him about a new world. But pray that His new world will start in your life.

> Spirit of God, teach us what is right and how to do Your will, through Jesus Christ our Lord. *Amen.*

August 25

The Great Love of God

And I pray that you...may have power, together with all the Lord's holy people, to grasp how wide and long and high and deep is the love of Christ.
Ephesians 3:17–18 NIV

It is impossible to stop growing when we are children. We do not have an option. Yet, the possibility of spiritual stagnation is common amongst us as Christians. A. J. Gossip writes that we come to Jesus Christ and He does for us what He promised and the thing works out.

The problem after, says Gossip, is that we settle down. Our own first-hand and irrefutable experience is behind us. He says, "instead of being incited to a hugeness of faith by what Christ has already done for us, we can't believe that there can be anything more, or even that He can work, for us, anything better. That first foretaste satisfies us." Gossip then compares our lives with someone camping out for life, but never pressing on to inherit what is there and meant for us.

Paul's prayer for the church is that we should constantly seek with other believers to experience the great love of God. We will never be able to grasp this on our own.

The poor condition of the church, family life, and our personal lives is the direct result of our lack of growth. We have become satisfied with the minimum on our Christian journey. Our faith is sometimes nothing more than an emergency parachute. Yet, the riches of God's grace is there for us to enjoy. May God free us from stagnation by His Spirit.

Lord God, do in and through us immeasurably more than all we ask or imagine, through the power of Your Spirit. Amen.

August 26

When God Calls...

> "Alas, Sovereign LORD," I said, "I do not know
> how to speak; I am too young."
> Jeremiah 1:6 NIV

I cannot recall how many times I have heard a sermon about this passage in Scripture. It motivated me and many others to take on the task of serving the Lord in ministry. Reflecting on that now, after many years in the Lord's service, I realize that I would probably not have been so keen to answer the call if I had known what Jeremiah's task was!

Jeremiah's task is terrible: "today I appoint you over nations and kingdoms to uproot and tear down, to destroy and overthrow, to build and to plant" (1:10 NIV). Planting and building are fine, but tearing down and uprooting is not!

No wonder Jeremiah feels that he is not up to the task. He looks at himself and finds some reasons to say no to this call. Why doesn't God choose a mature person with life experience? Jeremiah himself feels this way. In Jeremiah 1:6 (NKJV), he says, "Ah, Lord GOD! Behold, I cannot speak, for I am a youth."

The Lord's personnel policy is strange. Everywhere in the world powerful figures and personalities are sought for the job. But in God's work, He does not look for the strongest personalities and greatest achievers. He seeks for those who are weak in themselves, even the poor in spirit.

Lord, thank You that You equip us when You call us.

August 27

Vulnerable, But Useful

> But we have this treasure in earthen vessels, that the excellence of the power may be of God and not of us.
> 2 Corinthians 4:7 NKJV

Sometimes we believe that we must be perfect instruments to be in God's service. We think that our brokenness makes us useless. Brokenness does not make us less suitable to be used by God and to serve others. On the contrary, it makes us more suitable, because the focus is not on us. The treasure of God's grace will become more clearly visible in our lives when we are broken.

Maybe you feel like a clay pot. The cracks in our lives are often very visible. We feel ashamed. Remember that God's grace becomes more visible through your cracks! This is not about you, but about the treasure of God's grace in you!

Lord, let Your grace become clearer to others through the brokenness of my life, by the power of Your Spirit. Amen.

August 28

No Sinless People

Who can say, "I have kept my heart pure;
I am clean and without sin"?
Proverbs 20:9 NIV

People have amazing potential—especially to sin! There is no trustworthy person (20:6). Sometimes people get drunk (20:1). Some people will try to deceive us by advising us not to buy something because they want it for themselves (20:14). Other people earn their daily bread in dishonest ways (20:17). Still others deceive us with wrong scales (20:10, 23). There are people gossiping (20:19). Others want to avenge themselves about something that happened in the past (20:22).

Karl Barth said that sin is not confined to the evil things we do. It is the evil within us, the evil which we are. We could call it our pride, our laziness, or the deceit of our life. It is better, he said, to "call it for once the great defiance which turns us again and again into enemies of God and of our fellowmen, even our own selves."

Paul quotes Psalm 14 and 53 to emphasize our state, "There is none righteous, no, not one; there is none who understands; there is none who seeks after God. They have all turned aside; they have together become unprofitable; there is none who does good, no, not one" (Rom. 3:10-12 NKJV). Our best deeds are like dirty rags (Isa. 64:6).

The blood of Christ covers our worst deeds. Through Him we receive liberation, sanctification and salvation (1 Cor. 1:29-31).

Father, thank You for Your grace through the blood of Jesus Christ. *Amen.*

August 29

The Gift of Yourself

*To do what is right and just is more acceptable
to the LORD than sacrifice.*
Proverbs 21:3 NIV

The Lord is not interested in external worship as a substitute for love toward Him and our fellow human beings. The prophets are particularly outspoken about it. People should not worship the Lord in the temple while treating each other badly (Amos 5:21-24; Isa. 1:10-17).

We see it in Proverbs 21 as well. He says twice that the Lord does not want sacrifices but justice and righteousness (Prov. 21:3, 27). Almost every other saying in this chapter has something to say about it. If you bring sacrifices but you exalt yourself above others (21:4), deceive someone to become rich (21:6), do not show compassion (21:10), close your ears from the cry of the poor (21:13) and have a tongue that hurts others (21:23, 28), forget that the Lord feels happy about worship.

We cannot deceive the Lord. Jesus says that we should rather leave our sacrifices if our relationship with our fellow human beings is not right. Reconciliation comes before worship (Matt. 5:23-24). This is the sacrifice that God wants.

We can be very pious in the church, but it counts for nothing without justice and righteousness. When our relationship with God changes, there is also an altered relationship with ourselves, others, nature—yes, with everything.

Lord, let my actions towards my fellow human beings be worship before You, in Jesus' name. *Amen.*

August 30

Reflecting the Change He Brings

"I had concern for My holy name, which the people of Israel profaned among the nations where they had gone."
Ezekiel 36:21 NIV

The purpose of life is to honor God. Our life becomes senseless when we, who were called by this God, dishonor Him. Our lives darken the picture of God and turn it into a caricature. The Lord is judged by the life of His people.

This is what happened with Israel. It was a scandal for Israel to be in exile, but it was even worse for the God of Israel, because the nations said, "These are the LORD's people, and yet they had to leave His land" (36:20 NIV). The judgment about Israel was in its deepest sense a judgment upon their God. The living God, the creator of heaven and earth, the One who has chosen them to be His possession, was being dishonored by the people who did not worship the living God.

What is the future for people who have dishonored God's name? These are the surprising and overwhelming words of God. He gives a new beginning (36:25-28). He restores the relationship so that "you will be My people, and I will be your God" (36:28 NIV).

How can we remain the same?

Thank You for Your mercy, O God. Let my life honor You, through the power of Your Spirit. Amen.

August 31

Friends with Jesus

"As the Father has loved Me, so have I loved you. Now remain in My love. If you keep My commands, you will remain in My love. My command is this: Love each other as I have loved you. You are My friends if you do what I command."
John 15:9–10, 12, 14 NIV

Jesus chose us to be His friends (15:15–16). What a privilege! He shares everything His Father made known to Him with His disciples (15:15). They are His friends and confidants. Even more, as their friend, He already knows what price He will pay for them—His own life (15:13).

What does Jesus' friendship cost you? What does your friendship with Him look like? Jesus gives us clear guidelines. Our love should reflect His love: "Love each other as I have loved you" (15:12, 17 NIV). How will we be able to do it? Jesus says, "If you keep My commandments, you will abide in My love" (15:10 NKJV). To be a faithful friend to Jesus is to do what He says (15:14). To do what He says is to love other people as He loved us.

Who are your friends? True friends show their friends what God's love is like. This is how we are faithful to Him. Jesus' friendship with you is the starting point of great things. Listen to Him!

Lord, let our friendship reflect Your love and grace, in Jesus' name. *Amen.*

September

September 1

Darkness Shows Stars

> I know, O LORD, that Your regulations are fair;
> You disciplined me because I needed it.
> Psalm 119:75 NLT

Is affliction a sign of God's faithfulness? This is hard to swallow. We normally try to avoid hard times. It is part of our obsession with success. When we serve the Lord, we want things to go well.

Yes, of course, it is nice when the sun shines on our lives. Who does not want to prosper and enjoy life? However, when all goes well, one easily gets a one-sided image of God and life. We easily begin to think that prosperity is the only sign of the Lord's love. When the wheel turns and we get bad news about our health, or some or other disaster strikes, we wonder if the Lord still loves us.

The psalmist is convinced that we can also experience the faithfulness of the Lord in hard times. Sometimes God uses suffering, even though He is not the source of it, to teach us more about Him and His faithfulness. Faith is to know that we are safe in God's hands even in the worst of times. During those hard times, we begin to understand something of the Lord's grace.

We love the light because it shows us the way. But, we can endure the darkness because it shows us the stars. The darkness shows us the stars. Affliction shows us that God always cares for us. Nothing, yes nothing, can separate you from His love (Rom. 8:35-39).

Lord, open my eyes to the stars of Your grace in every situation, through Jesus Christ our Lord. Amen.

September 2

Rejoicing in Suffering

> Not only so, but we also glory in our sufferings, because we know
> that suffering produces perseverance; perseverance, character;
> and character, hope. And hope does not put us to shame.
> Romans 5:3-5 NIV

I visited one of the most beautiful wine farms in South Africa a few years ago. One of the best winemakers in South Africa works there. He told us a little bit more about his work. He remarked that they were picking grapes for a specific wine that specific day. He was very happy when he saw these grapes because they were the best he had seen. But he said that didn't mean they would necessarily produce the best wine. Many factors play a role in the process of winemaking. Some researchers claim that we need about eighteen percent "rot" for a good wine!

I immediately thought about the meaning of trouble and suffering in our lives. Paul says that we should rejoice in the "rot" of our suffering because, in the cellar of my suffering and affliction, I discover the best wines of perseverance, character and hope! Somewhere else he writes that when we are comforted in our troubles, we are also able to comfort others who are suffering (2 Cor. 1:4).

Lord, enable me to discover the wonder of Your grace in my circumstances today, through Jesus Christ our Lord. Amen.

September 3

Trust God

> "My ears had heard of You but now my eyes have seen You. Therefore I despise myself and repent in dust and ashes."
> Job 42:5-6 NIV

A man I know said that he is too tired to discuss religion. Everybody has their own philosophy. He therefore decided not to believe anything.

Job's friends also have their theology about God. Nothing Job heard from the ten discussions with his four friends could satisfy him. He also did not have an answer to his suffering. He did not doubt that it was undeserved and even blamed God for what happened to him.

God then confronted Job in the storm. He asked Job if he understood how creation works. Job realized that he was just a human being and God is God. All the talk about God did not lead to a personal experience with God. The result: Job repented!

What did Job repent of? He came to a point in which he renounced the requirement that we should understand everything. God is far greater than his questions. My own thoughts, theology and beliefs are limited. It is better just to trust God.

You may find yourself stuck in the questions that arise from your suffering. I can guarantee you that all your questions will not be answered.

Lord, I trust You irrespective of my circumstances, in Jesus' name. Amen.

September 4

Remember Your Purpose

*"You will do more than restore the people of Israel to Me.
I will make You a light to the Gentiles, and You will
bring My salvation to the ends of the earth."*
Isaiah 49:6 NLT

Someone who has been in prison for a long time and is released normally wants to catch up with family and friends to make up for the time that was lost. It is very normal to be self-centered in such a situation.

Israel was suffering greatly as a result of exile. They were there because their forefathers sinned. Now they hear the wonderful news that exile is over. They will return to their own land. The big temptation was to forget their calling. They thought the Lord was only interested in their salvation. However, God's purpose was never that they would keep the good news of God's salvation to themselves.

Isaiah emphasizes that all people are included in this salvation (49:1). The salvation that the Lord will bring will cause kings and leaders to bow before the living God (49:7). The nations will see that He is faithful. Israel is called anew to fulfill their purpose: They are God's servant, His light in the world.

Jesus calls us the light of the world. We cannot keep the good news of liberation to ourselves.

Lord, let us be a light to the nations so that Your salvation will reach every corner of this planet, in Jesus' name. Amen

September 5

Here I Stand

Now it happened as they journeyed on the road, that someone said to Him, "Lord, I will follow You wherever You go."
Luke 9:57 NKJV

Near Swakopmund in Namibia is a lonely train in the desert. It just stands there and does not move. It is called Martin Luther. Why? Because Martin Luther was immovable in his conviction about God's grace. He said: "Here I stand; I can do no other. God help me." Such commitment takes courage. He had to deal with hostility and even persecution. He defended the gospel at disputations. He refused to back down.

Jesus' parable refers to two attitudes towards following Him. Each time we hear the promise: I will follow the Lord, but I must first pay attention to a few things. In Luke 14, it is clear that family ties are one of the major reasons why people are reluctant to simply follow Jesus.

Some of the readers of Luke began to be tied up with earthly things. Their expectation that Jesus would return soon began to fade. Therefore, earthly commitments began to outweigh their commitment to Christ.

Jesus says that those who cling to earthly commitments do not really follow Christ. Christ did not cling to earthly things (Luke 9:58). Therefore, let go of what prevents you from following Him unconditionally.

Someone said that if God called you, you should not look over your shoulder to see who is following you. Likewise, do not look back and see what you are leaving behind. Follow Jesus unconditionally.

Spirit of God, empower me to follow Jesus unconditionally.

Amen.

September 6

When Love Rules...

Better to live in a desert than with a quarrelsome and nagging wife.
Proverbs 21:19 NIV

Do we have a male chauvinist speaking here? Some would say so. In some places in Proverbs, we get a rather negative view of women. She is compared with folly, a leaking roof (19:13; 27:15). Three times it is said that one cannot live with a woman who likes to quarrel (21:9, 19; 25:24).

Of course, there are such women. However, there are such men, too. They can complain, are negative and often quarrel. In many homes, it is nowadays the woman who keeps the household together. The point of these statements is not to point fingers, but to emphasize that a home is not a place of conflict, but where peace, love and harmony should rule. It must be a place of safety, security, forgiveness and tolerance.

Let us strive for this today so that nobody will feel it is better to be outside the home, go to work and make other friends just to avoid the conflict at home. Where love rules, there is no need for power struggles.

Spirit of God, make our home a place where family members want to be. Amen.

September 7

God Made You

> Rich and poor have this in common:
> The LORD is the Maker of them all.
> Proverbs 22:2 NIV

We often measure people's worth in terms of their possessions. Our society has become a rat race to get more and more possessions. We sometimes think like the bosses in a poem by Swiss theologian Kurt Marti. Many bosses, he says, want death to confirm their rule and their slaves' bondage—that they would remain bosses in their private graves and their slaves would remain slaves in their nameless graves.

What do you think of yourself? Do you find your dignity and worth in what you know, in your status, your income level, the things you own? Do you feel worthless because these things are missing?

Our dignity is not dependent on our wealth or poverty. We are God's people. God formed us with His own hands. Rich and poor, smart and unintelligent, beautiful and ugly, thin or overweight, white and black don't determine our worth before God. He made you.

God thinks so much of you that He sacrificed His Son in your place. Any boundaries that people draw to make us feel worthy or unworthy disappear when we look at the Cross. There we see the love of God for unworthy people.

Go and live today as someone whose dignity is determined by the fact that you are God's creation for whom Jesus died.

Lord God, thank You for making me and that I therefore have much value, through Jesus Christ our Lord. Amen.

September 8

After Action...Depression

> He sat down under a solitary broom tree and prayed
> that he might die. "I have had enough, LORD,"
> he said. "Take my life, for I am no better than
> my ancestors who have already died."
>
> 1 Kings 19:4 NLT

Someone said that the greatest people in God's kingdom can become despondent. Martin Luther very often felt this way, which led his wife to wear black clothes. When he asked her why she was wearing black, she replied: "It seems like God is dead by the way you are acting."

After the great victory over the Baal priests on Mount Carmel, Elijah was on top of the world. God gave a wonderful victory! However, his mood did not last long. He fled to the desert and was very depressed. Why? Jezebel, the king's wife, threatened to kill him before the day was over. It was terrible news for a man who was wholeheartedly devoted to God's cause.

Sometimes the forces around us are too much for us. Sometimes it makes us feel like we have no future. God does not leave us to ourselves. He reached out to Elijah in his despondency and distress. God provides Elijah with food and encourages him to get up and continue his work. God does not let us down. He promises His care and encouragement.

Lord, encourage me today, despite opposition, in Jesus' name.

Amen.

September 9

Lone Warrior?

> "I have zealously served the LORD God Almighty. But the people of Israel have broken their covenant with You. I am the only one left, and now they are trying to kill me, too."
> 1 Kings 19:14 NLT

When we are depressed, we often feel lonely. We feel that nobody cares what happens to us. The immense opposition we sometimes face in a community where God is not honored, can make us feel isolated and foolish. It feels like the whole world is against us. We feel that we are fighting a losing battle for our faith. The people who once stood with us now stand far away from us.

That is what Elijah experiences (19:10, 14). The bottom line of this is that he feels alienated from the faith community. Those who confessed in 1 Kings 18 that the Lord is their God are the people who broke the covenant with God and are now also seeking his life.

It is in such times that the Lord wants to open our eyes to the community of believers. The Lord said to Elijah that seven thousand people in Israel did not worship the image of Baal. He was not alone. Peter writes that we should resist evil, "because you know that the family of believers throughout the world is undergoing the same kind of sufferings" (1 Pet. 5:9 NIV). In this context, we can cast all our anxiety on Him because He cares for us (1 Pet. 5:7). The Lord gives us fellow believers. We are given to each other to carry us through difficult times.

Father, open my eyes for the fellowship of believers, in Jesus' name. *Amen.*

September 10

Who Is in Charge?

*"Go back the way you came, and go to the
Desert of Damascus. When you get there..."*
1 Kings 19:15 NIV

I am sure you know how difficult it is to change your own mood when you have gone through threatening and difficult situations. Elijah felt that he'd come to the end of his life and calling. He wanted the Lord to take his life and to be released from his task.

Elijah's attitude is surprising. Once he had trusted God with his whole heart. Fire came from heaven (1 King 19). The enemy was defeated! Then came the setback. After he fully lived, the man who stood steadfast in faith against the mighty ruler and his servants and helpers, now lies with his head in the sand of the desert, begging to die.

This is the painful reality of our existence if we lose vision. The "I" of Jezebel became greater than the "I" of God. Now the Lord turns this around. Jezebel may think she's in control, but it is not true. Elijah is instructed to anoint Hazael king of Aram. Aram was an enemy of Israel for a very long time. Elijah had to learn anew that the Lord reigns over all nations. He is in control of history.

Do not read too much into the forces around you. Do not let it discourage you or deprive you of your zeal. Jesus, our Lord, is the Lord of the world. Jesus sits at the right hand of God and reigns forever!

Lord, help me to see Your power, in Jesus' name. *Amen.*

September 11

Bumpy Roads—Good Shoes

*God is faithful; He will not let you be tempted
beyond what you can bear.*
1 Corinthians 10:13 NIV

Our journey with God is not always easy. Sometimes the road can be quite bumpy! Some people find it easier than others. I remember a classmate at university who said that his life was just easy—a good family, good parents and more than enough on a material level. When one is young, it is also often the case that life seems simpler. However, it does not take long before one realizes that life has its ups and downs. Sometimes there are more downs than ups! When we move into the world, we see how broken everything is.

Sometimes the devil uses the bad things in our lives to try to convince us that the Lord has forgotten us. You must never believe in that nonsense. God is faithful—always remember this!

This is what Paul says to people who are being tempted. Temptations come our way. We need to be alert. We need to understand that they are dangerous for our life of faith. However, God will not let us down. No matter how long the road feels, the Lord will also give us the outcome. Hold on to it! For God, no road is too long to be with us.

Father, thank You for walking with us! Open our eyes to temptations and let us trust in You alone! Amen.

September 12

Loneliness

*Turn to me and have mercy,
for I am alone and in deep distress.*
Psalm 25:16 NLT

What is poverty? A quick definition is impossible. Being poor and being rich differ from context to context. Mother Teresa worked for many years among the poorest of the poor in India. She knew how people suffered because of this poverty. Those who do not have food to eat, clothes to wear or a place to stay, suffer terribly. Our dignity as human beings is also connected to these realities. Sometimes these people feel worthless.

However, Mother Teresa also knew about a worse form of suffering. Having nothing is one thing. Having nobody is even worse. She writes that the worst suffering is to feel lonely, that no one needs you and that no one loves you. This loneliness destroys joy and hope. This loneliness sometimes makes people take their own lives.

The psalmist flees to the Lord with his loneliness. There are many reasons for his loneliness. Amongst others, he has to deal with his past and asks for forgiveness. He is at the right address.

However, people experience the Lord's presence and grace best when there are people who care and are merciful. I am sure you know of someone who is lonely today and feels rejected. The Lord is sending you there today.

> Father of the lonely, there are people who need Your presence today. Use me to make them aware of You in their loneliness, in Jesus' name. *Amen.*

September 13

Following the Master

> Jesus told them, "In this world the kings and great men lord it over their people, yet they are called 'friends of the people.' But among you it will be different. Those who are the greatest among you should take the lowest rank, and the leader should be like a servant."
>
> Luke 22:25-26 NLT

It is wonderful when people honor us. However, in this passage, Jesus warns the disciples about the dangers of the desire to be important. They wanted to be leaders. Jesus puts His finger on the problem with this desire. This desire can go wrong. Some people want to be important in order to dominate and control others. They misuse their authority. This desire can cause much hurt in the lives of others. This is not a Christian lifestyle. Christians follow their Master.

Jesus was a servant. He did more than just serve people with His time and teaching. He gave His life as a ransom for us. He gave His life to set us free (Mark 10:45). We are set free from the slavery of our sinful nature. We become like Jesus. Only those who are willing to serve are fit to be Christian leaders.

Happiness cannot be found in power or influence. Real happiness is to be servants, to open our lives to the healing, loving power of God, so that it can flow through us and be a blessing to everybody around us.

Father, let my life be a blessing, for Christ's sake. Amen.

September 14

Respect for Authority

*"Honor your father and your mother, as the
LORD your God has commanded you."*
Deuteronomy 5:16 NIV

There is a crisis of authority in our society. Even the authority that God has over our lives is rejected by a large portion of our society. Few authority structures are still maintained. People rebel against authority. The result is often chaos—uprisings on the streets, division in churches, broken relationships between parents and children. Chaos is the result of turning our backs on God. God established authority structures to ensure that there is order in society.

How can we help to bring order in chaos? It starts at home. The microcosmos where we learn how to handle and exercise authority is at home. If the authority of the parental home is not maintained, children will find it difficult to respect the authority structures in society. This is where we practice how to respect each other. This is where we practice how to submit to those who are wiser than us.

Not all households are successful in creating this atmosphere. One of the reasons is because parents have not been faithful to their calling. Parents are the bearers of the message of salvation. After the Ten Commandments are given in Deuteronomy 5 parents are instructed to teach all the Lord's commandments to their children. Moses teaches them to do this because the Lord delivered them and their children from Egypt. Without His deliverance, our lives would still be in chaos. This is the basis for order in our lives.

Father, help our families to be places where we can learn respect for order, through Jesus Christ our Lord. *Amen.*

September 15

Possessions and Service

*Blessed are those who are generous,
because they feed the poor.*
Proverbs 22:9 NLT

I often hear how we piously say: "Money is not everything. Yet, there are few things that compare with having enough money! If we have enough money, life is a bit easier."

Well, if we have money, we have to look at our attitudes towards money. It may happen that people cling to their money and possessions and give nothing to others. Another attitude towards our money is to exploit others to get more (22:16). What should our attitude to money and possessions be? Of course, we should not waste money. However, the purpose of our money and possessions is to help others (22:9).

Paul writes that if we are rich, we should not put our hope in it, but in God who provides everything. We should do good, be rich in good deeds, generous and willing to share (1 Tim. 6:17-18). Francis Bacon was correct when he said that money is like manure. It means nothing if it is not spread.

Let us learn again that God gives us our possessions and prosperity so that we can serve the world in need.

Father, teach us to serve others with our possessions, through the power of Your Spirit. Amen.

September 16

Representing God's Care

*So that your trust may be in the LORD,
I teach you today, even you.*
Proverbs 22:19 NIV

Proverbs 22:17-29 contain proverbs of so-called wise men. Many of these Proverbs also occur in Egyptian wisdom. However, there is a very big difference. The poet "interprets" this wisdom. Therefore, he says that he wrote it down so that people can learn to trust in the Lord (22:19).

It is a generally accepted value that one does not oppress poor people. However, we live these values because the Lord cares for these people (22:23). It is a generally accepted principle that one does not steal the land from people (22:28) because the Lord gave the land to people (Josh. 13-21). It is a generally accepted principle to do your work with dedication (Prov. 22:29). People of the Lord work and promote their skills so that God can be glorified. Paul writes, "Whatever you do, work at it with all your heart, as working for the Lord, not for human masters. It is the Lord Christ you are serving" (Col. 3:23-24 NIV).

We are not doing good just because we love people. We are doing good to each other because we actually stand in the Lord's place and look at the world. It can be said that only people who really hear, obey, and only they who obey can really hear. Our thoughts, prayers, conduct and focus are only right when it is born from trust in and obedience to the Lord.

Lord, teach me to look through Your eyes at the world, in Jesus' name. Amen.

September 17

God of Love

Beloved, let us love one another, for love is of God; and everyone who loves is born of God and knows God. God is love, and he who abides in love abides in God, and God in him.
1 John 4:7, 16 NKJV

Here the contrast with biblical love is so clear: "God is love" (4:16). It is His being. Everything He does is driven by His love.

Typical of this love of God is that there was no reason why God should have loved us. God so loved the world, the rebellious world, the world that crucified Jesus Christ, the world that rejected Him. Yes, "This is love: not that we loved God, but that He loved us and sent His Son as an atoning sacrifice for our sins" (4:10 NIV). He loved us before we could love Him.

Now we should love each other in the same way—sacrificing ourselves for others. Love is to go up to the altar. Then our communities, marriages, families and churches will be different. Love is like a candle—burning by consuming itself!

Where there is love, we really resemble God and show ourselves to be the children of God.

God of love, You live in us. Let other people see and experience it, through the power of Your Spirit. Amen.

September 18

God's Unending Love

> In this the love of God was manifested toward us, that God
> has sent His only begotten Son into the world, that we
> might live through Him. In this is love, not that we
> loved God, but that He loved us and sent His
> Son to be the propitiation for our sins.
> 1 John 4:9–10 NKJV

You are God's beloved. You should always remember this and embrace this thought. Irenaeus said that God created us so that He could have someone on whom He could pour out His love. God could not keep His love for Himself.

The people at the beginning of the world chose against God. God's love was not enough for Adam and Eve. They took it for granted and rebelled against it. They wanted to do their own will. It has become the pattern in the world. People did not want God's love. They fled from it, turning their backs on it. Now we are looking for love in so many other places that cannot give us the permanent security of God's love.

Still, God kept pouring out His love on us. God sent His Son for people like us. Even our rebellion and hostility against God could not stop Jesus, God's beloved, from giving His life for us. God made you to pour out His love on you!

A life before God is impossible without the realization that nothing can take away this love that God has for us. If rebellion and sin were reconciled, let's return to God and serve Him and others with love.

Spirit of God, fill us with love for You, in Jesus' name. *Amen.*

September 19

Sin, Satan and Self

> Now the serpent was more crafty
> than any of the wild animals the LORD God had made.
> He said to the woman, "Did God really say..."
> Genesis 3:1 NIV

Someone said that broken creation is the result of the unholy trinity: sin, Satan and self. Look no further for the cause of the trouble and suffering we are facing every day. After all, Satan deceived us into sinning. It is he who made us doubt God's word. It is his job to drive a wedge between us and God. He succeeded and since then we are by nature sinful. The fact that Satan deceived humans should not be an alibi to excuse us.

Once a drunk man knocked on my door and asked for money. I asked him if he was going to use the money for more alcohol. His answer was: "Sir, the devil makes me do it!" "No," I said, "don't blame the devil. It is your sin! It is your decision!"

However, this is not the last word about our existence. We are not given over to Satan, sin and self. Jesus came to save us from this unholy trinity. In Ephesians 2:1–10, Paul says that it was by grace alone that God saved us and made us His new creation. Let us turn around from the cul-de-sac and return to the ways of the Lord. Let us also rejoice in the victory that Christ achieved through His resurrection over sin, Satan and self (Col. 2:14-15).

Father, we praise You for the victory over Satan and our own brokenness, in Jesus' name. Amen.

September 20

Our Fault

"Cursed is the ground because of you."
Genesis 3:17 NIV

Some years there are droughts. Animals die and crops fail. The next year there are floods. Some countries have famine, while others throw tons of expired food away. Some nations have vaccines and let them expire while others struggle to get them. Is God behind everything? Did He plan it this way? If it is God's fault, Hans Küng is right when he says that our questions about this broken world not only reach heaven, but even accuse heaven and its God.

Before the Fall, we do not read of a broken creation. We read that God made everything very good. After Adam and Eve's sin, we begin to read of a cursed earth. In Genesis 3:17, the Lord tells Adam that the whole earth is suffering under his sin, yes, is cursed. And after the first fratricide (Gen. 4) and the earth swallowed up Abel's blood, God tells Cain that the land will not yield its produce when he cultivates it. Brother turned against brother. The one killed the other. This is not on God's account. It is on our account.

Yet, Jesus took this sin upon Him and shared in our suffering. God is there when people suffer. He cries with those who cry. In His ministry, He alleviated the pain and suffering of people. He promises a new heaven and earth when this reality will be replaced by God's perfect world without the problems we are now facing.

Father, forgive what we have done to Your creation, in Jesus' name. *Amen.*

September 21

Hope in a Broken World

> "Since you listened to your wife and ate from the tree whose fruit I commanded you not to eat, the ground is cursed because of you."
> Genesis 3:17 NLT

It is as if the biblical story gives an explanation for the brokenness that exists in the world. It wants to say that this was not part of God's plan for the world.

We see it around us. The droughts, famines, diseases, pests, hatred, polluted rivers and oceans, inequality between people and in marriages, discrimination and racism were never in God's mind. We, the people whom He commanded to live in obedience to Him, decided to walk our own path.

Our disobedience meant that we turned our back on God. When people do that, it also brings a distance between us, the people around us and creation. This is why we treat the earth as if it were our property to exploit and destroy.

Christ, the perfect, obedient One (Heb. 5) exchanged places with us, the guilty ones so that we could be changed. Paul says that Christians therefore sigh about the broken creation and long with the Spirit and creation for God's ultimate renewal of all things (Rom. 8:18–30).

> Lord, forgive us for what we have done and continue to do to the world around us. Let us take responsibility for making the world a better place, in Jesus' name. *Amen.*

September 22

God of Grace

*"But as for me, I know that my Redeemer lives,
and He will stand upon the earth at last.
And after my body has decayed,
yet in my body I will see God!"*

Job 19:25-26 NLT

When we look at the world around us, we see how people are losing everything—their belongings, children, parents, livelihoods, jobs and even their dignity. Nothing is fair.

Maybe you feel today like Job or Jesus, who suffered innocently. What did they do to deserve what they were going through? God Himself testified that Job was a righteous man. Yet, Job lost everything, except his life. On more than one occasion, Job wanted to die, but he could not. And then, when we do not expect it, we hear these words of faith from his mouth. This is faith: to believe in God when nothing makes sense (Hab. 3:17-19; Rom. 8:35-39). Faith is to hold on to God despite...

May you, by the grace of God, be able to hold on to the edges of His grace, even if everything goes wrong. You will experience His grace!

God of grace, I cling to You. Let me experience Your presence, in Jesus' name. *Amen.*

September 23

The Addiction of Wealth

> Do not wear yourself out to get rich;
> do not trust your own cleverness.
> Cast but a glance at riches, and they are gone,
> for they will surely sprout wings
> and fly off to the sky like an eagle.
> Proverbs 23:4-5 NIV

The context of these verses refers to the taking of someone else's land (23:10-11). Whoever wants to be rich soon wants to move boundaries by which people are harmed (22:22-23, 28).

But one can also move the boundaries in another way. When the urge to get rich becomes our passion we always risk losing our sense of values. Stingy people might give the impression that they love others, but they only give us food because they have manners. Meanwhile, they are hypocritical and calculate what your "friendship" costs (23:6-7).

Like life and health, wealth is temporary. The rich fool discovered too late that everything is God's gift. When he thought that he secured his future, God said to him, "'You fool! This very night your life will be demanded from you. Then who will get what you have prepared for yourself?' This is how it will be with whoever stores up things for themselves but is not rich toward God" (Luke 12:20-21 NIV).

Lord, liberate me from the urge to want more and more. Make me content with what I have, in Jesus' name. *Amen.*

September 24

Shave Every Day

> Always be zealous for the fear of the LORD.
> There is surely a future hope for you,
> and your hope will not be cut off.
> Proverbs 23:17-18 NIV

In Proverbs some themes previously discussed are again taken up in an independent section. One can end up in a dead-end street through bad influence. A whole lot of verses are devoted to a typical description of an alcoholic (23:29-35). It is someone whose physical appearance already describes his hopeless situation. However, drunkenness often goes with other things. In many cases, it is the result of the friends we have (23:19-21). When we mix with bad company, we will become bad company. If we seek the friendship of someone without a sense of values, we often lose our own values (23:26-28).

Therefore, the call is clear: Live in devotion to God (23:17), otherwise our vision of the future is distorted. It sometimes destroys our whole future. However, whoever trusts in the Lord and serves Him will always have a future and hope (23:18). Whoever serves the Lord will have insight, self-control and wisdom. It will keep you on the right path.

The struggle against sin, said Martin Luther, is like a man's beard. We shave today, look clean, and have a smooth chin; tomorrow our beard will be grown again, nor does it cease growing while we remain on earth. Sin cannot be extirpated from us as long as we exist. Nevertheless, we are bound to resist it to our utmost strength, and to cut it down unceasingly.

Spirit of God, bind me to You every day so that I shall walk the right path, in Jesus' name. *Amen.*

September 25

The Golden Thread of God's Faithfulness

Enoch walked faithfully with God.
Genesis 5:24 NIV

When the French Huguenots came to Southern Africa in the 17th century, my ancestors were among them. It may not be of any interest to you, but it matters to me. I started to research at the history and saw how many different families of ancestors make up my present family.

Genealogical registers are not always the most interesting reading material. However, it is very valuable reading material in the Bible. Amongst all the names in Genesis 4 and 5, we discover the golden thread of the faithfulness of God. God could have destroyed the human race after the fall because He is God. He could have wiped Cain and his descendants off the face of the earth because He is God. The intention that He had with human beings was a failure. He wanted us to fill and manage the earth properly. He wanted us to be bearers of His image. All of this was destroyed by the sin of Adam and Eve. Cain's murder of his brother Abel indicates how far we have fallen away from God.

In the genealogy of Genesis 4 and 5, we also discover how people, despite their unfaithfulness, are still called image bearers of God (5:1-2). Among them was Enoch, the son of the murderer Cain (4:17), who lived close to God. The sin of Cain did not mean the end of God's grace in Enoch's life.

God remains faithful, even if we are unfaithful or even if our ancestors were unfaithful. Let us live close to Him.

Faithful God, we thank You that there is no end to Your love, in Jesus' name. Amen.

September 26

Come, Lord! Make Everything New!

> And the One sitting on the throne said, "Look, I am making everything new!" And then He said to me, "Write this down, for what I tell you is trustworthy and true."
>
> Revelation 21:5 NLT

When I read these words, I long for this day of total renewal. The tears, pain, suffering, wars, oppression, child trafficking, modern-day slavery, famines and disasters, despotic leaders, emotional and physical abuse in households are just too much. We want it all to end.

In the beginning the world was without suffering. This world was without sin and without alienation from God. Suffering and sin did not belong in a world well created by God. The Bible also says that one day there will be a world without suffering and sin. Then we will no longer be estranged from God. When sin no longer exists, suffering will also be over.

The description of the new heaven and earth in Revelation emphasizes that the new order awaiting us will be of a totally different quality. We will not experience what we are experiencing now. Now there are tears. Then there will be no more tears. Now we are experiencing death. Then there will be no more death.

What makes the difference? God's presence. Where God is, death flees! In Jesus' victory over death, these things are already true. The final fulfillment will therefore definitely take place because God has promised it!

Father, thank You for Your promises that everything will change.

Amen.

September 27

The Best Choice

*Yet I am always with You; You hold me by my right hand.
My flesh and my heart may fail, but God is the strength
of my heart and my portion forever.*
Psalm 73:23, 26 NIV

Driving a car on an open road is not that difficult. I often have to drive abroad where we drive on the other side of the road. The traffic comes from the other side. It is challenging! We only really see if we can drive well when it is not an open road. When everything changes or when there is heavy weather and traffic, our driving skills are tested. There is a saying that goes like this: "A smooth sea never made a skilled sailor."

In the same way, it is easy to believe that there are no storms when life is easygoing and circumstances are favorable. When life's twists and storms show up, it gets harder. Holding on to the Lord when you have no prosperity, no income, no good prospects tests your faith.

Maybe your day is not starting well, or the past days have been like night. The poet of Psalm 73 struggles with the fact that he believes and yet experiences hardships. It brought a crisis in his life with God. Then he received a new understanding. God never left him in his troubled times. God was always there and will always be there. He holds his hand.

The Lord will never leave you! Hold on to Him!

Father, there is nothing that I desire, besides You. *Amen.*

September 28

Take a Break

"Observe the Sabbath day by keeping it holy,
as the LORD your God has commanded you."
Deuteronomy 5:12 NLT

Maybe you do not believe what you are reading now. Sabbath day? We don't do this anymore! Shops are open. Sports events are organized. Parties take place.

We should remember that the Sabbath is not the same as Sunday. We can easily become confused here. Sunday is the day of the resurrection of Christ. Paul says that the legalistic observance of the Sabbath is nothing but the observance of a shadow (Col. 2:16-17). The writer of Hebrews says that one can keep the Sabbath without sharing in the true rest (Heb. 4). Christ is our rest (Matt. 11:28-30).

Yet, as Christians, we have imported some of the ideas of the Sabbath into our Sunday. The Old Testament gives two reasons why the Sabbath day should be observed. In the version of the Ten Commandments in Exodus 20, God rested after creation (Exod. 20:8-11). Just as God rested, this is a day of rest for His people. On the other hand, God led them out of Egypt and they are no longer slaves (Deut. 5:12-15). It is therefore a day of celebration of our salvation.

Sundays give us the opportunity to break with our daily routine. It gives us time to rest. It also gives us the opportunity to be equipped for our life with God. Together with other believers, we can rest and celebrate our salvation. We must guard this day with zeal—without becoming legalistic.

Father, enable me to use Your day to celebrate Your salvation and to rest, in Jesus' name. Amen.

September 29

Let Go and Follow Him

> "If anyone comes to Me and does not hate his father
> and mother, wife and children, brothers and sisters,
> yes, and his own life also, he cannot be My disciple.
> And whoever does not bear his cross and
> come after Me cannot be My disciple."
> Luke 14:26–27 NKJV

It remains a miracle that anybody followed Jesus. In Luke 14, He speaks about a cross, self-denial, even that one has to deny one's family. Someone wrote that Jesus gives us no guarantees. He does not want to give us any false impressions, Jesus calls us not only to repentance, to the "letting go" of the false gods we come to Him with; but He goes one more difficult step farther: He also calls us to believe in Him alone as the decisive, absolutely unique, once and for all, full revelation of God to man.

This is extremely difficult for us because Jesus was careful to give men no external guarantee that He was, in fact, God in the flesh. Otherwise, He realized, we would not be worshiping Him, but would only be worshiping or trusting in the guarantee, whatever it might be. Are you willing to let go of everything and follow Him? It may cost us everything.

John Calvin said that the Lord is the King of kings. When He has opened His sacred mouth, He alone must be heard, before all and above all people.

Lord, teach me to follow You unconditionally, by Your grace.

Amen.

September 30

Surrender and Be Healed

*Commit your way to the LORD; trust in Him.
Be still before the LORD and wait patiently for Him.*
Psalm 37:5, 7 NIV

In one of the churches I served, we started prayer meetings on Friday mornings. The congregation never had such regular prayer meetings. We started these meetings because the congregation was under attack by people from the community. We experienced hostility and boycotting of our activities and projects. I have never experienced such a thing before. So, we prayed and prayed.

The psalmist is in a similar place in his life. Hostility, evil, undermining and open threats are part of his daily life. The psalm is like a prophetic voice. It gives him an alternative perspective on reality. The Lord is in control. Therefore, the psalmist should continue to do what is right and trust the Lord for the outcome.

I remember how one of the people in our prayer group read this whole psalm during our prayer meetings several times. I remember how the Holy Spirit spoke into our hearts and circumstances with these words.

While we cling to our problems and want to sort them out ourselves, our lives are closed to these promises. Peter says that we should cast all our anxiety on God because He cares for us (1 Pet. 5:7). Jesus invited us to rest in Him (Matt. 11:28).

Lord, heal me from my fears today, in Jesus' name. *Amen.*

October

October 1

Stop!

> Rescue those being led away to death; hold back those staggering toward slaughter. If you say, "But we knew nothing about this," does not He who weighs the heart perceive it?
> Proverbs 24:11-12 NIV

What would you do if you saw that your husband or wife was about to have an accident? Of course, our first response is to shout: "Watch out!" This cry can save us from an accident—even from death. In the same way, the Lord expects us to be an alarm for our fellow human beings.

Sometimes it happens that we clearly see how one of our friends or a member of the congregation is starting to go the wrong way. We can have the attitude of Cain and say that we do not have to look after our brother or sister. They are big enough to make their own choices. But the Lord asks us that we will not remain silent when we see someone stumbling and falling into sin. If we do not stop them, says the poet, those who are staggering toward slaughter will lose their lives (24:11).

Obviously, these words can also refer to those who are victims of injustice. We have to stand up for them. Jesus calls us also to care even for those who cause problems in our midst (Matt. 18). We need to talk to them to win them back. We received mercy. Let us show God's mercy (Matt. 18:21-35).

Lord, let us care for those going astray, in Jesus' name.

Amen.

October 2

Tell Them!

> Rescue those being led away to death; hold back those staggering toward slaughter. If you say, "But we knew nothing about this," does not He who weighs the heart perceive it?
> Proverbs 24:11-12 NIV

From the earliest times, we have been trying to evade this command. Like watchmen on the walls of a city, we must warn each other when we see the enemy coming (Ezek. 33:1-9). If we do not, we are responsible for the death of our fellow human beings. We cannot say that we did not know or that it does not affect us. We are called in the Bible to care for each other (Gal. 6:1-2). Jude writes, "Be merciful to those who doubt; save others by snatching them from the fire…" (Jude 22-23 NIV). Why should we do that? Because we have received mercy.

We want other people to have peace with God. A missionary wrote that all day he saw people who are dead to God, looking sadly out of hungry eyes. He said, "I want them to know my discovery! That any minute can be paradise, that any place can be heaven! That any man can have God! That every man does have God the moment he speaks to God, or listens for Him!"

Talk today with your parents, children, spouse, or friend who are far from God or straying from God's ways. Do not rest before you have started this task. God asks us to be instruments of His grace.

Lord, help me to talk to those who, even without knowing it, hunger for You, in Jesus' name. Amen.

October 3

He Finds Us

*One day Moses was tending the flock of his father-in-law.
He led the flock far into the wilderness and
came to Sinai, the mountain of God.*
Exodus 3:1 NLT

Francis Thompson wrote a poem called *The Hound of Heaven*. Some of the lines go like this: "I fled Him, down the nights and down the days; I fled Him, down the arches of the years; I fled Him, down the labyrinthine ways of my own mind; and in the mist of tears I hid from Him...But with unhurrying chase, and unperturbed pace, deliberate speed, majestic instancy..." God overtook him and made him His own.

Our failures do not stop God from doing great things in our lives. While refugee Moses is tending a flock of sheep in Midian and unsuspectingly chasing the flock into the wilderness, God overtakes him. Unbeknownst to Moses, he chases the flock in the direction of a place that will later play a major role in his own life. He does not know that it is God who speaks to him. He does not know it is a holy place. God makes this a place of perfect revelation which changes the direction of Moses' life. Even more, it changed the history of the nation of Israel.

Maybe you are plodding on in a meaningless life. The Lord has caught up with you today. It is time to surrender to Him and His will for your life. Today is the time and the place when God has overtaken you if you have fled from Him.

Lord, thank You that You chase us because You love us.

Amen.

October 4

The Faithful God

> "I am the LORD God of Abraham your
> father and the God of Isaac..."
> Genesis 28:13 NKJV

Some of us might have a family member whom we do not talk about too much because it can be embarrassing. Maybe he or she is in prison or did something that was a disgrace to the family.

Jacob is a refugee. Behind him lies a past full of deception. His future is very uncertain. Jacob was a perfect deceiver! Jacob cheats on his father and brother, steals his brother's blessing, and uses the name of the Lord for his own benefit (Gen. 27:20).

If Jacob were our brother, we would not have mentioned him in good company. Yet, Jacob is a perfect example of our own lives. We have been unfaithful to God. Maybe we did not cause a huge public scandal, but God knows how our secret sins have become an obstacle to the plans God had for our lives.

God's faithfulness cannot be curtailed by our unfaithfulness. We fall and make mistakes. We cause other people to avoid us. The Lord is not like that. He came for the sick. Jesus died for the deceivers, sinners, and the wicked (Rom. 5:6-10). If you are one of them, God speaks with love about you, so that you can start all over again. He is the Lord of new beginnings, like here in Jacob's case.

Father, thank You for always remaining faithful to Yourself, through Jesus our Lord. Amen.

October 5

You Will Never Walk Alone

"I am with you...I will not leave you..."
Genesis 28:15 NIV

Liverpool football club has an anthem that goes something like this: "When you walk through a storm hold your head up high and don't be afraid of the dark, at the end of the storm there's a golden sky...walk on through the wind, walk on through the rain...walk on, walk on with hope in your heart and you'll never walk alone..." The original song was meant to comfort someone who had lost a loved one.

The hope that we will never walk alone, finds a much firmer foundation in the promises of God. The promise that God is with us is repeatedly given to fearful and failed people throughout the Bible. Think of Moses the stutterer, Gideon the idolater, Jeremiah the young man, and Israel the deaf and blind people. Here it is given to Jacob, the deceiver.

Jesus is also called Immanuel. It means, "God with us" (Matt. 1:23). He is God with us, despite who we are. The disciples could not watch with Him in Gethsemane. They all ran away when He was taken prisoner. When they were fearful and in doubt after His resurrection, He stood among them with the promise: "I am with you always, to the very end" (Matt. 28:20 NIV).

In Jesus God stands beside us. Therefore, nothing can separate us from His love (Rom. 8:31-39).

Thank You, Immanuel, that we will never walk alone. Amen.

October 6

The Warmth of God's Love

"I will not leave you until I have done what I have promised you."
Genesis 28:15 NIV

In the movie *The Jazz Singer*, a song starts like this: "Love on the rocks..." The song is about love that grows cold. Almost no disappointment is greater than when love grows cold and relationships fail. It is painful and many people find it difficult to move on after such a disappointment.

God's love for us never grows cold. Through the ups and downs of our lives, His love is the one factor that never changes. I am trying to imagine how surprised Jacob would have been when he heard God saying, "I will not leave you until I have done what I have promised you."

God's love is connected to His character. In this passage, He is the covenant God, the One who made promises that He will not break—irrespective of the behavior of people. The Lord promised that He would not let Jacob down, while he deserved the opposite. While his future was very bleak, God broke open the door with the promise that He would do what He promised.

In Jesus, we see how love for us kept Him on the cross. Jesus is the fulfillment of all God's promises (2 Cor. 1:19-22). He never gets tired of loving us. His love is eternal—it never perishes.

The God of Jacob is also the God of your life. Therefore, this firm promise is also for you.

Father, thank You for the promise that You will not leave us, but will fulfill Your promises, in Jesus' name. Amen.

October 7

God Is Everywhere

> Then Jacob awoke from his sleep and said, "Surely the LORD is in this place, and I did not know it."
> Genesis 28:16 NKJV

Where is God? C. S. Lewis said that we may ignore it, but we can nowhere evade the presence of God. The world is crowded with Him. Sometimes the Lord is in places where we least expect it. How comforting! Just look at the history of Jacob. He is a champion deceiver. He cheated his brother (with the help of his mother) out of his birthright. Behind him is his dubious past. Now he is on his way into a very unknown future.

What happened at this low point? He hears words sounding like beautiful music, "I am with you and will watch over you wherever you go…I will not leave you until I have done what I have promised you" (28:15 NIV).

He did not expect it at all. So, he says, "Surely the LORD is in this place, and I was not aware of it" (28:16 NIV). By God's grace, the "wanted" fugitive is God's chosen.

We need a new understanding of God to free ourselves from the hopeless and pessimistic attitude that is so prevalent today. Jesus' name is Immanuel, God with us (Matt. 1:23). This same promise Jesus gives to His anxious disciples when He sends them to make disciples of all nations.

Lord, open my eyes to Your presence, by the power of Your Spirit. Amen.

October 8

End Result of Our Faith

> In all this you greatly rejoice, though now for a little while you may have had to suffer grief in all kinds of trials...and even though you do not see Him now, you believe in Him and are filled with an inexpressible and glorious joy...
> 1 Peter 1:6, 8 NIV

The Christians of Peter's time experienced marginalization and discrimination because they believed in Christ. Peter says that these trials are a joy. This is a strange perspective in a society where success and prosperity are the driving forces. If I could choose, I would not want to suffer to finally experience a little joy. After all, there are other ways to be joyful!

Yet, Peter wants to help them to have an alternative perspective on the suffering they endure for the sake of Christ. Their faith is being purified like gold in a fire. The end result is that it will bring praise, glory, and honor when Jesus Christ is revealed (1:7).

Why can we be so sure that it will be the end result of our faith? Peter emphasizes that God preserves our inheritance in heaven. That's not all. He also preserves us to the end (1:4–5). We will not lose our salvation. The resurrection of Christ is the guarantee for it (1:3–4)! What an unchanging and stable guarantee!

Lord Jesus Christ, thank You for the guarantee that we belong to You in all circumstances. Amen.

October 9

Watch Out for Them

An honest answer is like a kiss on the lips.
Proverbs 24:26 NIV

The last verses of Proverbs 24 are like an attachment to the chapter (24:23). The purpose of this section is very clear. Corruption undermines a healthy society. We are normally very judgmental if the people in high positions are corrupt. Yes, the population curses people in high positions who have accepted bribes or who show partiality (24:23–25).

Small corruption, however, is just as bad. It happens when I am not honest in what I say (24:26). Elsewhere, the poet says, "Those who flatter their neighbors are spreading nets for their feet" (29:5 NIV). It happens when I lie when someone asks my honest opinion, and I am afraid that my status or position will be affected by my honest answer. It happens when I spread false information about others. By doing this, I deceive people (24:28).

If we want to build a society with healthy values, we must start with the corruption in our own hearts. Paul says, "Love must be sincere. Hate what is evil; cling to what is good" (Rom. 12:9 NIV).

Lord, give us integrity and honesty, even if it is to our detriment, in Jesus' name. Amen.

October 10

In His Service

> Do your planning and prepare your fields
> before building your house.
> Proverbs 24:27 NLT

The poet speaks about lazy people and people who have the wrong priorities. It is easy to put the cart before the horse. Sometimes we look at our own interests, like a nice home, beautiful car, or overseas vacation, before we plan how we are going to afford it.

The worst form of irresponsibility is laziness. A lazy person does as little as possible. The poet says that it is the recipe for poverty (24:34). It does not take a very clever person to recognize it. A lazy person does not see it.

God gives us the wonderful opportunity to work. Let us do it as if we do it for Him. Paul writes in his letter to the Colossians, "Whatever you do, do it heartily, as to the Lord and not to men, knowing that from the Lord you will receive the reward of the inheritance; for you serve the Lord Christ" (Col. 3:23-24 NKJV). When this is our vision, we will have the right priorities in our work.

> Father who cares for us, give us the opportunity to work as good managers, because we are in Your service, by the power of Your Spirit. *Amen.*

October 11

Angels and Saints

*It is because of Him that you are in Christ Jesus,
who has become for us wisdom from God—that is,
our righteousness, holiness and redemption.*
1 Corinthians 1:30 NIV

"A man does not have to be an angel to be a saint," said Albert Schweitzer. The custom of celebrating the life of a saint exists in many churches. These churches remember the life and example of someone who has already died. This person serves as an inspiration for their lives.

You have probably heard someone saying, "Look, I'm really no angel, but I am not too bad!" In most cases, this means that I am not perfect. I still have some way to go before I am holy like an angel. You are not an angel. You are right. You also do not have to be one to be holy! God has declared you holy despite your sin. It is not only dead people who are saints. You are one too.

God did not just declare us righteous, because Jesus died and rose for us. We have also been declared saints by God, even if the church has not made us a saint! Jesus is our sanctification, says Paul. It is because of God's grace that we are united with the One who brought about our total salvation!

We have no reason to brag (1:29). Our sinlessness does not make us holy. The fact that we are not too bad also does not make us acceptable before God. Jesus' merits alone make us holy.

Lord, thank You for the full salvation we have received by Your grace, in Jesus' name. *Amen.*

October 12

Hope for Broken Lives

"As the Father has sent Me, I also send you."
John 20:21 NKJV

Martin Luther once said that Christians in this world must take care of two things: the Word of God and the work of God.

If you believe that the Lord is alive, this conviction flows through your mouth and actions. When Jesus appeared to His disciples one Sunday evening after His resurrection, He involved them in His plan for the world, "As the Father has sent Me, I also send you."

With what does He send them into the world? Jesus was God's missionary to the world. For John, Jesus' task was very clear. He is the Lamb of God who would take away the sin of the world (1:29). This He has now come to do. He proclaimed that His work was finished (19:30). Now He is risen, He is Lord over death.

Jesus' ministry must now be continued by His followers in the world. He immediately instructs them to be witnesses of His love. They must go and proclaim the forgiveness of sins to people, "If you forgive anyone's sins, they are forgiven. If you do not forgive them, they are not forgiven" (20:23 NLT). Through us, the followers of Jesus, people should experience the wonderful freedom of the forgiveness wrought by the blood of Jesus Christ.

God is sending you today to bring this message of comfort to people with broken lives. We share the Word of God, which is the word of grace and forgiveness. We do the work of God, continuing His ministry of grace in the power of His Spirit.

Lord, send me to be a messenger of Your grace, by the power of Your Spirit. Amen.

October 13

True Religion

> "Is not this the kind of fasting I have chosen: to loose the chains of injustice and untie the cords of the yoke...to share your food with the hungry and to provide the poor wanderer with shelter—when you see the naked, to clothe them?"
>
> Isaiah 58:6–7 NIV

Soup, soap, and salvation. This is what people need, the founder of the Salvation Army, William Booth, said. The one cannot be without the other. It is a package of God's care. There is no sense in giving someone the gospel, without caring for their needs. There is no sense in giving someone food and shelter without sharing the good news of Jesus.

Isaiah said that this is part of the lives of godly people. In his last speech William Booth, said: "While women weep, as they do now, I'll fight; while little children go hungry, as they do now, I'll fight; while men go to prison, in and out, as they do now, I'll fight; while there is a drunkard left, while there is a poor lost girl upon the streets, while there remains one dark soul without the light of God, I'll fight—I'll fight to the very end!"

He understood something of Isaiah's words. He understood what it means to follow Christ. True religion is not about getting caught up in all sorts of religious rituals. True religion is when you are involved with those who need you. This is what Jesus did through His life and ministry.

Lord, use me today as Your instrument of care, in Jesus' name. Amen.

October 14

Meaning in Suffering

> In all this you greatly rejoice, though now for a little while
> you may have had to suffer grief in all kinds of trials. These
> have come so that the proven genuineness of your faith.
> 1 Peter 1:6-7 NIV

One of my friends said that the COVID-19 pandemic challenged the message of the church significantly. What kind of message have we been proclaiming? Did it help people during this traumatic time of loss and uncertainty?

It is grace to look back on your hardships and find meaning in them. When one suffers, one usually finds no meaning. However, the Bible is full of people who looked back and said that the Lord used the hardships in their lives to shape them. Peter is one of them. He knows that suffering works like a furnace that purifies gold (1:7).

Why do we only discover meaning when we look back? The challenge is to have hope and see meaning even while we are in the furnace of life. Henri-Frédéric Amiel asked: "You desire to know the art of living, my friend? It is contained in one phrase: make use of suffering."

Hard times expose the impurity of our faith life. It teaches us to no longer trust in ourselves but to build our hope on God's faithfulness alone. His faithfulness, says Peter, means that the resurrection of Christ has given us a new life (1:3-4). This is what carries us through every trial!

Lord, enable me to discover meaning in my suffering, by the power of Your Spirit. Amen.

October 15

Praise Him!

Praise the LORD, my soul, and forget not all His benefits.
Psalm 103:2 NIV

One of the most beautiful contemporary songs of worship is based on Psalm 103. The song *10,000 Reasons (Bless the Lord)* was co-written by Matt Redman and Jonas Myrin. It's about the eternal love of God, from morning to evening, until the end of our lives. An eternal song of praise is fitting for all those who believe in the Lord and experience His love. This psalm sings about God's grace. He forgives our sins and saves us from death (103:3-4). He gives new strength when ours is failing (103:5).

To explain this love of the Lord, the poet says that we should understand ourselves well. We are sinful and perishable (103:14-16). Against this background, we hear of the Father. He does not always remain angry (103:9). He does not keep score of our debt (103:10). He removes our sin (103:12). He has mercy on us like a good father (103:13). His love never goes away (103:17).

Our Lord is worthy of all our praise and worship. "The LORD has established His throne in heaven, and His kingdom rules over all" (103:19 NKJV).

Bless the Lord, O my soul! *Amen.*

October 16

Freedom in Suffering

*Who shall separate us from the love of Christ?
Shall tribulation, or distress, or persecution, or famine,
or nakedness, or peril, or sword? Yet in all these things
we are more than conquerors through Him who loved us.*
Romans 8:35, 37 NKJV

Viktor Frankl was in a Nazi concentration camp during World War II. It is impossible for us to imagine what kind of suffering these people went through. The horrendous experiences are well documented.

How can we keep on going when there is no hope? Frankl said that those who lived in concentration camps can remember the people who walked through their dormitories to comfort others. They even gave their last piece of bread to others. Although they were not many, they were proof that while everything can be taken away from you, you can still choose your own attitude in any circumstance.

Paul's words reflect something of this freedom. Christians' paths may be rocky, but our God gives us the promise that nothing that happens to us can separate us from His love. It determines our attitude when we suffer. It gives us stability even when everything is hopeless.

Maybe things are bad for you today. What determines the outcome of your life? God's promises or the negative things around you and in you?

Father, instill in me the freedom to know that I can never be separated from You, even when everything is hopeless, in Jesus' name. Amen.

October 17

On the Guest List!

Then the angel said to me, "Write this: Blessed are those who are invited to the wedding supper of the Lamb!" And he added, "These are the true words of God."
Revelation 19:9 NIV

Guido de Brés was one of the authors of an important document after the Reformation. It later became known as the Belgic Confession. People like him wanted to make the truth of the Word of God known at a time when this truth was obscured. This action caused massive problems for him. Authorities wanted to kill him. Eventually, he was caught and sentenced to death. He was beheaded. A few hours before this terrible death, he said: "It appears to me that my soul has wings to ascend into heaven, for I have been invited to the wedding feast of my Lord, the Son of God."

These words echoed the words we read in Revelation 19:9. The church of Christ is a suffering church. When we are faithful to God, we should expect resistance. Has anyone threatened you because you are faithful to God? Nothing can change your future. We have the assurance and receive the comfort that nothing can change the promises of God. Our future is secure. We are on the guest list for the celebration of the final victory over death, on our way to a feast with the Lord.

To live in God's presence and for His truth is to know that you have a future, even if people threaten to take it away from you. After all, God says so. Is it necessary to be afraid?

Father, thank You for inviting me to the feast of Your victory, in Jesus' name. Amen.

October 18

Why Am I Working?

A little extra sleep, a little more slumber, a little folding of the hands to rest—then poverty will pounce on you like a bandit; scarcity will attack you like an armed robber.
Proverbs 24:33-34 NLT

Why are you working? To earn money or to honor God? Are you stealing from your employer by your (lack of) productivity? These are questions that every Christian should answer. Wisdom is the fruit of the Spirit. It is not complicated. It is wisdom in the affairs of our daily lives. Part of this wisdom is to be freed from the unhealthy value of earning the most money for the least work.

It is our calling as Christians to set an example when we work so that we can try to restore good values in society. A Christian's work must be done in such a way that people will discover that we are in Christ's service (Col. 3:23-24). If we are in our Savior's service, we work harder and with greater dedication than people who just work to earn money. Look carefully after the job God has given you. This is His way of meeting your needs. If you do not use it, you and your family may fall into poverty (Prov. 24:34).

In a letter to Polycarp in the first century, Ignatius of Antioch wrote, "Toil together one with another, struggle together, run together, suffer together, lie down together, rise up together, as God's stewards and assessors and ministers. Please the Captain in whose army you serve, from whom also you will receive your pay."

Lord, make me committed to my work, through the power of Your Spirit. Amen.

October 19

Unreserved Kindness

> If your enemy is hungry, give him food to eat; if he is thirsty, give him water to drink. In doing this, you will heap burning coals on his head, and the LORD will reward you.
> Proverbs 25:21-22 NIV

If someone who has caused you massive harm needs help, what will your reaction be? Paul quotes the words of Proverbs 25:21-22 as a description of the Christian lifestyle (Rom. 12:20). Someone who has discovered that God loved His enemies (Rom. 5:6-10) and who experiences His compassion (Rom. 12:1) acts differently to others.

Human love has boundaries. Christian love crosses borders. This is why we give bread, clothes, water, and love to people who cannot afford to give anything in return. Then our deeds are like our words—like golden apples (Prov. 25:11).

Jesus said that people of the kingdom love their enemies (Matt. 5:43-48). Loving with boundaries is what unbelievers do. When we help our enemies, it may bring a change of heart (Prov. 25:22). Perhaps they may be so surprised that their attitude might change.

Compassion means seeing your friend and your enemy in equal need, and helping both equally. It demands that you seek and find the stranger, the broken, the prisoner, and comfort him and offer him your help. Herein lies the holy compassion of God that causes the devil much distress.

Father, make me sensitive to people in need because You helped me in my distress, in Jesus' name. Amen.

October 20

The Mark of a Christian

Let us not love with words or speech but with actions and in truth.
1 John 3:18 NIV

Impossible! Do you want to tell me *he* is a Christian? I would never have believed it!"

I am sure you have heard these words or even said them about someone. Well, this is exactly what John is saying in his letter. Love is a sign of being a Christian. In 1 John 3:16-18, he gives an example. God went to great lengths to show His love for us. He brought a sacrifice. A sacrifice is something you give away, even if it is the most precious thing you have. Jesus gave His life away.

This love must also be shown through our lives, he says. Sacrifices are normal for Christians. If we see someone in need, we are willing to give up some of our own possessions to help. If we do not, John asks the straightforward question: How can the love of God be in that person (3:17)? In other words, do you want to tell me the person is a Christian?

Impossible! It is impossible for a Christian to turn his or her back on the needs of our fellow human beings. It does not mean solving the problems of the world far away from us. Sometimes the need is just in front of us, working for us or with us.

Victor Hugo remarked: "You may give without loving, but you cannot love without giving."

Lord, open my eyes and make me willing to help those in need, in Jesus' name. *Amen.*

October 21

Please Help!

> How long, O LORD, must I call for help? But You do not listen!
> "Violence is everywhere!" I cry, but You do not come to save.
> Habakkuk 1:2 NLT

Imagine that your city is under siege for 900 days. You cannot get out. People are starving. They eat anything they can get. This was the situation of the old Leningrad, now St Petersburg, in Russia during the Second World War.

Now imagine the prayers of people in that city. Habakkuk's words express what so many people prayed for in contexts of extreme violence. Habakkuk consists of a prophet's complaints and God's answers about the suffering of the people. Violence and oppression are the order of the day. Not the good people, but bad ones rule (1:4). It is a lawless society, and justice disappeared. God also does not answer with good news. Things will get even worse. The prophet finds it difficult to accept that God sees the injustice in the world but apparently does nothing about it (1:3).

Jesus Christ is Lord, we say. It is one of the most wonderful Christian confessions from the very beginning. This is why we expect things to look different in this world. There should be less trouble, less suffering, and hardship. Where is God in my suffering?

The New Testament says that Jesus became part of this broken and suffering world. He is there when we suffer. Therefore, with the prophet, we can call on God to change the situation. We can lament even more because we know that He has something better in mind than this broken world.

> Lord, how long are You going to wait to dispel the injustice?
> *Amen.*

October 22

God Hates Violence

Your eyes are too pure to look on evil; You cannot tolerate wrongdoing. Why then do You tolerate the treacherous? Why are You silent while the wicked swallow up those more righteous than themselves?
Habakkuk 1:13 NIV

When we look at what is going on in the world, we might wonder why God does not intervene. There are many passages in the Bible where people argue with God. Habakkuk is one of them. The prophet does not give up. He is not going to leave the matter of injustice there. After he complained earlier, he got an answer that the time of judgment was not over.

In his second lament, he approaches the matter somewhat differently. He knows that God is holy and can be trusted (1:12). If God is holy, He cannot use a sinful nation like the Chaldeans to punish His own people (1:13). It is unacceptable that these nations can catch people like fish in hooks and nets, take away their possessions and rejoice about their hardship (1:15). How can God just watch and do nothing?

If you have something on your heart take it to God. He is the living God and listens to our complaints. We can argue with God. He listens!

Lord, You are alive. Please bring an end to injustice, in Jesus' name. Amen.

October 23

The Song of Faith

*Though the fig tree does not bud and there are no
grapes on the vines...yet I will rejoice in the LORD.
The Sovereign LORD is my strength.*
Habakkuk 3:17–19 NIV

In a letter to a soldier in World War II, Helmut Thielicke wrote that faith does not make us blind. The opposite is true. Believers see much better than non-believers.

Habakkuk looks at the situation around him. All the means of life are gone—fig trees do not show any promise of bearing fruit. There is nothing to be seen in the vineyards. No produce is seen. Farmers have no animals. It is a terrible reality. Such a hopeless situation often leads to hopelessness. It is like someone in a dark forest. We only see the trees, not the light.

Yet, the prophet sees more than this terrible reality. Faith is this "yet". Despite everything, there is joy because we see further. Faith enables one's eye to see things in us, around us, and above us that the natural eye cannot see. This clairvoyance is only born in those who blindly believe, says Thielicke.

The journey of faith does not mean that we always know what awaits us in this life. It is not a road where there will be no problems. The assurance that things will change does not mean that they will happen immediately. Adoniram Judson once remarked that the future is as bright as God's promises. It is also as bleak as the prospect of those who do not trust Him.

Father, give me eyes of faith, in Jesus' name. *Amen.*

October 24

God's Child

> See what great love the Father has lavished on us, that we should be called children of God! And that is what we are!
> 1 John 3:1 NIV

Adopted children often search for their biological parents. When they find them, there are two basic reactions. The first is thankfulness for the parents who adopted and raised them. When they look at the circumstances in which they could have grown up, they are happy with what they had! The other reaction is happiness that they could meet their biological parents. They know their origin!

How do you know you are your parent's child? Have you had blood tests taken? Most of us will not go that far. We are sure that we are children of our parents. From an early age, we were taught to call our parents Mom and Dad. They put it in our mouths, as it were. We could do nothing to deserve it.

John says that God calls us His children. This is how much He loves us. We were not His children before, but now we discover our real being, our origin! We are born of God! Martin Luther remarked that we are not allowed to believe that we are lost.

There are people who no longer have parents, are disappointed in their parents, or never knew their own parents. We have the certainty and comfort that the Lord who made us with His own hands and bought us through the blood of His Son, calls us His children. That is what we are!

Thank You that I am Your child, through Jesus our Lord.

Amen.

October 25

Worship Means Obedience

> Come, let us worship and bow down. Let us kneel before the LORD our Maker, for He is our God. We are the people He watches over, the flock under His care.
> Psalm 95:6-7 NLT

It is wonderful to hear that we are cared for by the Shepherd of our lives. We agree with Psalm 23 that the Lord is our Shepherd. Jesus is our Good Shepherd (John 10). Nothing can snatch us from His hands.

This idea is comforting and is taken up by Psalm 95. The people have an identity. They are like sheep led and cared for by the caring God (Ps. 95:7). They worship the saving Creator God (95:1-7). They should bow before Him in grateful acknowledgment of His love.

Yet, there is a difference. In Psalm 95:8-11 we find a reference to Exodus 17:1-7. The people rebelled against Moses because they did not have water in the desert. However, their rebellion was essentially a rebellion against God's guidance. As a result, this generation did not enter the Promised Land.

Worship is not something we do one day per week or on special occasions. It does not help that we worship the Lord, fall on our knees before Him, and confess with our mouths that He is the King, Caretaker, and Shepherd of our life, while not listening to His voice. Worship means following God's guidance. Worship means being obedient. Worship is loving God in our everyday life.

Lord, we worship You and follow You, our Shepherd and Guide.

Amen.

October 26

His Name Is Holy

"You shall not take the name of the LORD your God in vain."
Deuteronomy 5:11 NKJV

I know a man who uses bad language. He does not care who is around: women, children, or anybody else. The misuse of the Lord's name is part of it. It is disgusting. This commandment was given to God's people. It seems it was a danger even amongst them. God's people can also misuse and abuse the Lord's name.

How does this happen? When church people like you and I do not act like Christians in society. It happens when people make promises to God in the presence of the congregation and do not keep them. It happens when we as Christians are not honest.

In short, we can say that each commandment of the Ten Commandments indicates a way of life that will honor the name of the Lord! Every time people who were liberated by Christ live or act contrary to these commandments, the name of the Lord is misused. Every time people in the world known as God's people slander others, tell lies, harm their fellow man, commit adultery, steal, or live as if God is not the only Lord, His name is abused.

Paul writes, "whatever you do, whether in word or deed, do it all in the name of the Lord Jesus" (Col. 3:17 NIV). We are His representatives. We act and live in His name. The misuse of the Lord's name is to live in such a way that it is dragged through the mud.

Lord, help me to remember today that I am representing Your name. Amen.

October 27

Friends with Hostility

> Like one who grabs a stray dog by the ears is someone who rushes into a quarrel not their own. Like a maniac shooting flaming arrows of death is one who deceives their neighbor and says, "I was only joking!" Without wood a fire goes out; without a gossip a quarrel dies down. As charcoal to embers and as wood to fire, so is a quarrelsome person for kindling strife.
>
> Proverbs 26:17–21 NIV

Constant quarreling when it is none of your business, deception, and gossiping about others is like looking for trouble with a stray dog, a maniac with flaming arrows, and like charcoal to embers. It is easy to imagine what will happen in these three images. It is dangerous and causes massive destruction and pain.

There are many such people. They are friends with hostility. If they can "stir" things they are happy. They like to cause division between people. It does not matter whether the disagreement has anything to do with them, they like to be part of it.

Do we really understand what these things do to people around us? People like it if someone spreads gossip (26:22). Our words break people and destroy their dignity. Our words can take away their will to live.

This is so different from the teaching of our Savior, Jesus Christ. We should treat people the way we want to be treated. If this principle guides our actions, the world will be a much better place.

Spirit of God, teach me to live by the principles of the kingdom of God, in Jesus' name. *Amen.*

October 28

It Will Come Back to Bite You

> Whoever digs a pit will fall into it, and he who
> rolls a stone will have it roll back on him.
> Proverbs 26:27 NKJV

The poet is concerned about people with two faces (26:23–26). These people say one thing in your presence, but something different behind your back. Even when they seem to have good intentions, they have evil intentions in their hearts.

Hypocrisy is engraved in many of us. Most of us wear masks. Yes, there may be people who always have honest intentions, but it is definitely the exception.

Gossiping and hypocrisy are like digging a hole for others. It is like rolling a stone over someone. Unfortunately, it is not one-directional. Eventually, these kinds of actions will come back to haunt us. Eventually this hole and stone are for us, not for others (26:27).

Do not hurt others. God does not like it. Paul writes that Christians should not wear masks, "Love must be sincere. Hate what is evil; cling to what is good. Be devoted to one another in love. Honor one another above yourselves" (Rom. 12:9–10 NIV).

Spirit of God, free me from the inclination to hurt others. Make me a sincere instrument of peace, in Jesus' name. Amen.

October 29

Life and Morality

> Who may worship in Your sanctuary, LORD? Who
> may enter Your presence on Your holy hill?
> Psalm 15:1 NLT

A political leader in the United Kingdom resigned from his position as a member of parliament a few years ago. Although he loved his political party, as a Christian he could not in good conscience accept the stance of his party on some moral issues.

In Psalm 15, it is clear that God's presence requires a very strong moral-ethical attitude to life. Like Psalm 24, the question of who may come into God's presence was asked by the temple-goers. The lifestyle that suits it is then spelled out. We therefore have to confess that we therefore have no right to be in God's presence. Can any human being be in God's presence without being destroyed? Apparently not (Exod. 34; Heb. 12:14-29). No separation is possible between God's presence in the temple and the presence of God in everyday life. The way we treat our fellow human beings and our morality is our daily worship.

We are all sinners and there is nobody who can claim that he or she fulfills all God's requirements, except Christ. As we think about His death and resurrection, we also accept that we can only enter into God's presence through the blood and perfect obedience of Christ (Heb. 10:19-25). By His Spirit, He dwells in us to bear the fruit of love for our fellow human beings (Gal. 5:22-23).

Fill me with Your Spirit, Lord. *Amen.*

October 30

Away with Religion

"Away with the noise of your songs! I will not listen to the music of your harps. But let justice roll on like a river."
Amos 5:23–24 NIV

The well-known preacher Charles Spurgeon said that the Christian faith is meant to be bread for everyday use, not cake for special occasions. The meaning is simple: We should live out our faith in everything we do, everywhere we are, and in all relationships. Our whole life is lived in the presence of God.

Apparently, the people in Amos's time separated their worship services from their lives. While singing, sacrificing, and celebrating, they misused their fellow human beings (5:7–13). God was not satisfied. This is why the prophet utters such harsh words. God wants our worship services on Sundays to be the launching pad to the worship service of life. When we come in contact with our fellow human beings, they still need to be able to read the message of Sunday in our lives, eyes, and hands. When we detach our daily lives from what happens on Sundays in worship, we are not serving the Lord sincerely and with integrity.

We serve God sincerely when we see our family life, our work, our sports, and leisure as places where God's will should be done. Only then do our worship services on Sundays make any sense.

Lord, make my life a worship service, by the power of Your Spirit.

Amen.

October 31

No Performance Please!

> God has united you with Christ Jesus. For our benefit God made Him to be wisdom itself. Christ made us right with God; He made us pure and holy, and He freed us from sin. Therefore, as the Scriptures say, "If you want to boast, boast only about the LORD."
> 1 Corinthians 1:30-31 NLT

We live in a society where we have to perform. Nothing is free. You have to earn promotion, favor, and even love. Some people apply this sick mindset to our journey with God. It has a devastating influence on our spiritual life: achievement-reward, prayer-healing, confession-forgiveness. Unconsciously, or even consciously, we think that God will show us His mercy and grace based on our performance. Or, when we suffer, we think that we have not been thankful enough, devout enough, or good enough.

When we think that God responds with His love based on our actions, we do not understand the gospel. There is only one achievement that counts before God and that is the achievement of His Son, Jesus Christ. Only Jesus was perfect enough, good enough, devout enough. His perfection covers our imperfections.

We can only boast about Him. That is why our performance can never be a condition of God's grace. John Calvin said that we should not fix our eyes on our shattered condition, repentance, or tears, but should keep both our eyes alone on God's love and grace. If God's grace were to depend on any condition or achievement on our part, there would be nothing more miserable than our own condition.

God's grace is grace. God's gift is a gift! God's love is free.

Father, thank You for Your unconditional grace, through Jesus Christ our Lord. *Amen.*

November

November 1

The Whole Law

> Let no debt remain outstanding,
> except the continuing debt to love one another,
> for whoever loves others has fulfilled the law.
> Romans 13:8 NIV

To live loving others is an incredible way of life. It is a total change of attitude—something our world needs every day. Yet, this is what a Christian should be like. There are many ways we try to show that we are children of the Lord. Sometimes people stick the symbol of fish on their cars to indicate that they are Christians. Sometimes they give their businesses names that come from the Bible. It is meant to be a testimony.

These are all wonderful ways of publicly stating that we are loyal to Jesus Christ. However, love is the only real way Christians show that they are children of God. Everything God intended us to be is summed up in this one word.

Paul says that love is the one action that sums up everything that is written in the Ten Commandments. Of course, Christian love is different from the love that many people sing about. The songs we hear often sing of a romantic love that is grounded in what the other person offers and is for us. The other person's qualities determine, as it were, the quality of my love.

Our love is determined by the unconditional love that God has for us. It is not based on our qualities. It is simply because God loves us.

Lord, let me show Your unconditional love today, in Jesus' name.

Amen.

November 2

Radiating God's Kindness

Be kind and compassionate to one another.
Ephesians 4:32 NIV

I am often amazed at how friendly the cashiers at the grocery stores in my town are. How do they keep it up? Mother Teresa said that it is amazing to see how many good things can be achieved by a simple smile. We often say: "It costs nothing to be friendly." To be friendly and kind might change someone's life.

We should, however, distinguish between genuine and superficial kindness and friendliness. Christians should never be accused of not being genuine. Love wears no masks, Paul says (Rom. 12:9). Christians smile and are friendly and kind especially because God has smiled over our lives. In Ephesians 4, Paul emphasizes how we have moved from darkness to light, from a life in selfishness, bitterness and hatred to a life of service, forgiveness and caring for our neighbor.

God's love is not based on our looks, intelligence or position in society. He is friendly because He loves us unconditionally. Our kindness to one another is thus symbolic of God's kindness to us. He forgave us and gave us a new chance in life. We reflect this by being kind and compassionate to people around us.

Yes, kindness may not cost anything, but Christian kindness, goodwill and care have cost something. Jesus laid down His life to show us what it means. As people who have been sealed as God's possession by His Spirit (Eph. 4:30), we will do everything to radiate something of His love for others (5:1-2).

Lord, let my friendliness and smile radiate Your goodwill and love today, in Jesus' name. Amen.

November 3

Instruments of Peace

> The LORD said, "What have you done? Listen! Your brother's blood cries out to Me from the ground."
> Genesis 4:10 NIV

There is at least one person in our lives that we find hard to love. We find it much easier to be bitter and even hate that person. Sometimes he or she did something to us that changed the course of our life or caused almost irreversible damage. We need to be healed from this. Hatred and bitterness chains us to the past.

The story of Cain and Abel follows directly on from the story of the fall of Adam and Eve. It is clear: When our relationship with God goes wrong, our relationships with others also go wrong. This story is ours. Even though God pleads with us not to sin (4:6-7), we often walk out of worship and kill our brother or sister (4:8). Maybe not with our bare hands, but with our words, our eyes and our unloving actions. We judge, hate and scold each other and deny each other God's grace and forgiveness.

Jesus Christ's death not only brought peace between God and us but also between people (Eph. 2:11-22). As a reconciled community, Christians must take the lead in the community and banish lovelessness and hatred. We must never be at peace when there is no peace. We need to do everything to bring reconciliation between people.

Father, make me an instrument of Your peace, in Jesus' name.

Amen.

November 4

Choosing Friends

> An open rebuke is better than hidden love!
> Wounds from a sincere friend are better
> than many kisses from an enemy.
> Proverbs 27:5-6 NLT

Sometimes we say jokingly to each other, "With a friend like you, I don't need an enemy!" It is usually when our friend unexpectedly disagrees with us.

We all need friends who stand by us through thick and thin. William Arthur Ward wrote, "Flatter me, and I may not believe you. Criticize me, and I may not like you. Ignore me, and I may not forgive you. Encourage me, and I will not forget you."

If we are serious about this, we must also be prepared to be formed by our friends. Friends are like iron that grinds on the iron in my life (27:17). Friends smooth the sharp points in my life. I also help my friends to get rid of the sharp points in their lives.

How do we do it? We do it by encouragement, love, reprimanding and sometimes by hard words which may even cause hurt. We do it, however, because we love each other and because we know that we can contribute to Christ's image being seen more and more in each other's lives. Jesus, who calls us His friend, says that we should be willing to be pruned to bear more fruit (John 15:1–17). Sometimes God uses our friends to do this pruning.

Lord, thank You for friends whose love also includes pruning in my life, in Jesus' name. Amen.

November 5

A Friend for the Gospel

> An open rebuke is better than hidden love!
> Wounds from a sincere friend
> are better than many kisses from an enemy.
> Proverbs 27:5–6 NLT

We said that we sometimes have to correct our friends and be corrected by them. Does it mean that we should disagree just because we do not like what our friend says?

Paul had to disagree openly when Peter associated himself only with the Jews. He did not disagree just because they just had different views about the matter. Peter was clearly hypocritical. Paul pointed this out and rebuked him because the gospel was at stake (Gal. 2:11–21).

Maybe we disagree too much about petty little things, while we do not disagree when the gospel is at stake. This is the principle: We help each other to become more like Jesus, so that the gospel of Jesus Christ may be honored and advanced. When someone's growth to become more like Christ is at stake, we have to take a stand. When my own relationship with Christ is at stake, I want a friend to help me on the way. Yes, when the integrity of the gospel is at stake, we need to take a stand—even if it is our best friend who is in the wrong.

Friends like this are God's gifts. They keep us from falling. They keep us on the road of the gospel. Are you such a friend?

Lord God, thank You for friends who help to form my life, through the power of Your Spirit. Amen.

November 6

Heaven Is Where God Is

No one has seen God at any time. If we love one another, God abides in us, and His love has been perfected in us. God is love, and he who abides in love abides in God, and God in him.
1 John 4:12, 16 NKJV

When we read the words of John, he reminds us that the Lord can be seen. How? Years ago, there was a very popular song, containing these words: "Heaven is a place on earth." These words make us think. Can heaven be experienced on earth?

When people love one another, God becomes visible in the world. This is when people begin to experience something of heaven. Love is the best proof that God lives in us. And when God lives in us, He becomes visible through love.

This love has a special character. John describes it as sacrificial. Our love should reflect the love of God who gave His son as a sacrifice for our sin. Jesus gave Himself up. This is true love. The opposite is of course also true. When we do not show love, God is not seen. Through our lack of love, we are responsible for people not seeing God. Where love is lacking, it is the best proof that people do not know God, says John.

Heaven can be a place on earth today when you show the sacrificial love of Christ! God is where this love is shown.

Lord, give me this love, by the power of Your Spirit. *Amen.*

November 7

Only One True God

> Hear, O Israel: The LORD our God, the LORD is one.
> Deuteronomy 6:4 NIV

Many Jews have a small box at their door. In this box there is a copy of the words of Deuteronomy 6:4. They do this because Deuteronomy 6:9 (NLT) says: "Write them on the doorposts of your house and on your gates."

These words in Deuteronomy 6:4 describe the unique Lord whom they worship. He delivered them from bondage in Egypt. He led them through the wilderness and gave them land. He gave victories over mighty kings. No other God could do that! He is the living, faithful God.

Yet, these words cannot be read in isolation. We cannot confess who He is, without responding to it. The response is simple: We love the Lord. This love demands my life, my all. It fills my mind, heart, emotions and takes up my strength! It fills my life in such a way that I share it with the people around me.

It fills my life in such a way that I live according to it from morning to night. My children can see God's presence in my life (6:7). The way I act and think is a testimony to my household that I love God above all else (6:8). Yes, my home is recognized by it (6:9)!

This is the result when the Spirit convinces me of God's love. He is the only Lord! Let the Spirit lead you to total surrender!

Lord, take my life and let it honor You, by the power of Your Spirit. Amen.

November 8

No Other God

"You must not have any other god but Me."
Deuteronomy 5:7 NLT

Who or what is our God? Do we have other gods than the One true and living God? Our attempts to capture God in an image is modern. We try to place Him in a box. We create our own little gods, and the one true and living God should fit into our schemes.

The implications of this commandment are clear. Nothing can replace God. Yet our hearts are like a factory that produces idols. We can try to fill the hole in our heart with success, beautiful things, sports, fun and many other things. It will, as Ecclesiastes says, come to nothing (Eccles. 2:1–11). We can also try to shape God so that He is the way we want Him to be. It will come to nothing.

Have you deceived yourself with your gods? There is only One true living God. We see His face in Jesus. We see Him as the One who liberated us from false Gods and gave us a new life by forgiving us.

Spirit of God, deliver me from idols in my life, in Jesus' name.

Amen.

November 9

Stealing Dignity

> "You shall not steal."
> Leviticus 19:11 NKJV

Powerlessness is one of the worst emotions one can experience. We feel powerless when there is no one who stands up for us. It makes one feel terribly lonely.

God knew we would feel that way. This is why God is very concerned about the powerless people of society. In Leviticus 19, there are instructions on how the rights of these people should be protected by the faith community. The community must ensure that the poor have enough to eat (19:9-10). The poor and foreigners did not own land so they could take what remained in the fields after harvest. All that remained on the land belonged to them (Deut. 24:19-21). Also, the laborer, someone who lived day by day from hand to mouth, must be protected from exploitation (Lev. 19:13). The dignity of the deaf and blind must always be respected (19:14). According to God's law, injustice should never be committed against a fellow human being (19:15). People should not be slandered and thus be hurt (19:16). People who choose for life also choose for the protection of their fellow human beings.

Theft lies on different levels. We can steal each other's stuff. We can also be passive about the needs of our fellow humans. It is theft. We can pay people poorly. It is theft. We can damage people's dignity. It is theft. We can harm people's futures through our gossiping tongues. It is theft. We can deprive people of hope through our conversations. It is theft. You shall not steal!

Lord, keep me from stealing, in Jesus' name. *Amen.*

November 10

Do Not Fake Anything!

"Do not lie. Do not deceive one another."
Leviticus 19:11 NIV

John Owen wrote that sometimes first truth is lost in a church and then holiness. Sometimes the decay or hatred of holiness is the cause of the loss of truth; but where either is rejected, the other will not remain in the church.

This is also true of our personal lives. There is an unbreakable link between truth, integrity and holiness. People should be able to trust us. Paul writes that our love should be without masks (Rom. 12:9).

God gives clear instructions on how we should respect one another. In Leviticus 19, we see quite a few references to deception (Lev. 19:11-12, 36). Deception, of course, begins deep in one's heart. We deceive when we are hateful and hold things against someone, while the opportunity exists to settle the matter with each other (19:17-18). What do we actually do when we act like that? We have no integrity.

Why can Christians not live like this? At the end of each paragraph in Leviticus 19 we read: "I am the Lord!" He set them free. He is the holy God who set us apart for Himself to serve Him (11:44-45; 20:7-8). This means that every relationship, every action, every conversation about our fellow human beings, every business transaction, every feeling of hatred, every gossip story, does not in the first place damage the honor of people. It harms God's holiness! Everyone who harms God's people harms Him.

Spirit of God, let my motives be pure and teach me to live with truth and integrity, through the power of Your Spirit. Amen.

November 11

Gold Can Blind You

"You shall not covet your neighbor's house."
Exodus 20:17 NIV

Sometimes my wife and I used to drive through the suburbs to see new houses. Some of these places were enormous. It was someone's dream house. Then we also dreamed! What would our dream house be like?

To dream is not wrong. Dreams can go wrong when they begin to fill our horizons, our passions and time. For many, wealth and possessions have already meant their downfall. The moment we begin to put something other than God in the center of our lives, we have already started to fall away from Him. Later on, we do not need God.

I once heard someone say that gold dust is valuable. Yet, it restricts our sight when it gets in our eyes. It is clear: When our vision is clouded by our search for more, it makes us blind. The modern word for it is materialism. Greed is the biblical word. It is the same as when someone worships an idol (Col. 3:5). The pursuit of more possessions has become almost synonymous with our modern lifestyle.

Unfortunately, people's efforts to have more are not just about money. In this commandment, the relationship aspect of greed clearly emerges. When I want someone else's husband or wife, it destroys another family's life. When I gamble, I am impoverishing my own family.

The Christian value of contentment with what you have is something that our society and Spirit-filled Christians need to learn anew.

Father, thank You for what I have received from Your hand. Make me content with what I have, in Jesus' name. *Amen.*

November 12

Our Time and God's Time

> This is what the LORD Almighty says: "These people say,
> 'The time has not yet come to rebuild the LORD's house.'"
> Haggai 1:2 NIV

Priorities. How do we decide what is most important in life? There are so many things that demand our attention.

Haggai was a prophet among people returning from decades of exile. They were very excited to return to their land and to rebuild their lives. According to records from that time, the Persian government allowed them to build the temple and even provided materials for it. However, the excitement dwindled as life became easier and other things began to demand attention.

The result was that the people decided it was not the time for the temple to be built. It is not a sin to choose your time right, but their priorities were not right. While the cause of God was in ruins, their houses were lavish and everybody focused on their own interests (1:4, 9).

Now they were experiencing hard times. Haggai says that they are using their suffering as the reason why they cannot pay attention to God's cause. He turns their argument against them: It is because their priorities were wrong that they are suffering (1:5-7).

God has given us the task of putting His kingdom above all, but we are building our own kingdoms and taking care of ourselves. Every time we hear: "Now is not the time..." No, now is the time! Jesus said that when our primary concern, or first priority, is the kingdom of God, He will look after the other concerns we might have.

Father, today I choose to make Your kingdom my first priority.

Amen.

November 13

Loyalty

Whoever keeps the fig tree will eat its fruit;
so he who waits on his master will be honored.
Proverbs 27:18 NKJV

I read an engaging story of a factory worker who became friends with a minister. After attending a church service where his friend preached, he told the minister that he was touched. He realized that he had to work a lot harder and better. The minister was excited and waited for the right moment to share the gospel with his friend. Then the man went on to say that he would also have liked to hear how to act at work in a factory where the boss cheats people, uses child labor and treats people like pigs.

It is not so easy to look after the interests of your employer if there is so much injustice. Ye, we must work to provide for ourselves (27:23-27). Sometimes it means that we work in very unfavorable circumstances. Many people struggle in their work environment. They feel that they make no positive contribution to anything.

However, as Paul says, we are not working for people (Col. 3). We are working as Christians. Yes, if there is injustice, we need to speak about it and maybe even leave our jobs. If we do not leave it, we should work as if we work for the Lord. In small things people will see our witness.

Spirit of God, give me wisdom in my workplace, in Jesus' name.

Amen.

November 14

Your Influence

*Whoever keeps the fig tree will eat its fruit;
so he who waits on his master will be honored.*
Proverbs 27:18 NKJV

Perhaps we should also remember how people in the early Christian community had to do their work in a pagan environment. Their entire existence as workers (slaves) was built on injustice. They worked for people who owned them and could demand anything from them.

Look what Paul said to them, "Slaves, obey your earthly masters with deep respect and fear. Serve them sincerely as you would serve Christ. Try to please them all the time, not just when they are watching you. As slaves of Christ, do the will of God with all your heart. Work with enthusiasm, as though you were working for the Lord" (Eph. 6:5–7 NLT).

Perhaps, through our small contribution at the factory or in the office, we can radiate a testimony that may affect the unfair boss to see something different in us. Peter writes, "Slaves, in reverent fear of God submit yourselves to your masters, not only to those who are good and considerate, but also to those who are harsh. For it is commendable if someone bears up under the pain of unjust suffering because they are conscious of God. If you suffer for doing good and you endure it, this is commendable before God. To this you were called, because Christ suffered for you, leaving you an example, that you should follow in His steps" (1 Pet. 2:18–21 NIV).

Father, enable me to deliver my best where You placed me, through the power of Your Spirit. Amen.

November 15

A Discerning Heart

"So give your servant a discerning heart to govern your people and to distinguish between right and wrong."
1 Kings 3:9 NIV

What would you have asked if God offered you the same as He offered Solomon? "Ask for whatever you want me to give you" (1 Kings 3:5 NIV). This is a generous God. It sounds like the words of Jesus in Luke 11:9 (NIV): "Ask and it will be given to you."

Solomon faced the massive challenge to take over from the greatest king of Israel, his father David. He admitted that it was impossible for him to fulfil this massive task. To lead God's people in his father's place was impossible without God's help. He calls himself a young child.

Solomon's prayer is remarkable in more ways than one. This is not a long prayer. It contains only one request: "Give me a discerning heart." In the Hebrew language, it is a "hearing heart". Solomon could certainly have compiled his grocery list before God. He could ask for victory over his enemies, wealth and a long life. It was the king's privilege. Instead of more time, more money and more power, he rather asks the Lord to make him obedient to use his time, money and power correctly.

When we pray, God stands before us with full hands. Are you asking for more power, money, time? Rather ask for obedience! Prayerful dependence on Him every day is the only way.

Father, give me a hearing heart, by the power of Your Spirit.

Amen.

November 16

Reformation

This is what the LORD Almighty, the God of Israel, says:
"Reform your ways and your actions."
Jeremiah 7:3 NIV

Hypocrites deceive others. They pretend to be good, but inside they are bad or sometimes even evil. They smile at us, while their hearts burn with hatred. Let us not point a finger at others. Let us search our own hearts. We can have beautiful worship services, praise courses and prayer seminars, but our eyes are closed to the injustice and need in the world.

The people in Jeremiah 7 think they can deceive the Lord. They have divided their lives in compartments. One day they serve the Lord and the other they live as they please. They expect God to deliver them from a crisis, but they serve other gods (7:6, 9, 18). They want God to keep His promises, but they take false oaths (7:9). They desire that God should comfort them, but the people without rights around them cry out to God because of their injustice (7:6). They cause sadness and destruction in the lives of people through murder, adultery, theft and the oppression of orphans and widows. The time has come for them to test their lives and actions.

What God asks of us is not outward appearance and beautiful worship, but obedience (7:22-23). Worship means dedicating yourself to God and the world. True worship, true religion is to care for those in need (James 1:27). We live before God when we dedicate ourselves to those in need.

Lord, free me from deceptive hypocrisy, in Jesus' name.

Amen.

November 17

A Life Before God and Each Other

> "Do not trust in these lying words, saying, 'The temple of the LORD, the temple of the LORD, the temple of the LORD are these.'"
> Jeremiah 7:4 NKJV

Someone wrote that we can describe the thoughts and theology of the reformer Martin Luther as a life before God (*coram Deo*). Essentially, our whole life, from morning to evening, from Monday to Sunday, at home, when we play sport or relax, is a life *coram Deo*—a life before God, in the presence of God.

The prophet speaks to people who loved to go to the temple and perform all kinds of religious acts (7:2). At the temple gate, however, they hear: "Your religion is false!" They hear that they are using the temple to hide like robbers (7:11).

Why? The people misunderstood God's presence (7:4). The tabernacle and temple were like God's dwelling place to them. Zion was God's eternal abode (Ps. 46:5-8; Ps. 132:13-14). The temple therefore became a place of security and trust (Jer. 7:14). The people thought that temples provide security—as if God's presence provided security when one lives as if God had no claim on your human relationships.

They found out that the temple is the last place where they are safe! God has the exclusive right over their lives. Their everyday lives were just as important as their acts of worship in the temple.

God's presence is not limited to Sundays or so-called holy places. Our whole life is lived before God, in the presence of God.

Lord, make me aware today that I am always in Your presence, in Jesus' name. Amen.

November 18

Continue Jesus' Ministry

"Heal the sick, raise the dead, cure those with leprosy, and cast out demons. Give as freely as you have received!"
Matthew 10:8 NLT

Sometimes we get up in the morning, have breakfast, go to work, come back, eat, watch something and go to sleep. It becomes a deadly routine. We begin to ask what the sense of it all is. Why am I a doctor, nurse, clerk, auditor, psychologist, pastor, bank manager or stay-at-home-mom?

We need perspective. According to Matthew, Jesus' ministry had a specific program. In Matthew 4:23-25, he says that it consisted of two aspects, namely the proclamation of the gospel and the doing of miracles. Immediately the Sermon on the Mount begins (5-7) and miracles follow (8-9). Jesus preached and cared for the needs of people. He gave bread when people were hungry, cast out demons when people were possessed, healed and even raised the dead when it served God's purposes. He gave rest to those who carried heavy burdens.

He gives the same command to His disciples here. God's comprehensive help in every form of need should be shared. The Lord has given so many gifts of grace. Every profession contributes to God's bigger plan of making the world a better place. If you are a doctor, nurse, clerk, housekeeper, psychologist, pastor, bank manager or raising your children at home, you are in God's service. Your contribution is so important to show God's compassion. It is making the world a better place.

Lord, enable me to serve You today by what I am doing, in Jesus' name. *Amen.*

November 19

Other's Sin as a Mirror

> "Let any one of you who is without sin
> be the first to throw a stone at her."
> John 8:7 NIV

The religious leaders brought a woman to Jesus who had clearly transgressed the law of God. The law was clear. This person had to be killed. If Jesus decided that the law of Moses was not important, it would give them a reason to say that He was against the law of God. If He gave the command that she should be stoned, it would undermine the message of grace.

We are quick to point out the sins of others. It is easy and clear to see. What was their purpose of pointing out the woman's sin? Why did they not apply the law?

Jesus surprises them with His answer. The woman's sin became a mirror. They suddenly had to look at themselves. These watchdogs against immorality with dubious motives had to walk away in shame.

No one can honestly say that we are not guilty of sin. Other people could easily drag us before God and people when they know our life's story. Remember, all sin is the same. Your "small sins" are the same as the sin of the woman before Jesus. Let us take our own sin seriously, so that we may confess it before God and judge others less.

> Lord, I confess my own sin before You. Please help me to be less judgmental, in Jesus' name. *Amen.*

November 20

We Are Lights, Not Ornaments

> "You are the light of the world. A town
> built on a hill cannot be hidden."
> Matthew 5:14 NIV

A Christian man received a job offer and accepted it. At his farewell party, a colleague told him that they often wondered why he was such a nice person—helpful, hardworking and loyal. Their conclusion: He must be a Buddhist!

This is the danger when we think that we can show that we are Christians just by being good people without making Christ known through our words. Maybe the world sings about us, "Twinkle, twinkle little star, how I wonder what you are…"

A light is made to shine. If it does not shine, it's just an ornament. We become an ornament if we are invisible and inaudible. A follower of Jesus can hide His discipleship as little as a light can hide its rays. Yes, we are not always God's "spotlights", but remember that the darkness of the world cannot extinguish a candle's light. Christians belong in the middle of the world like a lamp in the middle of a room.

A soldier's glowing cigarette in World War II revealed his group's position to the enemy. It was the difference between life and death. The question is not how big our light is, but whether it is visible. It can mean the difference between life and death for people.

Lord, let the light which shines from my life help people to see You, in Jesus' name. *Amen.*

November 21

Domino Effect

*His divine power has given us everything we need
for a godly life through our knowledge of Him
who called us by His own glory and goodness.*
2 Peter 1:3 NIV

Sometimes we talk about a domino effect, referring to a chain reaction of events. One thing happens and then this event sets off a chain of similar events. Like a row of dominoes that get knocked down one after the other.

Peter says that God's power in our lives is the one thing that should have a domino effect on our lives with God and one another. He gives us everything we need to live a godly life, which is the effect of His power in our lives. His power leads to the amazing effect that we share in His divine nature (1:4).

What kind of life is this? Peter says, "For this very reason, make every effort to add to your faith goodness; and to goodness, knowledge; and to knowledge, self-control; and to self-control, perseverance; and to perseverance, godliness; and to godliness, mutual affection; and to mutual affection, love" (1:5–7 NIV).

What a chain reaction!

*Lord, thank You for the wonderful effect of Your power in my life.
Amen.*

November 22

Prayer and Everyday Life

*If anyone turns a deaf ear to my instruction,
even their prayers are detestable.*
Proverbs 28:9 NIV

There is a close relationship between our relationship with God and the way we act towards our fellow human beings. The prophets call the people away from their temples and altars. Before they go to worship and sacrifice, they are called to reconcile with others (Isa. 1:10-17; Jer. 7; Amos 5:21-25). Jesus says that we must leave our gifts at the altar and make peace with our fellow human beings (Matt. 5:23-24).

Proverbs 28 refers to people hurting each other if they do not listen to God's instruction (Prov. 28:2-3, 6-7, 10-12). People who ignore God often ignore other people. The Father closes His ears to people who think that they can pray while attacking other people's dignity (28:9).

Paul writes that chaotic relationships are the result of people without God's Spirit: disorder, hate and separation, division and controversy (Gal. 5:19-21). Where the Spirit rules, when we live in step with the Holy Spirit, community is created. New life, new relationships, driven by the love that the Spirit poured into our hearts come into being (Gal. 5:22-25).

William Barclay was right when he said that when the new power (Holy Spirit) enters our life it enables us to be what by ourselves we could never be, and to do what by ourselves we could never do.

Father of mercy, fill me with Your Spirit. *Amen.*

November 23

Open the Floodgate of Confession

> Whoever conceals their sins does not prosper, but the
> one who confesses and renounces them finds mercy.
> Proverbs 28:13 NIV

Confession of sin is like opening the floodgate of a dam. It releases pressure. When we do not confess our sin, the waters pile up behind the dam, creating immense pressure on the wall. When the floodgate of confession is opened, the waters subside and the pressures diminish.

We should not try to explain our sin. We can only confess it. The moment we try to explain our sin, we find excuses for what we have done. Later on, we believe ourselves.

We hear about the pressure of sin also in Psalm 32. It is like a burden. It takes all our energy away like in the heat of summer (Ps. 32:3-4). Confession changes everything. Psalm 32:5 (NIV) says, "Then I acknowledged my sin to You and did not cover up my iniquity. I said, 'I will confess my transgressions to the LORD.' And You forgave the guilt of my sin." Confession of sin brings liberation. The chains fall off. The jail doors are open.

We have an address to go to with our sin and broken lives. It is God's grace, "If we confess our sins to Him, He is faithful and just to forgive us our sins and to cleanse us from all wickedness" (1 John 1:9 NLT). We receive what we do not deserve—His forgiveness and deliverance.

Lord, thank You for the grace of forgiveness in Jesus' name.

Amen.

November 24

Made in God's Image

So God created mankind in His own image, in the image of God He created them; male and female He created them.
Genesis 1:27 NIV

Over the years, many jokes have been made about how difficult it is to understand women. The movie *What Women Want* is a good example. As a man, looking back over my own life, I would say that the same things apply to men. We are also difficult to understand. We don't even understand ourselves!

Many jokes about the differences between men and women have some elements of truth. Unfortunately, due to the cultural situation in biblical times, the woman was often seen as the property of the man. Many jokes are plain chauvinistic and the result of discrimination against women and reflect the imbalance in society.

When God created the world, He indeed made a distinction between male and female. Anybody trying to diminish this distinction is out of line. Yet, the distinction does not mean inequality. According to this verse in Genesis, God created male and female to reflect His image! One is not more an image of God than the other. In other words, in our togetherness as God's image, we express what God wanted to make known about Himself in this world.

It is not necessary to have all kinds of extra-biblical arguments to try to convince people that men and women are equal. Just as God made man as His representative, so He made woman. We are equals!

Lord, thank You for creating us as equals. *Amen.*

November 25

Loving the World

> Jonah ran away from the LORD and headed for Tarshish.
> Jonah 1:3 NIV

Imagine the most brutal person or country you can think of. God speaks very clearly and says to you that you should go there. You have to tell them that God is going to destroy them because they are wicked. Maybe you will be happy that God has this in mind, but going there yourself to deliver the message is a bit too much.

Jonah felt this way. He took the boat in the opposite direction. To better understand Jonah's response, we need to know something about Nineveh. It was the capital of the Assyrian empire that took control of Israel in 722 BC. Nineveh meant violence, domination, hardship, murder, slavery. How, then, can God expect a prophet to go and preach God's Word to such wicked people?

This story is not about a prophet who was swallowed and spit out by some kind of a fish. It has a much more important message. It challenges us with God's heart of love. Even Nineveh is not outside God's grace. There is even a chance for the most brutal person or group in the world.

God loves the broken world. He makes us the messenger of His grace and mercy to the most unacceptable people in our lives—those who have hurt us and destroyed our hope and future. What is most important for you, your own interest or God's heartbeat for the world? Do you love the world as God does?

Lord, make me faithful to Your call to share Your message of hope with all people, by the power of Your Spirit. Amen.

November 26

No Revenge, But Grace

> "You have been concerned about this plant. And should
> I not have concern for the great city of Nineveh?"
> Jonah 4:10-11 NIV

I don't know if you ever had the feeling of satisfaction when something bad happens to someone who did bad things to you. Finally, they get what they deserve!

This is what Jonah felt about Nineveh. They were heartless and ruthless enemies of God's people. He did not want to go to Nineveh in the first place. When he eventually went, he would have been very happy if the message that they would be destroyed would come true. Then they repented! What a pity!

Now he sits outside the city and complains about a worm and about the east wind that caused a plant to die. He is still waiting for God to destroy the city, but unfortunately, they repented. It is not right that God is gracious.

We are like Jonah. We are concerned about our own well-being. We are not worried about the world in its distress because of sin. We would like God's wrath to come on the sinner, rather than His grace—especially those who caused us harm. Revenge sounds sweeter than grace. I do not worry about my unfriendly neighbor across the street who never sees the inside of a church. As long as I am saved and God takes care of me, I am happy. Let them get what they deserve!

John Henry Jowett wrote that God does not comfort us so that we can be comfortable, but so that we can be comforters.

Lord, make me concerned about others—friend or enemy—who does not know You, in Jesus' name. Amen.

November 27

Authentic Lives

But mark this: There will be terrible times in the last days.
2 Timothy 3:1 NIV

Chaos. I am not speaking about a teenager's room. I am speaking about our society. We should expect this kind of society when our relationship with God is not what it should be. Then it becomes chaos. Paul says that total chaos prevails when people only seem to be serving God but have forsaken the true God (3:1-5).

The terrible times Paul speaks about are a mixture of wickedness, idolatry and lovelessness. Families are not spared in the process either. Children are disobedient to their parents. The past will always matter, because nobody will forgive. Chaos!

Maybe we should ask ourselves today how Paul's words expose the things in our lives making life difficult for others and for ourselves: "For men will be lovers of themselves, lovers of money, boasters, proud, blasphemers, disobedient to parents, unthankful, unholy, unloving, unforgiving, slanderers, without self-control, brutal, despisers of good, traitors, headstrong, haughty, lovers of pleasure rather than lovers of God, having a form of godliness but denying its power" (3:2-5 NKJV).

What kind of society do you want? It does not help to complain about how bad the world is. We should make a difference where we are—in society, families, relationships and the ethical standards.

Authentic lives by Christians are needed. The light shining from our lives can bring order in chaos. Henry Martyn said: Let me burn out for God! When we burn, we shine!

Spirit of God, free me from myself so that I can be a good witness in my community, in Jesus' name. Amen.

November 28

He Cannot Lie

Whoever believes in the Son of God accepts this testimony. Whoever does not believe God has made Him out to be a liar.
1 John 5:10 NIV

One of my friends said that his attitude towards all people is the following: Trust but verify. It simply means that he wants to see if someone is trustworthy. I understand my friend's reluctance to trust everybody. People are not always trustworthy.

Most of the time, however, we believe what people say. In the future it may become clear that they lied to us, but our basic attitude is to trust. John takes up this basic attitude of trust. "We accept human testimony," he says (5:9 NIV).

Then he makes this surprising and beautiful conclusion: there is no risk if you believe God's Word because God will not lie to us. In 1 John 5:9-13, he says that we may believe God when He says that we are His children. His testimony is true. God loves us so much that He calls us His children (3:1).

I know that it is difficult these days to discern what is true. There is a lot of fake news. One should not just believe everything. One thing is true—always true—God gave us eternal life through His Son, Jesus Christ. If we don't believe it, we are saying in God's face that He is lying.

Do you believe the doubts of your heart and the words of people who make you feel bad about yourself? No, you are God's beloved! Believe it!

Thank You that I can trust Your words of life, in Jesus' name.

Amen.

November 29

King of Kings!

*I will exalt you, my God the King;
I will praise Your name for ever and ever.*
Psalm 145:1 NIV

Mobile phones were supposed to make communication easier. We can call our family or friends any time and people can reach us when they need to speak to us. Now it has become a burden to many people. They do not want to be reached! They check who phones and then decide if it is important enough to answer.

God is completely different. The King does not decide if someone is important enough to be answered. On the contrary. We do not struggle to get an appointment with Him. He does not stand at a distance. The whole psalm sings the praises of the King of heaven and earth who has been and is close to His people through the ages. This merciful King looks after people with His mercy (145:8-9). This King is fair (145:17). He listens to suffering people (145:19). He stands beside the oppressed (145:14). He delivers them from the hands of their enemies (145:20).

In Jesus, this King came to live amongst us. He left His royal existence and came to live with ordinary wounded people (Phil. 2). We can never praise Him enough every day (Ps. 145:2). His kingship will last forever (145:13). Everyone should know that this King cares and listens to the least important people in society. All people should know: God listens. Through Jesus we stand in the throne room of our Father with all our needs (Heb. 10:19-25).

King of kings, thank You that I am important to You. *Amen.*

November 30

Don't Be Trapped

*Evildoers are snared by their own sin,
but the righteous shout for joy and are glad.*
Proverbs 29:6 NIV

Sin. What is it? Sin is not necessarily something we do, but rather what we are. We are sinners. In our being we are corrupt. This is why we mess up almost everything we touch.

Kings can abuse their power and think only about themselves (29:2, 4). When a wicked man rules, everything in a country goes bad (29:16). Ordinary sinful people like us resist God and His teaching (29:1). We do not worry about the poor (29:7). We become angry and offend each other (29:9, 11). This is why we cause conflict between people (29:22). Yes, all that is mentioned here shows how deeply we are able to fall without God. Sin, as the poet says, is our greatest danger. It is like a snare in which you get stuck.

When God gives us His wisdom, when He makes us righteous, we act differently. The rights of the simple, the poor and the people on the margins of society are important to us. We discover that there is a joy in our lives that we did not know before. The song of God's wisdom plays in our lives. It makes our lives meaningful and full of good deeds to those who need our love.

Do you know this joy? It is the fruit of the Holy Spirit.

Father, make me a righteous person so that my life may be a song, through the power of Your Spirit. Amen.

December

December 1

Perfect Wisdom

"Every word of God is flawless; He is a shield to those who take refuge in Him."
Proverbs 30:5 NIV

The wisdom of Agar very strongly links up with the wisdom of people who lived around Israel. He picks examples of life. One can learn a lot about life by being a good observer. Several times he says we should notice three, no, four things. This means that he could name many other things, but that these few examples clearly illustrate the point he wants to make.

The leach wants everything for itself (30:15). Certain things in life are incomprehensible (30:18). Some things make life unbearable (30:21). Little creatures have great wisdom (30:24). Example after example is stacked up to make these points. It can be seen in everyday life. Just look out for it. Awareness is extremely important.

Creation contains some form of order. Yet, we need more than that. We need God's Word to teach us. Psalm 19 says God's Word is perfect and reliable. It makes us see our sin, but also guides us on the right path. Paul says that wisdom is one of the gifts of God's Spirit. Someone said that we are young only once, but we can stay immature indefinitely. We become wise when God's Spirit gives us greater wisdom through His Word. Only then do we really see!

Spirit of God, open my eyes to the simple lessons of life, in Jesus' name. *Amen.*

December 2

Holiday!

> Anyone who enters God's rest also rests from their
> works, just as God did from His. Let us, therefore,
> make every effort to enter that rest.
> Hebrews 4:10-11 NIV

Sometimes we live from weekend to weekend. We just want to rest. Someone said that the worst Friday is when you realize that it is only Wednesday! When does one really rest from your work? Most people will give one answer, weekends and holidays!

Holidays and rest are not the same for the author of Hebrews. Rest is a deeply spiritual exercise. In the Bible, rest is often seen as the point when people have reached a goal. At the end of His creative acts, God rested (Gen. 2:2-3). We do not really find rest when we rest over weekends or when we are on holiday. We can come back from vacation and still be exhausted because we have not experienced resting in God. We find rest when we come home to the place where God gives us rest (Heb. 4:10).

If we do not find rest with Him, we follow the example of disobedient Israel who never entered the Promised Land—the goal that God wanted them to reach. Just before Matthew recounts Jesus' words about the Sabbath in Matthew 12, he makes clear who Jesus is. Jesus says, "Come to Me, all you who labor and are heavy laden, and I will give you rest" (Matt. 11:28 NKJV). We find real rest, reach our real purpose in life, when we come to Jesus.

Lord Jesus, give me the rest I long for, by the power of Your Spirit. *Amen.*

December 3

Our Rock

> Truly my soul silently waits for God;
> from Him comes my salvation.
> Psalm 62:1 NKJV

I am afraid of heights. There is a cable car going up Table Mountain in Cape Town, but I prefer to walk up the mountain. Anything temporary—cable cars or lifts—makes my hands sweat. I prefer to have solid ground underneath my feet.

Solid ground is what the psalmist is speaking about. The poet contrasts two possibilities. You can decide to rely on people. This is, of course, a terrible gamble. His life is like a wall that can collapse at any moment. People are like grass that perishes quickly. If you put a person on a scale, he weighs even less than nothing (62:9)! This is a truth that the Bible emphasizes all the way. People are temporary. We cannot rely on ourselves or other people. The best of the best will perish.

In contrast, God is like a rock. Whoever trusts in Him has stability and certainty in life—even if life is very uncertain. God is the one fixed point in our lives. He is like a shelter when the storms of life rage. No problem is too big or too small for Him to handle. Therefore Psalm 62:8 (NKJV) says, "Trust in Him at all times, you people; pour out your heart before Him; God is a refuge for us."

I like solid, immovable ground. When I walk on it, I think of God.

Thank You, Lord, that my worried and tired heart finds rest in You. Amen.

December 4

He Knows Your Thoughts

You have searched me, LORD, and You know me. Before a word is on my tongue You, LORD, know it completely.
Psalm 139:1, 4 NIV

When I was a theological student at Stellenbosch University, we did practical work in hospitals, nursing homes and psychiatric institutions. We then had to write verbatim reports on our conversations with the patients. One of the most difficult situations was when I had a conversation with a stroke patient who could not answer me, because his speech was impaired. His reactions of joy or sadness could mean just the opposite.

What a comfort Psalm 139 is to us! The turning point of the whole psalm is found in verse 5 (NIV): "You hem me in behind and before, and You lay Your hand upon me." The Lord is above, below, behind and in front of us. We are His. Therefore, the psalmist can praise God because this Lord knows us and our thoughts (139:1-2, 4). He knows what goes on in our hearts. Before we can speak, the Lord knows what we are going to say (139:4).

For someone who can no longer put his or her thoughts into words, it is comforting to know that the Lord knows and understands us so well that we do not even need words. Wordless prayers are not silent before God, says Charles Spurgeon.

What a comfort to all of us. Sometimes it is hard for me to put my thoughts into words when I speak to God. Sometimes I can just say: "Lord, You know me, my heart and my unspoken thoughts and longings."

Lord, thank You for knowing me. *Amen.*

December 5

Darkness Is Light for God

*If I go up to the heavens, You are there; if I make
my bed in the depths, You are there.*
Psalm 139:8 NIV

After the first human entered space, the astronaut Yuri Gagarin reportedly said that he was looking everywhere, but could not see God. Some Christians were very concerned about this remark. According to reports, they sent a telegram to the Swiss theologian Karl Barth asking for his comment on this. Barth replied: "Just read Psalm 139 and do not panic!"

Psalm 139:7-12 emphasizes that God is everywhere. There is panic and comfort in these words. Of course, it can scare one to think that God also knows the dark places of our lives. Often, we try to hide from God. This is impossible. The comfort, however, is that it does not have to be a threat to us.

The beautiful truth is that God is present in every situation of our lives. He is everywhere: east, west, north, south, in my workplace and school, home, bedroom, dark places, hospitals and nursing homes. He is there when I suffer. Most of all, even in the depths, an idiomatic expression of death, God is present. He is Immanuel, God with us.

In Jesus, God came to share our lives in every place—dark or light. His Spirit lives in us. We are never alone! What a comfort to know that God is everywhere.

Lord, thank You that You are always present in my life. Amen.

December 6

God's Work of Art

> For You created my inmost being; You knit
> me together in my mother's womb.
> Psalm 139:13 NIV

Horace Walpole said that people are often able to do much bigger things than they think they can handle. We are sent into the world with a large credit balance, but do not use it very often.

What is this credit balance? When I read Psalm 139, I always want to fall on my knees and worship God. The psalm says that God knows us and that He is always with us. Why? The answer is simple: He was there when I was created. He formed me in my mother's womb. He is lovingly involved in my life (139:13-16). He is involved in my origins and future (139:15-16). All my days, my whole life, are in His hands (139:16). He is like someone standing around me and wrapping me in His love (139:5). How would He not know me, walk with me and love me?

Unfortunately, we think all sorts of other things define our lives. The great temptation is to use the apparent failures and disappointments in our lives to convince ourselves that we are not worth receiving love.

What do you think about yourself? Is your self-esteem determined by your negative self-talk, or by the voice of God you hear today?

Listen carefully: You are loved. You are God's own possession! He will always love you!

> Lord, thank You that You walk with me, know me, love me because You made me. *Amen.*

December 7

My Life Is in His Hands

*All the days ordained for me were written in
Your book before one of them came to be.*
Psalm 139:16 NIV

Your time to die is your time. Someone joked, just don't be on the plane when it is the pilot's time!

In Greek mythology, Zeus's goddesses controlled people's fate. The so-called Fates (Moirai) were a group of three weaving goddesses (Clotho the spinner, Lachesis the allotter and Atropos the inevitable) who assigned individual destinies to us at birth. The first one spun the thread of life, the second determined the length and the last one cut the thread.

We do not believe in Greek mythology. We believe the Bible as the final authority in all things. God is in control of our lives and watches over us. Our lives are safe in God's hands. God knows everything, is everywhere and made us with His own hands, says the psalmist.

God is involved with us from before the beginning to the end of our lives. Even after our death, we belong to the Lord (Rom. 14:8). Paul says that not even death nor any other power can ever separate us from God's love (Rom. 8:35-39).

Father, thank You for being involved in my life, in Jesus' name.

Amen.

December 8

World Mission

"Therefore go and make disciples of all nations."
Matthew 28:19 NIV

One of the worrying things about the church in the western world is the decrease in numbers. Many churches struggle to survive financially, because there is a lack of people attending. It is a common thing these days to see that old church buildings have been converted into cafes or shops or even big mansions. A place where there once was a vibrant, living congregation gathering to worship, now becomes an empty building.

Granted, some churches in other parts of the world are growing rapidly in numbers. However, the number of followers of Jesus in churches should not increase by taking on members from other churches. It is not real growth.

Why not? Our purpose is not to make people church members. Our calling is to make disciples of all nations. This means that our city or town, our country or continent is not the limit. World mission is the task of every believer. We must have a passion for one thing—that every human being will be a disciple of Jesus Christ. Why is this not the case? Someone wrote that the church is full of "undiscipled" disciples.

Being a disciple of Jesus Christ means two things. We were baptized into membership of God's people. It means that Father, Son and Holy Spirit rule over our lives (28:19). Secondly, we are constantly following the teaching of Jesus (28:20) Are you a disciple of the Lord? If you obey the words of the Lord, you will have the world on your agenda.

Lord, make me eager to spread the gospel to all people.

Amen.

December 9

Contentment

Give me neither poverty nor riches,
but give me only my daily bread.
Proverbs 30:8 NIV

Rich and poor constantly feature in Proverbs. Sometimes poverty is the result of laziness. Sometimes it is the result of injustice. Sometimes rich people are the culprits.

In these verses of Proverbs only one thing is actually requested. What is it? That God will not be dishonored! How does that happen?

When we are too rich, we may become independent from God (30:9). Our wealth becomes our god because we say that we don't need God. Paul says that money is the root of all evil (1 Tim. 6:6–10). Some people wanted more wealth than they needed and walked away from God. We need to be content when we have food and clothing (1 Tim. 6:8). When we are too poor, there is another danger. Poor people, in order to survive, sometimes steal (Prov. 30:9).

The poet prays for balance. Give me just enough! If he has enough God will prevent him from dishonoring His name.

It sounds simplistic, but it is not. A life in which nothing consumes us—riches or poverty—makes room for God. Having enough means that we are depending on God for every day of our lives. Give us TODAY our daily bread, Jesus taught us to pray. If we have more than what we need, we share it with those who need it.

Lord, make me content with Your gifts, in Jesus' name. Amen.

December 10

Listen to Wisdom

> Speak up for those who cannot speak for themselves;
> ensure justice for those being crushed. Yes, speak up for
> the poor and helpless, and see that they get justice.
> Proverbs 31:8-9 NLT

It is as if my own mother is speaking here. Lemuel's mother (Lemuel means 'dedicated to God') warns her son, who is a king, about two things: women and substance abuse. She knows that a deceitful woman can cost a king his throne. She also knows of another danger, namely the influence of excessive drinking. By drinking too much our judgment is affected.

Lemuel's mother is concerned about these influences. She understood what it meant when God placed people in a position of authority. A king must protect the rights of those who have no rights (Ps. 72). If they give in to these temptations, they "forget what has been decreed, and deprive all the oppressed of their rights" (Prov. 31:5 NIV). A king had to be a voice for those who could not speak because they were not in the position or had the right to speak (31:8-9).

Proverbs began with what the purpose of the book is. It must give people a sense of what is right and just and fair (1:3). Not only kings, but all people should be like this. Keep your eyes open to what can prevent us from walking from God's ways. Listen to the wisdom of our Spirit-filled mothers, fathers and friends who already know life.

Lord, open my eyes to those things that could cause me to leave Your ways, in Jesus' name. *Amen.*

December 11

Honoring God through the Poor

> Whoever oppresses the poor shows contempt for their Maker, but whoever is kind to the needy honors God.
> Proverbs 14:31 NIV

There is one thing that is worse than stealing from someone who is poor. You would maybe say that stealing from a poor person is deplorable. How can we take something from someone who has nothing? Well, you could say that to have and not to give is often worse than to steal.

This is a constant temptation to all of us. We easily forget that what we have is a gift from God. Yes, we have worked for it, but who gave us the energy and opportunities? God Himself. The very breath in our lungs is a gift from God. Who are we to think that it belongs to us? When we look down on the poor and refuse help, we dishonor the God to whom we owe our very existence.

This is constantly highlighted in the book of Proverbs. When we mock the poor, we show contempt for our Creator (17:5). Yes, "the poor plead for mercy, but the rich answer harshly" (18:23).

Other people's poverty can also be caused by us when we are stealing from our fellow man with poor salaries and withholding mercy from those in need.

If you read this today, you had the means of doing it. Some people wonder today where their next meal will come from. You can change that.

Lord, make me generous and merciful, in Jesus' name.

Amen.

December 12

I Cling to You

*If we confess our sins, He is faithful and just to forgive us
our sins and to cleanse us from all unrighteousness.*
1 John 1:9 NKJV

I failed again. There is no hope for me. This time God will not forgive. We all know that Jesus paid in full for our sins. Yet we remain trapped in the thought that it was not really enough.

We were also taught that way. First John 1:9 has often been used in the past to say: "If you have truly repented, if you are truly sorry enough for your sin, if you meet this condition, God will forgive you. God will forgive you on the basis of your true confession."

Who of us can claim that he or she has met all the conditions for God to forgive? The good news is that God does not forgive our sins on the basis of the authenticity of our confession. If this is true, we are forgiven on the basis of merit. God is faithful and just. He forgives because Jesus is the atonement for the sins of the whole world and intercedes on our behalf like an advocate (2:1–2).

Lord, thank You that Your grace is enough.

December 13

The Courage to Confess

If we confess our sins, He is faithful and just to forgive us our sins and to cleanse us from all unrighteousness.
1 John 1:9 NKJV

Imagine two scenarios. Your parent is someone with a heart of love and forgiveness, even if you have done something very bad. When you do something wrong, you have the courage to go and say you're sorry. You know that your parents will forgive you and you can move one. The other scenario is this: You know that your parents are hard people who do not easily forgive. They always demand that you should do something that would be almost like a punishment for your wrongdoing.

God is like this first parent. He is not hard but loving. We can be absolutely sure of God's forgiveness. Why? Because God is faithful and just, says John. We can be absolutely sure that our sin is forgiven every time we confess it. God knows that we are struggling with our sinful nature. He knows that we need His constant forgiveness. He thinks about His great love for people who confess that they have come to the end of themselves, who confess that they are not without sin (1:8, 10).

Because God's love is so great, it gives us the freedom to confess our sins before Him. Precisely by doing this, we are also saying that we can no longer continue on our old paths. Augustine remarked that the confession of evil works is the first beginning of good works.

Lord, I confess my sin and devote myself to You anew, in Jesus' name. *Amen.*

December 14

Our Advocate

*He Himself is the sacrifice that atones for our sins—
and not only our sins but the sins of all the world.*
1 John 2:2 NLT

When I was little, I was always afraid of the dark. The light had to be kept on until I fell asleep. When I woke up at night, my mother told me, I wanted the light on again. We are sometimes like a child in a dark room being woken up by a nightmare. We feel that the darkness engulfed our thoughts. Full of anxiety, we then call on our mother for help.

The good news of God dispels the darkness of our life crises as lights illuminate a dark room. As a mother takes her child in her arms and tells the child that everything is alright and always has been, God assures us like a good mother that our dark days have not cancelled His love for us. On the darkest day in human history—the darkest Good Friday—when the Son of God was killed by sinners, the light of God's love for people, ordinary people, shone at its strongest. The sin of the whole world was reconciled. Yours, too!

Ordinary people, said Lewis B. Smedes, realize that they are too weak to know how to deal with reality. Ordinary people make mistakes, fail and are guilty before God. God does not want us to fail and sin, but if we do, our Advocate, the righteous Jesus, stands on our behalf before God and defends us.

Thank You, Father, that Your Son, the Righteous One, is our Advocate when we fail! Amen.

December 15

Bury Their Mistakes

...forgiving each other, just as in Christ God forgave you.
Ephesians 4:32 NIV

We sometimes go to a cemetery because we want to keep the memory of a person alive. We take flowers or plant something to show that we love the person. Every visit to the grave makes us aware of one fact: The past is past forever. Nothing can change that. Death is death. Even the most loving person made mistakes and sinned. Yet, how we wish that we could just spend one hour with our loved one again! Death is irreversible.

The same is true of our sin! Yet, something else is also irreversible. God's forgiveness! Our sins were buried in the tomb after Calvary. When Jesus went into death, He took our sin with Him. The past is wiped out. Our sins are buried.

Henry Ward Beecher said we should make a big cemetery in our backyard where we can bury the mistakes of our friends. When the stamp of the gospel of Jesus Christ is imprinted on our lives, we do that, because our sins are buried!

Yes, what other people did to us was hurtful and left a mark. We can decide to chain ourselves to the past. We can decide to be bitter. We can hate. However, we are the only prisoners in this exhausting exercise!

We can also decide to be released from our past and the past of what people did to us. Whose sin are you going to finally bury today?

Lord, give us the strength to forgive, in Jesus' name. Amen.

December 16

True Wisdom

She speaks with wisdom, and faithful instruction is on her tongue.
Proverbs 31:26 NIV

Sometimes Proverbs 31:10-31 is read at funerals when people think about their mother or a wife that died. This woman is someone who cares for her family (31:14-15, 21-22), a good businesswoman (31:16, 18, 24) and someone who cares for those who have no rights (31:20). We can only say: "What a woman!"

Yes, there are incredible women, but this one is perfect. Probably the poet sketches an image of the ideal woman. The book of Proverbs describes wisdom as a woman (Prov. 8). It is incredible to think that a woman was the symbol of wisdom in a world in which women were marginalized in many ways.

This wisdom does not flow in our blood. Wisdom is born in a relationship with God, "Charm is deceptive, and beauty is fleeting; but a woman who fears the LORD is to be praised" (31:30 NIV). Real beauty is when God places His wisdom in our hearts.

Just as the book started, it ends. Wisdom is born out of a relationship with God (2:6). Brother Lawrence said that there is not in the world a kind of life more sweet and delightful than that of a continual walk with God. Those only can comprehend it who practice and experience it.

> Lord God, I am like a fool in everything I do. Give me Your wisdom, through the power of Your Spirit. *Amen.*

December 17

Emptiness?

*Everything was meaningless, a chasing after
the wind; nothing was gained under the sun.*
Ecclesiastes 2:11 NIV

In the Turkish television series *As the Crow Flies*, an obsessed young woman does everything to destroy a very successful television celebrity. In an argument about success, fame and wealth, the celebrity's best friend said that this young woman doesn't know that when you reach the top, there is nothing there. It reminds me of a reporter who asked Jack Higgins, a highly successful thriller writer, what kind of knowledge he now has that he would have liked to have had if he were a boy again. His answer was, "When you get to the top, there is nothing there."

The author of Ecclesiastes teaches us the same truth. This is the wisdom he gained: Nothing in the world satisfies. He experimented with everything. He tried the proverbial "wine, women and song". He tried projects, had slaves, and endless wealth. Nothing satisfied.

We often read in the media about so many people who are seriously unhappy in spite of their wealth, comfortable life and having everything that we so often pursue. Thomas Wolfe wrote that we have reached the pinnacle of success when money, compliments and publicity have become unimportant.

This is partly true. The greater truth is this: Only God can fill the hole in our heart which we try to fill with meaningless things.

Lord, fill my life with Your presence so that I will be content, in Jesus' name. *Amen.*

December 18

Eyes of Faith

> How long, O LORD? Will You forget me forever?
> How long will You hide Your face from me?
> Psalm 13:1 NKJV

Even the most committed Christian sometimes feels that God does not answer prayers. Sometimes we pray for the healing of a person and then the person dies. Sometimes we ask God to intervene in a situation, but it is as if God is silent. These are times of disorientation and doubt.

Every Christian experiences this at one time or another. It is as if one is shouting in your heart: if only there were someone who understood me, who heard me, who experienced what I experienced! If you're looking for someone like that, you've found him. The psalmist feels that way.

In the first two verses of Psalm 13, the poet asks four times: how much longer? He feels disoriented due to his circumstances. He feels the Lord is absent.

And then, as if something happened after his lament, we see a change of tone. His disorientation turns to a new orientation: "I trust in Your unfailing love; my heart rejoices in Your salvation. I will sing the LORD's praise, for He has been good to me" (13:5-6 NIV). It is very clear that the poet experienced some kind of answer.

We don't know what happened, but this surprising change of tone gives us hope. There is hope in the most hopeless situations. God opens our eyes of faith so that we do not have to doubt His faithfulness. The power of God surpasses all our circumstances and weaknesses.

Father, give us eyes of faith, in Jesus' name. *Amen.*

December 19

Spirit-Filled Love

Love never gives up, never loses faith, is always hopeful, and endures through every circumstance.
1 Corinthians 13:7 NLT

Many successful people are not happy. The big underlying issue is the lack of sincere love. Who really loves me just for who I am? Who loves me not for my money, contacts, position, reputation or for what I can mean to them, but just me?

Without sincere love we are lonely. This should never be the place where Christians find themselves. When Paul speaks about the gifts of the Spirit, he explains that no gift means anything without love.

The radical difference between Christian love and human love is clear. Our human love is conditional. We accept someone as long as they meet our standards. We will accept someone's mistakes if they do not go against our beliefs. We will not hold someone's mistakes of the past against them, provided they do not do it again. We love people we love.

Christian love is not a conditional or comfortable love. It is not love based on qualities or the merits of others. It is love which patiently covers and tolerates others' shortcomings and weaknesses (13:4, 7), which remains kind when the other one is conceited or boastful (13:4), which does not revolve around our own preferences and interests (13:5), which forgives the mistakes of others. It is unconditional, sacrificial love.

If we love each other this way, nobody has to be unhappy because of a lack of love.

Lord, teach me to love unconditionally, in Jesus' name.

Amen.

December 20

Getting Ready for Eternity

Love never fails. But where there are prophecies, they will cease; where there are tongues, they will be stilled; where there is knowledge, it will pass away.
1 Corinthians 13:8 NIV

How do we get ready for eternity with God? Paul says there is a way. It is to love in the power of God's Spirit.

Why is love the way to get ready for eternity? Paul made a list of spiritual gifts in 1 Corinthians 12 and ended the chapter with an extended list. The Spirit fills us with these gifts for the sake of Christ's body. Then he says, "And yet I will show you the most excellent way" (12:31 NIV).

What is this? Love. He repeats some of the gifts and compares it with this most excellent way. No spiritual gift has any value or meaning without love.

Then he ends the chapter by comparing faith, hope and love—the trilogy of the Christian life. There is no use for faith and hope because when we are forever in God's presence they will be fulfilled. But love is truly divine. It is something of heaven. Are you ready today to exercise for heaven? We have the opportunity today to get ready for the day when we will all enjoy the communion of love with God and one another.

Father, let my life overflow with Your love, by the power of Your Spirit. Amen.

December 21

We Love Because Jesus Is Lord

*Three things will last forever—faith, hope,
and love—and the greatest of these is love.*
1 Corinthians 13:13 NLT

Many think that we have to perform to be loved. We have to be good enough for love. If someone is not performing well enough, we cast them aside. This love does not last.

How different is Christian love! Paul explains this in 1 Corinthians 13. People love to read this passage at weddings. It is a high ideal of what love should be. Unfortunately, many people do not realize that this passage speaks about much more than an ideal of love. It speaks about the reality of love that is given to us by the Spirit of God. It speaks about love which is a reality when people say: "Jesus is Lord" (12:3 NIV).

This love is not focused on other people's achievements or mistakes. Contrary to the Greeks' conception of love, this love is not about what I can get, but what I can give. We love, not because of the qualities in others, but despite what they cannot offer us.

To love this way is only possible when we stand under the lordship of Christ and are filled with the Spirit of God. This love will last for all eternity!

Spirit of the living God, fill me with Your love which will last forever.

Amen.

December 22

The World Will Know

*"By this all will know that you are My disciples,
if you have love for one another."*
John 13:35 NKJV

I read about someone who was a "pastor" in a satanic church resigning from this position. The reason why he stepped aside is astonishing—the love he was shown by Christians! This is the power of love! He said that he was broken—like many of his "congregation"—but experienced how four Christians showed him what unconditional love meant.

The fact that only four Christians showed him this love, is the most painful thing I could read. Why only four? Jesus says that love for one another is a new commandment. It is new because it is self-sacrificing like the love of Christ. He laid down His life for us.

As a sign of this, at the beginning of John 13, He washed the feet of His disciples. Among these disciples are Judas and Peter—the traitor and the one who would deny Jesus. At the end of this act of love, He says to His disciples that they should do the same—love sacrificially (13:15).

A young man once told an old man that he was going to stay in the desert so that he could become more and more like Jesus. The old man replied: "If you want to be like Jesus, whose feet are you going to wash in the desert?"

Jesus, give me a loving heart, especially to the Judas' and Peter's in my life, by the power of Your Spirit. Amen.

December 23

No Peace—For His Sake!

> "Do not suppose that I have come to bring peace to the earth. I did not come to bring peace, but a sword."
> Matthew 10:34 NIV

Division! This is what Jesus came to bring. No, it cannot be. Is He the Prince of Peace that Isaiah wrote about earlier? How can the Prince of Peace cause discord? How can the Prince of Peace say that He will bring enmity into families? The Prince of Peace demands undivided love. Matthew calls this undivided loyalty a pure heart (6:19-24). We have a treasure in heaven.

When we serve our Lord, we will not always speak the language that the world wants to hear. Sometimes this will mean that we even have to go directly against our family. Christians cannot compromise on the kingdom of peace that God wants to establish. This peace is not just a soft word here and there or that we should keep quiet for the sake of peace. His followers will sometimes struggle in the world. They will be brought before governments and even accused by family members (10:16-25).

Whoever loses his life for the sake of the Prince of Peace will find life. We don't have a choice. People who belong to the Lord and have come to know the Prince of Peace love Him more than our family, even our life (10:37-39). Christians follow Jesus, even if He asks for your life.

Lord, help me to realize that it is worth serving You—even if it costs everything, for Jesus' sake. *Amen.*

December 24

Light of the World

> "...a light for revelation to the Gentiles,
> and the glory of Your people Israel."
> Luke 2:32 NIV

Have you ever been in a situation where you were totally caught by surprise? Everything was going as it always does. You just went through a routine. Then suddenly something very special happened. God revealed Himself.

This is what happened here. The routine of circumcision was part and parcel of the life of believers in the Old Testament. It was a sign of the covenant given to all male babies on the eighth day. Everyone went to the temple to see the new covenant children. Simeon, an old man with an unfulfilled promise in his heart, feels that he too should go to the temple.

When Simeon took the baby Jesus in his arms, he realized that today's circumcision service was not another service. The Son of Joseph and Mary was more than their Son. He was the fulfilment of the long-awaited promise. For Simeon, it was the end of his life's journey. He was satisfied. He was ready to die. He understood that the birth of this Son was the fulfilment of God's promise of a Savior to the nations. Jesus would become the light of the world.

In Jesus, God opened up His heart for the world. From now on, everyone who believes in Him will receive eternal life as a gift. Jesus, God's light for the world, was also sent for you. Now you have to carry this good message as light to all people in darkness!

Father, thank You for Jesus, the Way, Truth and Life for all people! Amen.

December 25

Such Love

"God so loved the world that He gave His only begotten Son."
John 3:16 NKJV

Faith without works is like a body without breath (James 2). We sing about love more easily than we do it. It has been said that love without action is like clouds without rain.

It is actually a criticism against the way we show love. God is not like this. He *gave* His only Son. Christmas teaches us that God's love is real love.

The bells and pretty Christmas trees do not tell the real story of Christmas. Jesus came to teach us that love is not an upward movement to better positions. Rather, His love is a downward movement to a position of human weakness. The manger, the stable and the cross are clear signs of this. This is exactly what makes Christmas a unique Christian celebration. We do not ascend to God. He comes to live with us.

The voice of God's love is still despised by many people. However, different places in the Bible make it clear that Christmas opened God's heart to the world. Therefore, John can say that God's being is love (1 John 4:8). Nothing can close His heart to the world.

Lord, thank You for not closing Your heart to us, in Jesus' name.

Amen.

December 26

Peacemakers

*They will beat their swords into plowshares
and their spears into pruning hooks.*
Micah 4:3 NIV

Wars, hostility, sanctions, nations standing up against nations and the formation of power blocks are just a few examples of what is constantly going on in our world. For some reason some countries with power can do whatever they want, while others have to suffer the consequences of these power games.

I wonder if anyone still believes the words of Dwight D. Eisenhower: "Every gun that is made, every warship launched, every rocket fired signifies in the final sense, a theft from those who hunger and are not fed, those who are cold and are not clothed. This world in arms is not spending money alone."

Micah dreams about a time when weapons of war will become agricultural instruments. Hostilities and strife will end. Weapons that were used to destroy people's lives will become instruments of building up, restoration and creating a peaceful life.

Yes, I know that wars and hostilities are part of our broken world, but Jesus calls us to be peacemakers. Children of the Lord dream with the Lord about a time when the needs of the world will count more than our own urge to rule. Therefore, we must resist all forms of hostility and support all actions aiming to bring peace. Anne Frank said that this is the wonderful thing about life: No one has to wait for a single moment before we can start improving the world.

Lord, make me a peacemaker, in Jesus' name. *Amen.*

December 27

We Are Privileged

*It is a sin to belittle one's neighbor;
blessed are those who help the poor.*
Proverbs 14:21 NLT

We do not suffer alone. Others are also suffering. It is said that if all our suffering were thrown into one heap and we had to divide it equally, most people would have picked up their own suffering again and gone home.

Many of us are privileged. I know that even the privileged suffer pain and emotional distress. Every person's pain is very personal. We need to respect people when they suffer, irrespective of their background.

A few years ago, a well-known car company ran an advertisement about everything that can go wrong with a person in one day. The main character is late, his books fall when he carries them to the car. The electric gate stops working. Everything is going wrong. Luckily, he has a car that works!

Maybe we easily complain when things do not go right for us. Maybe things in your life have gotten really bad. Yet, let us reflect today on the pain and suffering of others. Is ours really that big compared to theirs? Think about people in warzones as we see at the moment. Let us not lose perspective. God is with us in our struggles. Let us pray that others will also experience God's presence.

Teach me to have perspective in my suffering, in Jesus' name.

Amen.

December 28

Stop Hearts from Breaking

Do not withhold good from those to whom it is due, when it is in the power of your hand to do so. Do not say to your neighbor, "Go, and come back, and tomorrow I will give it," when you have it with you.
Proverbs 3:27-28 NKJV

I don't think we need to look too far to see the pain and suffering around us. Sometimes we see parents who don't have enough to feed their family. Sometimes we see people on the streets who have lost hope. Sometimes we see victims of conflict and war, domestic abuse, children broken by bullies or parents.

There are people who shout every day that someone should help, but there is no one. Even creation longs for good treatment. It suffers from overexploitation and pollution. Suffering affects the whole cosmos. When watching the media, we are often overwhelmed by the dire needs of the world. We do not know where to start. In the end, we do nothing.

What difference can we make? Emily Dickinson said: "If I can stop one heart from breaking, I shall not live in vain; if I can ease one life the aching, or cool one pain, or help one fainting robin unto his nest again, I shall not live in vain."

What can you do today to make someone's life better? Go and do it now!

Holy Spirit, open my eyes and heart for those who need me today, in Jesus' name. Amen.

December 29

Teach Us, Lord!

Teach us to number our days, that we may gain a heart of wisdom.
Psalm 90:12 NIV

Someone wrote that the greatest loss a person can suffer in life is this: To survive the hour of your pain without being able to make any permanent profit from it.

A teachable spirit is a gift from God. This is what the poet of this psalm asks: "Teach us to number our days, that we may gain a heart of wisdom." He looks at his own life and the reality of life. What does he see? He sees our sinful nature and knows that we all have secret sins (90:8). Life, he says, is fragile and short. We are mortal human beings (90:3-6, 10). Death is a definite item on the agenda of human life.

I have met very few older people who have told me that life was long. Most of the time they say that life is short and passes very quickly. Their children and grandchildren grew up so fast.

Whether you are ready to die is not the issue of the psalm. The question is whether you are ready to live! The poet prays for wisdom to live (90:12). Wisdom is to realize who God is. While we are like grass and flowers that wither, God's love and goodness is eternal (90:1-2).

Wisdom is to know this. Your life is a loss when you do not become wiser. Your life makes sense when you get to know the eternal and faithful God, in Jesus, the wisdom of God (Col. 2:1-2).

Lord, teach me how to live with wisdom, in Jesus' name.

Amen.

December 30

Living Hope

It is by His great mercy that we have been born again, because God raised Jesus Christ from the dead. Now we live with great expectation.
1 Peter 1:3 NLT

A comedian made a joke about the weather in the United Kingdom. Most times the weather person will say that the weather will be good for most of the United Kingdom. However, he would then add: "...except for Scotland and Northern Ireland." Living in Northern Ireland or Scotland means that the weather will be more unpredictable, colder or windier than the rest of the UK. Nothing is certain. It is hard to plan!

Rain can come any time in every season. This uncertainty leads people to think that hope is something very uncertain. We hope that tomorrow will be better than yesterday. We hope the economy improves. It is quite uncertain. However, as Christians our hope is not an uncertain matter. Why? Because it is not anchored in the uncertainty of our changing circumstances, but in the resurrection of Christ. It is the guarantee that we have a future with God.

Peter therefore says that we have a fixed inheritance in heaven. Although our circumstances vary, this inheritance is not something that can perish (1:4). We do not just have an inheritance. We, too, are protected by the power of God, even though we sometimes experience hard times (1:5-6). Nothing can take God's protection away from us. We like to say to each other: "Where there is life, there is hope." That is not entirely true. We should rather say: "Where there is hope, there is life!"

Lord, thank You for this living hope, through Jesus Christ our Lord. *Amen.*

December 31

Justice at Last!

*He will judge the world in righteousness
and the peoples with equity.*
Psalm 98:9 NIV

A tree that took a thousand years to grow can be cut down in a short while. Something can destroy what we have worked on for a long time. One of my friends said that one's reputation and standing in the community can change overnight. Governments can destroy our hope overnight.

We need hope. As Christians we have an endless hope, not a hopeless end. This psalmist expressed what Christians should be eager to express even more emphatically, namely that the Lord will rule over the world. He has a firm hope that the Lord will rule over the earth with justice and fairness at some stage (98:9).

Who came to reveal the style of fairness and justice more than the Son of God in His ministry? The world did not want Him and killed Him. After His resurrection He ascended into heaven and now sits at the right hand of the Father. He is Lord! He will come again as ruler to restore the fairness and justice of which we see so little in the world.

Christians can never stop reading from the book of Psalms. It is the prayer book of the church! But it also helps us to articulate our praise, worship, confession, complaint, and questions, and also our hope!

> You are king, Lord, over all the earth. Make us instruments of Your righteousness and fairness as well, by the power of Your Spirit.
>
> *Amen.*

About the Author

Annes Nel was born in Lambertsbaai in South Africa. He was odained as a minister in 1985 and served in two congregations before becoming a senior lecturer and later an associate profesor at two universities in Namibia and South Africa.

Since 2007, he has been working for the Presbyterian Church in Ireland and has been a lecturer in Systematic and Practical Theology at a training center for ministers and Christian leaders since 2019. His passion is to equip people as disciples of Jesus Christ and to help them understand the basics of the gospel of Jesus Christ.